Francesca Zappia

ELIZA

AND HER MONSTERS

Greenwillow Books

An Imprint of HarperCollinsPublishers

Eliza and Her Monsters
Copyright © 2017 by Francesca Zappia

The text of this book is set in Joanna MT.
Book design by Sylvie Le Floc'h

Library of Congress Control Number: 2017934160
ISBN 978-0-06-229013-7 (hardcover) — ISBN 978-0-06-269310-5 (proprietary edition)
18 19 20 21 PC/LSCH 10 9
First Edition

Greenwillow Books

For my friends, online and off
And for Jack and Norm

I took a deep breath and listened to the old brag of my heart.

I am, I am, I am.

—Sylvia Plath, *The Bell Jar*

PROLOGUE

Eliza Mirk is the kind of name you give to the creepy girl who clings to her ex-boyfriend for weeks after he's dumped her because she refuses to accept that he hates her guts. Eliza Mirk is a low-level villain with a secret hideout in the sewers. Eliza Mirk belongs in a comic book.

But Eliza Mirk is me. I don't think I'm desperate or deluded enough to hang on to an ex-boyfriend after he's broken up with me, I wouldn't go near a sewer with a ten-foot pole, and unfortunately I do not live in a comic book. I do live kind of a comic-book life, though, I guess.

I go to school during the day, and at night I cast off my secret identity to become LadyConstellation, creator of one of the internet's most popular webcomics, *Monstrous Sea*, and fearless mother of a fandom. My superpower is the ability to draw for hours without realizing what time it is or that I haven't eaten in too long. I succeed in disappearing in my disguise, and I excel at standing out in my true form.

Why LadyConstellation? you may ask.

Because, I reply, my favorite culture in *Monstrous Sea* comes from a people who have stars in their blood. These people—Nocturnians—instinctively chart stars. That is their calling in life. That is what they feel they must do, as I feel I must tell their story.

LadyConstellation is the one charting this story, drawing lines between plots and characters and places like the Nocturnians draw connections between stars. She is fearless, like the Nocturnians; she is mysterious and aloof, like the Nocturnians; and like the Nocturnians, she believes in the mystical, the supernatural, and the unknown.

LadyConstellation is the hero who defeats Eliza Mirk once a week and celebrates with her many admiring fans. She is beloved by all, even the villain, because without her the villain wouldn't exist.

I am LadyConstellation.

I am also Eliza Mirk.

This is the paradox that can never be solved.

NOCTURNIAN CONSTELLATIONS

Amity's constellation
non-Nocturnian

???

FAREN
the king crow/
the first Nocturnian

REIRAL
the Undercliff,
the Soul Bluffs

LUCIS
the life light

this star is
also called
Lucis

NOX
Queen Mother
of Night,
Mother of
Nocturnians

BYRAL
The Beak,
the thief that
steals the life
light from the
hand of NOX.

GYURHEI
Devourer of the light.
(Rises from the sea every
1,000 years to swallow
the sun)

THE BEST THING YOU'LL READ TODAY

*Posted at 10:46 a.m. on 02-19-2014 by **Apocalypse_Cow***

go here. read this. thank me later.

http://monstroussea.blogspot.com/

CHAPTER 1

The origin post is open on my computer when I shuffle over to it in the morning. Overnight, another three hundred comments have cropped up. I don't know what they say anymore—I haven't checked in months. I know some are from fans. A lot are from trolls. I don't look at the post for the comments. I look because it is my daily reminder that all of this—all of my life—is a real thing.

My beginning is time-stamped in history.

I smooth down my tangle of hair, yawn, and rub sleep from my eyes. When I blink, the post is still there, sitting happy near the top of the Masterminds subforum for webcomics. You'd think, after two years, it would have fallen. It hasn't.

I close the browser before I betray my own rules. I do not

read comments. Comments are explosives for mental walls, and right now I need those walls up. I open Photoshop to find the file I was working on last night, a half-finished page from *Monstrous Sea*. All the line work is done. I started on the colors but didn't finish, and I still need to add the text. Still, I'm ahead of schedule. This will be a whole chapter kind of week. My minimum for each week is one page; usually I average three. I always have something to post.

I skim over the comic page, skipping from panel to panel, double-checking the characters and settings. I lay out the rest of the colors in my head, then the light sources and the shadows. The text. The flow of the action looks okay, but in the bottom panel I drew Amity's nose too narrow again. It's always noticeable in close-ups of her face, and it's always her nose. I'll have to fix it later. I don't have time now.

Like it agrees with me, my alarm clock goes off, and I jump. Even when I know it's coming, even when I'm staring right at the thing. I shuffle back to the other side of the room to hit the button before it wakes up Church and Sully in the next room. Stupid middle schoolers get to sleep in an extra half hour, and they think they're kings.

Amity

Mom already has two hard-boiled eggs and a glass of fresh-squeezed orange juice ready for me when I get downstairs. I don't know when she hard-boiled those eggs. She certainly didn't do it last night, and it's the crack of dawn now. She sits at the island counter in her running outfit with her bouncy ponytail, reading some health article on her tablet. A few strands of hair are out of place, and water splashes in the shower down the hall. She and Dad are already back from their early morning run. Heinous.

"Morning, hon!" I know in some universe she must be speaking at normal volume, but it is not this universe. "Made you breakfast. Are you feeling okay? You look a little gray."

I grunt. Morning is the devil's time. And Mom has told me I "look gray" at least once a week for the past year. I drop onto the island stool in front of the eggs and juice and begin eating. Maybe I should try coffee. Coffee might help. Coffee might also send me into spiraling bouts of depression.

Under Mom's elbow is today's issue of the *Westcliff Star*. I pull it over and turn it around. The front-page headline reads REMINDERS PLACED AT WELLHOUSE TURN. Below that is a picture of the sharp turn in the road past Wellhouse Bridge where wreaths of flowers, ribbons, and toys decorate the ground. That's local Indiana news for you: they have nothing, so they fill their pages with the reminder that Wellhouse Turn kills more people every year than great white sharks. Also local Indiana news: comparing a turn in the road to a shark.

I finish the first egg. Dad comes out of the back hall smelling like a pack of spearmint gum and wearing slightly different running gear than what he wears when he goes out with Mom, which means these are his work clothes for the day.

"Morning, Eggs!" He stops behind me, puts his hands on my shoulders, and leans down to kiss the top of my head. I grunt at the nickname and stuff egg in my mouth. Hard-boiled heaven. "How'd you sleep?"

I shrug. Is it too much to ask that no one speak to me in the morning? I have just enough energy in my mouth to eat delicious eggs; there's none left to form words. Not to mention that in twenty minutes I have to get in my car to go to school for seven hours, where I'm sure plenty of talking will happen, whether I like it or not.

Mom distracts Dad with her health article, which is apparently about the benefits of cycling. I tune them out. Read about how the Westcliff High band bus driver fell asleep at the wheel and drove off Wellhouse Turn last summer on their way back from regionals. Chew. Before that it was a guy driving with his son in the winter. Drink juice. And before that, a woman taking her two kids to day care early in the morning. Chew more. A group of drunk teenagers. Finish off the egg. A lone girl who hit the wrong patch of black ice. Finish off the juice. They should put up a barrier to keep people from flying off the turn and down the hill to the river, but no. Without Wellhouse Turn, we have no news.

"Don't forget, your brothers have their first soccer game this afternoon," Mom says when I drop off my stool and take my plate and cup to the sink. "They're really excited, and we all have to be there to support them. Okay?"

I hate it when she says "Okay?" like that. Like she expects me to get angry at her before the words are ever out of her mouth. Always prepared for a fight.

"Yeah," I say. I can't muster any more. I return upstairs to my room for my backpack, my sketchbook, and my shoes. I jump up and down a few times in an attempt to get more blood flowing to my brain. Eggs eaten. Energy up. Ready for battle.

I resist the urge to go back to my computer, open up the browser, and check the *Monstrous Sea* forums. I don't read comments, and I don't check the forums before I leave for school. That computer is my rabbit hole; the internet is my wonderland.

I am only allowed to fall into it when it doesn't matter if I get lost.

Amity had two birth days. The first was the same as anyone's, and she didn't remember it. She didn't spend much time dwelling on the fact that she didn't remember it, because she had learned years ago that nothing good came of dwelling. The second birth—or the rebirth, depending on what mood she found herself in—she remembered with stunning clarity, and imagined she would for the rest of her life.

Her second birth was the day the Watcher took her as its host.

CHAPTER 2

Some people have called *Monstrous Sea* a phenomenon. Articles here and there. A few critics. The fans.

I can't call it that, because I created it. It's my story—it's the one I care about more than anything else, and it's one that a lot of other people happen to enjoy—but I can't call it a phenomenon because that is pretentious, and narcissistic, and honestly it makes me queasy to think of it that way.

Is it strange to be nauseated by recognition?

Lots of things about *Monstrous Sea* nauseate me.

The story is at once very easy and very hard to explain. I've never tried to do it in person, but I imagine if I did, I would end up vomiting on someone's shoes. Explaining something online is as simple as pasting a link and saying, "Here, read this." They click. Read the intro page. If they like it, they keep reading. If not, oh well, at least I didn't have to talk.

If I did have to explain the story without the very handy reference of the story itself, I imagine it would sound something like this:

"On distant planet Orcus, a girl and boy fight on opposite sides of a long war between the natives and colonists from Earth. The girl and boy are hosts to parasitic energy creatures whose only weakness is each other. There's lots of ocean, and there are monsters in that ocean. Stuff happens. Colors are pretty."

There's a reason I'm an artist and not a writer.

I began posting *Monstrous Sea* online three years ago, but it blew up when the origin post appeared on the Masterminds site. People actually saw it. They started reading.

They *cared*.

That was the weirdest thing. People other than me cared about it. They cared about Amity and Damien and the fate of Orcus. They cared whether the species of sea monsters had names. They cared if I put the pages up on time, and how good they looked. They even cared about me, who I was, though they never got past my username. The fans didn't, the trolls didn't, the articles and critics didn't. Maybe the creator's anonymity made it more of a phenomenon. It certainly kept me from getting too nauseated to work. I get emails from agents and publishers about putting

Monstrous Sea into print, but I delete them right away; traditional publishing is this huge, terrifying thing I have to fend off with a stick every once in a while so I don't get overwhelmed by the thought of a corporate machine manhandling my baby.

I didn't make *Monstrous Sea* to be a phenomenon—I made it because it was the story I wanted. I make it now because there's something inside of me, crushed around my heart, that says I must do it. This is what I was put on Earth to create, for me and for my fans. This story. This is mine, and it is my duty to bring it into the world.

Does that make me sound pretentious?

I don't care.

It's the truth.

MONSTROUS SEA FORUMS

USER PROFILE

LadyConstellation **

Admin

AGE: 00

LOCATION: Nocturne Island

INTERESTS: Riding sea monsters, charting stars, exploring clockwork palaces.

Followers 2,340,228 | Following 0 | Posts 5,009

UPDATES

View earlier updates

Oct 14 2016

> Don't forget, new Monstrous Sea T-shirts are on sale this week! We've got Amity and Dallas, Damien and the dread crows, and plenty of sea monsters. Go check them out! monstroussea.com/store

Oct 15 2016

> Wow, you really ate up those T-shirts. More on the way! (Plus, don't forget the next compendium!)

Oct 17 2016

> I think you guys are really going to like tonight's pages.
>
> . . .

Oct 18 2016

> Hehehehehe told you you'd like them. >:D

Oct 19 2016

> Yes, yes, I know, I'm evil.

Oct 19 2016

> You liked the shirts so much, they're going to be on sale
> this week too! Hot off the presses!

Oct 20 2016

> Excited for Dog Days tonight! Hope to see everyone in
> the chatroom.

When asked what the rebirth had felt like, Amity could only respond with "Painful." A creature of pure energy had crawled inside her and rearranged her very genetic structure. How else could it feel? But the people of Nocturne Island were persistent, and deeply spiritual, and the Watcher was one of their great guardians, so eventually she changed her answer to "Enlightening."

CHAPTER 3

School feels more like a punishment than ever.

I just don't *care*. I stand at my locker this fine October morning and stare down the hallway. A homecoming banner decorates the mouth of the hallway, reminding students to buy tickets for the football game this Friday night. Someone put that banner up there. God, someone *made* that banner. Someone painted it and everything. Students pass me wearing outfits for this particular day of homecoming spirit week, which happens to be hippie day. Lots of peace signs and tie-dye floating around. So much school spirit.

I barely finish my homework every night; how does anyone else have the willpower to care like this? The people having the most fun, dressed in the most ridiculous costumes, are seniors like me. How? Why? These are legitimate questions: I feel like someone told a joke and I missed the punchline, and now everyone's laughing without me.

I stand by my locker in stretched-out jeans and a baggy sweatshirt, counting the minutes until I have to give up and go to homeroom. A group of boys wearing tie-dye headbands and rose-colored glasses crowd up to the locker beside mine; one of them throws it open so hard it smacks me between the shoulder blades. The boy who did it starts to apologize, then sees that it's me and loses his voice to a badly concealed snort. I turn away and ignore them until they leave again, when one of the others pulls his hood up and acts like a cave creature, his back hunched and his hands held out in gnarled claws. The other boys laugh, as if they aren't still within my sight. I yank my own hood down.

I don't understand this place, but I only have to survive it for seven more months—seven months until graduation, until college. And college, as I have heard it from several respectable sources in the *Monstrous Sea* fandom, is so much better than high school it's laughable.

I want to be there. I want to be in the place where high school is the joke, and I don't have to be near people if I don't want to, and nobody cares what I wear or look like or do.

When the boys disappear around the corner and all attention fades away from me, I turn back to my locker. Freshman year, I festooned it in graphics and fanmade art for Children of Hypnos, my favorite book series. A few early *Monstrous Sea* sketches hid in the corners, but that was before *Monstrous Sea* was even a thing. Now my locker is empty aside from my school stuff. I stuff my stats and history books in my backpack. Wedge my sketchbook under my arm. The backpack gets slung over my shoulders, and my dignity tucked safely away.

On to homeroom.

"Eliza. I need to borrow you for a little while." Mrs. Grier has a bad habit of grabbing the first student who walks through her door when she needs something, and today I'm the unlucky plebe she gets her happy teacher hands on. She beams at me, looking the picture of joy in an unseasonal yellow sundress and earrings shaped like bananas.

I ease my arm out of her hand so it doesn't seem like I don't want her to touch me. I don't mind Mrs. Grier. Most days I like her. I wish I had her for an actual class instead of just homeroom, because she doesn't make me talk if I don't want to, and she counts showing up to class as your entire participation grade.

"We have a transfer student new to the school today," she says, smiling, and steps sideways. Behind her is a boy a little taller than me, football-player big, wearing jeans and a Westcliff High T-shirt. He hasn't even been here a day, and he's already got the school spirit. He scrubs a hand through his short dark hair and glances at me, expression blank, like he doesn't quite see me there. My stomach turns. He is exactly the kind of person I try to avoid—I like being invisible, not having someone look at me like I should be.

"This is Wallace," Mrs. Grier says. "I thought you could give him a few tips about the school and help him with his schedule before we leave homeroom."

I shrug. I'm not going to say no to her. "No" usually makes more problems than it solves. Mrs. Grier smiles.

"Great! Wallace, this is Eliza. You can go ahead and sit next to her."

Wallace follows me to my seat in the back of the room. He moves slow, sits slow, and looks around like he's still asleep. He glances at me again, and when I don't say anything, he pulls his phone out of his pocket and starts going through texts.

I didn't want to say anything to him, anyway. The school isn't that confusing—I'm sure he's smart enough to figure it out on his own.

I curl up my legs in the desk chair, set my sketchbook against them so no one can see the inside, and begin work on the next *Monstrous Sea* page. I forget Wallace. I forget Mrs. Grier. I forget this whole school.

I'm gone.

I get through the day the way I always do: by disappearing so well the teachers never see me, and by resisting the temptation to check the *Monstrous Sea* forums on my phone. I've heard it's much easier to get through school when you have friends to talk to, but all my friends are online. I used to have offline friends. Or at least I thought I did. Growing up, I had friends in school and in my neighborhood, but never good friends. Never friends who invited me to sleepovers or movies. I got invited to a couple of birthday parties, but sometimes I think that was because my mom badgered other moms. I was a weird kid then, and I'm weird now. Except now neither I nor any of my classmates is under the delusion that we have to interact with each other on a more than superficial basis.

Dad likes to say thinking I'm weird is normal. "Well, Eggs, you're just going to have to trust me when I say that's a thing a lot of kids your age think." Maybe he's right. All I know is, last year Casey Miller saw me walking behind her in the hallway and actually *squealed* in fear before she skipped away. She halfheartedly apologized a second later, of course, but it was a packed hallway during passing period—who gets scared by another student behind them? I know a week before that, I walked into gym late because of particularly nasty period cramps and scored my entire class ten minutes of stair laps that to this day have earned me the sort of looks that should be reserved for murderers. I know a few months before that, Manny Rodriguez invited some of his swimmer friends to cut me in the lunch line, only to have them refuse because they were afraid I'd call down a demon on them.

Is that the kind of person I seem like? A cultist? A religious fanatic? Am I so weird I should be the bad guy of the week on a prime-time television crime show?

My parents wonder why I don't have more friends, and this is why: because I don't *want* to be friends with these people. Even the nice ones think I'm weird; I can see it in their faces when they get paired with me for projects. I'm the person you pray the teacher doesn't call for your group. Not because I'm a terrible student, or because I make you do all the work, but because I dress like a homeless person and I never talk. When I was really little, it was endearing. Now it's strange.

I should have grown out of it.

I should want to be social.

I should desire friends I can see with my eyes and touch with my hands.

But I don't want to be friends with people who have already decided I'm too weird to live. Maybe if they knew who I am and what I've made, maybe then they wouldn't think I was so weird. Maybe then the *weird* would just be *eccentric*. But the only person I can be in this school is Eliza Mirk, and Eliza Mirk is barely a footnote in anyone's life. Including mine.

By the seventh-period bell, I have a whole new page of *Monstrous Sea* ready for inking, but my mind is on the page at home I still have to finish. New pages go up on Friday nights, always, like TV shows or sporting events. My readers like consistency. I like giving it to them.

I toss the books I don't need back into my locker and make my way to the parking lot, sticking close to the walls and shrinking until I barely feel myself there. Most people are already in their cars, clogging the lot. I make my way out the school's front doors, digging through my bag for my keys.

That kid Wallace sits on one of the benches on the front walk, phone in one hand and screen turned up like he's waiting for a message, a pen in the other hand so he can write on the sheaf of papers on the binder in his lap. Still looks like he's falling asleep. He might need a ride home. Or maybe he's just smart and knows it's better to wait until the parking lot clears out to try to leave. I stop outside the doors and watch him for a moment. I could offer him a ride, but that would be strange. Eliza Mirk does not offer rides, and no one asks her for them.

When he starts to look up, I turn away and hurry out to my car.

CHAPTER 4

Apocalypse_Cow: are you working on the next page right now?

MirkerLurker: No—finished one earlier. Now sitting in the car going to my brothers' soccer game. Only have my sketchbook.

emmersmacks: Bummer

emmersmacks: Hey did you get my care package

MirkerLurker: No! You sent another one? You didn't have to do that, Em!

emmersmacks: :DDD I love sending stuff to you guys!! Besides this ones got good stuff in it

Apocalypse_Cow: when do they not have good stuff in them?

Apocalypse_Cow: also where's MY care package???

emmersmacks: Oh calm down youre getting one too dummy

emmersmacks: E youre going to be around for the Dog Days livewatch right

MirkerLurker: Duh. The day I miss Dog Days is the day I eat my own foot.

Apocalypse_Cow: *takes screenshot*

Apocalypse_Cow: let it be known on this day that if eliza ever misses dog days, she will eat her own foot.

emmersmacks: Masterminds would love that one

emmersmacks: Creator of Monstrous Sea eats own foot over teen soap opera

Apocalypse_Cow: tacky teen soap opera.

MirkerLurker: Tacky teen soap opera? Yes. Wildly entertaining? Also yes.

emmersmacks: Amen

"Are you texting your boyfriend again?" Sully nudges up against my side, putting his chin on my shoulder. At his words, Church pulls away from the car window on my other side and leans in too. I slam my phone facedown on the sketchbook in my lap.

"Stop reading over my shoulder," I snap. "And it's not my boyfriend. It's just Max and Emmy."

"Oh, just Max and Emmy," Sully says, making air quotes. "Sure." Church snickers and copies the air quotes a second later.

"Be nice back there," Mom chirps from the passenger seat. Dad makes a sound of agreement.

We pull into the parking lot of the gym where Sully and Church play indoor soccer. The half-hour drive went fast thanks to Max and Emmy, but I don't look at the phone again until the two nightmares climb out of the car. Then I follow Mom and Dad into the building, with my nose in the phone.

> **Apocalypse_Cow:** but seriously tho, dog days is the worst
>
> **emmersmacks:** Not worse than the second season when Chris got with Ben
>
> **Apocalypse_Cow:** chris got with jason in the second season, not ben
>
> **emmersmacks:** Says the guy who doesnt watch Dog Days
>
> **Apocalypse_Cow:** . . .
>
> **emmersmacks:** Ah how the mighty have fallen

I snicker. Dad looks over his shoulder at me. "What's so funny, Eggs?"

I turn off the phone and press it to my sketchbook again. Annoyance pings over my humor, little dark spots in the lightness. "Nothing."

Until I'm sure neither Mom or Dad are looking back again, I keep the phone down and my eyes up. This gym is more like a warehouse than anything. A big empty room with movable walls as dividers between different courts. Volleyball, basketball, tennis. The place is huge. In the center is a walled-in soccer field with bleachers and everything. I take a picture and send it to the chat.

> **MirkerLurker:** This place is actual hell.
>
> **emmersmacks:** My sister hangs out at one of those gyms
>
> **emmersmacks:** They make me want to shower
>
> **Apocalypse_Cow:** that is weirdly specific, ems. sorry for your luck, e.
>
> **MirkerLurker:** When I die here, bury me with my art.
>
> **Apocalypse_Cow:** songs will be sung. potential mourned. someone will have to notify the fans, of course. as head security admin for the ms forums, i accept this responsibility.
>
> **emmersmacks:** When did you start calling yourself Head Security Admin
>
> **emmersmacks:** All you do is ban trolls

"Oh, Eliza, look." Mom's hand brushes my shoulder. I look up and find her examining a poster on a board by the gym entrance. Dad and the boys have already taken off toward the soccer field, where the teams warm up for their game. "They're starting tennis lessons soon. I really think you'd love tennis—it's a solitary game, and it's great exercise."

"No," I say, and go back to my phone. She gives up immediately.

We've evolved this process steadily over the years. When I was little and didn't have a say in the matter, my parents signed me up for every sport under the sun. Little League Baseball. Soccer. Basketball. Volleyball. I hated all of them because I didn't—don't—have any coordination and I didn't—don't—like to talk, so I didn't play well, so my teammates wanted me gone. The first time I told my dad I wanted to quit softball, he flipped out and didn't speak to me for a week. Mom tried to reason me back into it.

It would build character. It would help me make friends. It would be good exercise.

I refused. Then I quit all the other sports too. Casting them off was like casting off a set of old, heavy armor. Church and Sully loved sports, so some of the focus fell away from me, but Mom and Dad still tried. If I said no, they kept trying. I kept saying no.

Now we are at that place where they suggest something and I say no and that's the end of it.

I follow Mom to the soccer field and perch beside her at

the foot of the bleachers. Dad stands on the sidelines, coach's clipboard in hand, talking to a group of gangly fourteen-and-under boys in sky-blue uniforms. I take my pencils and eraser out of my pocket and crack open my sketchbook.

"I wish you wouldn't take that everywhere," Mom says. "Why can't you watch your brothers play?"

I look up at her, then at the field, then back down at my sketchbook. There's no answer I can give her that she wants to hear, so I won't give her one at all.

Faren and Damien are supposed to be identical, but for some reason I really suck at that

We get home in time for *Dog Days*. I scramble out of the car over a sweaty Church, grab a water bottle from the fridge in my rush to my room, turn on the small TV on the crook of the desk beside the computer, and flip the channels until I find the one I want. The opening credits are starting. I wake up the computer and hurry to the website.

Monstroussea.com is not only the first place to find all the *Monstrous Sea* pages I've done up to this point, it's also the link to the largest fan forums for the comic and a chat page where once a week I show up under my pen name to watch *Dog Days* with the fans. This is the only time LadyConstellation speaks live.

LadyConstellation: I'M HERE! Nobody worry, I'm here!

moby66: Yay!

GirlWho: yayayay

hustonsproblem: We thought you wouldn't show up!

A flood of other comments follows those. Usually there are so many people in the chat I can't actually reply to any of them. I blurt out things about the show and let them respond. They hold conversations with themselves. Mostly the point is that I'm there, and we're watching the same thing, and for once no one is talking about *Monstrous Sea*.

I love *Monstrous Sea* as much—probably more—as them, but

even I need something simple to talk about every once in a while.

A private chat comes up on my phone, where I'm still logged in to my MirkerLurker account.

Apocalypse_Cow: looking forward to this one! will spencer find out jane's a lesbian and is also dating his ex??

Max will never admit it to the public, but he loves watching *Dog Days* as much as the rest of us. Only Emmy and I know, but right now Emmy's too busy frolicking with the other fans in the main chat.

I send some senseless emojis to Max and start commenting in main chat through the opening scenes of *Dog Days*, where Spencer does indeed discover Jane has come out as a lesbian and is now dating his ex-girlfriend Jennifer. I can't tell if this is mindless plot twisting or if the show is actually trying to make some statement about gay rights. I send that to chat. They love it.

At the first commercial break, I scan into the computer the new *Monstrous Sea* page I sketched out in school today and bring it up in Photoshop to start the good line work. My pen display waits for me like a prized stallion ready to launch out of the gate, its screen duplicating the screen of my computer. I pull my smudge guard—an old glove with the thumb, index, and middle fingers cut off—over my right hand, to keep the pen display screen from getting gross, and to let my hand move smoothly across it.

Nothing ruins a piece faster than poor hand movement.

Line work is my favorite part of any page. Colors are second, but line work has a subtlety matched by nothing else. Good lines will make or break a picture. Bonus, this page will have some really awesome lines: right now, Amity and Damien are in the middle of the Battle of Sands, where Orcians and Earthens clash for control of the capital city of the desert lands.

Monstrous Sea involves a lot of elemental-type powers, very anime, so most fights have great lines. Especially when Amity and Damien are there, because they fight with crystals and fog. Angles and curves. Delicious.

The commercial ends before I get a chance to really do anything. I set down my pen and turn back to the chat to find a few noticeable newcomers among the flock.

LadyConstellation: I hope no one caused any trouble during that commercial break.

rainmaker: Define "trouble."

Fire_Served_Cold: Trouble: n. def: This guy.

rainmaker: Smooth.

Fire_Served_Cold: I try.

Below that quick exchange come a flurry of excited "rainmaker!!"s and a few "The Angels are here!"

The Angels they refer to are the group of five fans who took names based on the Angels in *Monstrous Sea*, the guardians of the planet Orcus. I've never really interacted with rainmaker and the other Angels of the fandom, but I've seen them around the boards. It's kind of impossible *not* to see them around the boards. They're almost as popular as I am.

The music on the TV hits a crescendo. I turn in time to see Jane find out she's pregnant with Spencer's baby before it cuts to another commercial. They really are going for an issues episode here. Back to main chat.

> **LadyConstellation:** Another pregnancy?! This show already kept a baby, gave a baby up for adoption, and had an abortion! How will they tackle this problem and still stay relevant to REAL TEEN LIFE?
>
> **rainmaker:** Hahahahaha

The reply pops up immediately, and a strange warm feeling flutters in my chest. Other people laugh, but rainmaker's response is the one that does it. He's the most-read fanfic writer for *Monstrous Sea*. I've seen some of his stuff. He's really funny. Like, really fucking funny. Like, I couldn't make *Monstrous Sea* that funny if I tried.

So him laughing at something I said feels like winning a lottery.

Then he replies with this:

rainmaker: PLOT TWIST it was actually Jennifer's baby. Jane was cheating on Spencer long before this. When the baby is born, they name it Janifer and live a happy lesbian life in the suburbs and never think about Spencer again.

I nearly spit water all over my computer screen at "Janifer." The rest of the threads going on in the chat, all the other voices, fade into the background and my eye only catches rainmaker's when it appears.

Fire_Served_Cold: Wait, how did two lesbians have a biological child together?

rainmaker: Um excuse you no one said it was biologically Jennifer's. Blood=/=family. Amirite? Anyone?

LadyConstellation: Sorry, I'm still trying to process "Janifer."

rainmaker: Liked that one, did you? ;)

Oh god, a winky face. The most provocative of all emoticons. A blush creeps over my face and I rub my cheeks to hide it, even though there's no one here to see. What a confident, cocky bastard. Boys at school never do this to me—I don't know if it's because I can see their faces or because they can see mine or what. I only have feelings like this for people I meet online, and honestly, rainmaker's the first one to drudge them up in a good long while. It's like in this whole chat, he's only talking to me. Like two people sitting next to each other on a couch in a crowded party.

Now, here's the new issue:

Do I say anything back?

My fingers hover over the keyboard. A commercial for acne medication flashes on the TV, then a commercial for the show coming on after *Dog Days*. I type:

LadyConstellation: Oh, you know it. ;)

What a cop-out. At least I got the winky face in there. Maybe it sounds coy enough to make up for the complete lack of cleverness. It's stupid because that's what I like about the internet—that it gives you time to think about what you want to say before you say it. But my brain isn't working right, I'm not sure it's wise to publicly flirt with someone as LadyConstellation, and I don't even know who rainmaker is. He could be some forty-year-old living in his parents' basement with Cheeto dust on his fingers and a collection of vintage Star Wars T-shirts that no longer fit his ever-expanding stomach.

I turn back to my line art. My shaking hands go still against the screen of the pen display, and the lines come out smooth and bold. Drawing gives me something to do as I think about that winky face, and the winky face I sent back.

Amity, with her cloud of white hair and her sharp orange eyes, comes into being against the blank background one line at a time. There's no color on her yet, but I see it in her every time I draw her. I've always wondered what it would be like to be the person whose color comes through even when standing still. To be someone so vibrant, others can't help but notice you. It's not Amity's eyes or her hair or even her skin that do that. It's just her.

I save the mass of knifelike orange crystals growing along Amity's right arm—pulled back, ready to strike down her foes— for later. The show is back on.

Rainmaker hasn't said anything else in the chat. I pop in every now and then to comment on the show, but for the most part I sit back, stop thinking, and enjoy a group of pretty twenty-somethings pretending to be teenagers, making astronomically bad decisions and learning from their mistakes. Every once in a while, a troll account will take over the chat window with screaming caps or strings of emoticons, and the account Forges_ of_Risht appears to block them.

A message from Max appears on my phone.

Apocalypse_Cow: forges, reporting for duty with the banhammer.

MirkerLurker: Excellent work, soldier.

Apocalypse_Cow: see, there's a reason you hired me for this job.

MirkerLurker: Yeah, so Emmy doesn't have to do that and take care of the website.

Apocalypse_Cow: har har.

MirkerLurker: But really, great job. No one wields the banhammer quite as well as you.

Max sends more emojis. A lady dancing the salsa. Nail painting. A lightning bolt. He routinely pesters Emmy to make emojis part of *Monstrous Sea* forum chat capability, and she refuses because she thinks it's funny.

Emmy says something in the *Dog Days* chat that sets off a flood of replies so fast I can't scroll back up to see what the original comment was.

Max and Emmy aren't the only two people who help run the forums, but they are the best. And they're the only ones who know me not as LadyConstellation but as Eliza. Before Max was my bouncer, even before he shared the link to *Monstrous Sea* on Masterminds that drew in the fans, he was an anal-retentive plot theorist on the Children of Hypnos forums. And Emmy—before Emmy built monstroussea.com and the forums and the shop where I sell my merchandise, she was the life of the Children of Hypnos party, an eleven-year-old with enough fangirl energy to power a small city.

If it weren't for them finding my fan art, none of this would have happened. It was both of them separately who found my dead art thread on the Children of Hypnos forums, and it was in that thread where we carved out a little space just for us.

I do have friends. Maybe they live hundreds of miles away from me, and maybe I can only talk to them through a screen, but they're still my friends. They don't just hold *Monstrous Sea* together. They hold *me* together.

Max and Emmy are the reason any of this exists.

After the second birth, she had felt the Watcher sitting in her mind, its eyes turned on her. Inside her, of course, it had no eyes but her own, yet that was how it felt. A lump of burning coal in the back of her head. Sometimes it clung to her shoulders, though she could turn to her reflection and see nothing there. She didn't know now if those had been hallucinations left over from post-rebirth sickness, or if she'd simply grown used to the sensation. Either way, she no longer felt it. And the Watcher hadn't spoken to her since that first day, when it had made the bargain with her.

Her body for its power.

CHAPTER 5

Over the next few days, I finish two more pages. I could go faster—I can finish a page in a day if I try—but the quality will start to deteriorate, and that's the last thing I want at this point. We've already gone through so much of the comic, it should only be getting better from here, not worse. I sketch out the pages in school, doing as much of the line work foundation as I can before it ever gets on the computer. I do these in class when no one is watching, or at lunch while I sit by myself in the drafty courtyard outside the cafeteria. Soon it'll be too cold to sit out here at all, and I'll have to find a table inside, which should be fun considering all of the tables are taken every day I walk in.

On Friday, the day of our homecoming game, everyone is

dressed in typical Westcliff gold, adorned with football jerseys and face paint and gold ribbons tied in ponytails. In the main hallway, there are five different homecoming banners encouraging the football team to GO FIGHT WIN. On my walk to fourth period, it is banner number three that detaches from the wall as I walk beneath it. The world goes dark. I smack at the banner to get it off, and snickers erupt in the hallway behind me. The banner falls to the floor.

Travis Stone and Deshawn Johnson, the only two students in this school who scare me even on a good day, lean against the lockers nearby and watch me struggle. Travis Stone looks like a vulture in sagging jeans and a buzz cut, and Deshawn Johnson is a kid who half the time is too cool to hang out with Travis and the other half the time not very cool at all. Ten years ago they were two sweet little boys at my grade school who played tag with me on the playground, and they would've helped me with this banner instead of watching.

"Nice hair," Travis says. I brush a hand over my head and find an ungodly amount of glitter trapped there. The look on my face sends Travis and Deshawn into new rounds of laughter.

In the bathroom, attempts to remove the glitter fail. All I manage to do is fill a sink with gold glitter dandruff and get a few other girls to give me strange looks, like I did it to myself. All hope of happiness and a bright future dies.

I walk outside at the end of the day to a gloomy sky, a sharp breeze, and lines of cars vying to leave the parking lot. In a few hours everyone will be back here for the football game, crammed together in the stadium behind the school, shouting their support to the chilled night air and huddled together with their friends. There will be class floats paraded around the perimeter of the football field. There will be a moment of silence and a short memorial for the band members who went off Wellhouse Turn last summer. There will be football jerseys and parties and revelry deep into the night.

I rearrange my backpack on my shoulders and hold my sketchbook in both hands. There are too many cars. I bet college doesn't have parking issues like this. I bet college is great.

I turn and find Wallace sitting on that same bench again. He has sat there every day this week. I found out yesterday that his last name is Warland, which seems appropriate for someone of his size and stature. Capable of inflicting destruction wherever he goes.

Today, Wallace Warland is not alone. Flanking him are Travis Stone and Deshawn Johnson, forever and always the bane of my existence. Running into my long-forgotten friends once a day is bad enough—twice is asking for trouble. Deshawn stands by the bench with his arms crossed, and Travis lounges beside Wallace like they're old buddies. Wallace sits stiffly, with his hands covering the papers he's always writing on, his eyes stuck on the sidewalk somewhere to the left of Deshawn's shoes.

Wallace did not strike me as the kind of person to begin a friendship with the likes of Travis Stone, at least not High-School-Dickbag Travis Stone. Curiosity makes my feet inch a little closer, pretending I'm debating going to my car. I pull out my phone and stare at the black screen.

". . . must have typed this. No one can write that good. What is this again?"

Travis tries to take one of the papers. Wallace clamps his hand down.

"What'd you call it? Fan . . . fan . . ."

"Fanfiction," Deshawn says.

No way in the nine circles of hell. No way is Wallace Warland writing fanfiction. Fanfiction of *what*? What does Wallace Warland enjoy so much he writes fanfiction about it? Can you have fanfiction about professional sports teams?

"Lemme see." Travis tries to take the paper again, which makes Wallace lock down tighter.

"I think it's for that online thing," Deshawn says, peering down at the paper. "That sea thing."

All the hair on the back of my neck prickles. My heart rate ratchets upward. They are not talking about *Monstrous Sea*.

Wallace Warland cannot write *Monstrous Sea* fanfiction.

"Leave him alone." I've spun and headed toward them before I can stop myself. My voice comes up from some black reserve of courage inside me, a place usually saved for speech class, or going to the dentist on my own. My face crumples in on itself; my legs shake. My heart beats like I just sprinted a mile.

Travis and Deshawn both turn to me and smile—well, Deshawn doesn't really smile, and all of Travis's smiles look like leers. God, I remember when those smiles used to be nice. Wallace stares at me, expression unreadable. Does he realize how futile this is? Maybe I can at least give him a few seconds to run. The only thing I can't do is stand idly by while a fan—if not a fan of *Monstrous Sea*, then definitely a fan of something—gets ridiculed for what he likes. LadyConstellation wouldn't stand for that, and for this exact moment now, neither do I.

Travis fakes surprise. "Oh my god, Murky can actually speak."

We've been in school together since the second grade. He knows I can speak fine, unlike some of our other classmates, who believe I am an actual mute.

"Leave him alone, Travis." My voice is already too weak for this. Emergency courage reserves depleted.

"Why're you standing up for him, Murky? Does someone have a crush?"

My face flames instantly. I press the edge of my sketchbook into my thighs. I know this is his go-to to make a girl either stop talking or get so flustered she can't make a rational argument. He started using it in middle school, when I became too weird for anyone to hang out with. If I can push through it, maybe I'll knock him off his game.

"No. Shut up," I warble. "I just—you . . . let him write what he wants. Whatever it is, it's none of your business."

"None of my business? I'm not trying to hate on him for it, Murky, I just want to read it! What's your problem?"

"He obviously doesn't want you to read it!"

Wallace stares at me the whole time I'm saying this, and heat seeps into my ears too. So I'm distracted when Deshawn slips my sketchbook out of my hands.

"Hey!"

I reach for it, but he backpedals away, opening it up to look at the pictures. Some of the loose pages flutter in the cold breeze but don't come free of the pages.

"Whoa, these are really good," Deshawn says. "Trav, I think she's into the sea thing too."

He snaps the book closed and Frisbees it over my head, out of the reach of my fingers when I jump for it, to Travis, who has stood up off the bench. Travis grabs it out of the air, sending a few of the loose pages sailing off into the wind, and opens it up.

"Oh, this is why you stood up for him. You guys like the same thing!"

"Give it back!" No one is supposed to look in that sketchbook. It's the one I bring to school, so it's safer than some of the others I have, but there are still *Monstrous Sea* things in there—like unfinished comic pages—and it might give away who I am. Plus I just don't like the idea of Travis Stone's goopy eyes on the things I've drawn.

I didn't let him see my drawings even when we were friends, and I'm not going to start now. I rush at Travis to get it back, but he tosses it to Deshawn.

I won't be caught in a game of monkey in the middle. Not as a senior in high school. I *won't*. But Deshawn stands there holding it, rifling through the pages, and he won't move until I do. Tears blur my vision. *Great.* Now I'm crying too. Let's make the situation worse. I ball my hands into fists and move toward Deshawn. As soon as I get close enough, he laughs and throws the sketchbook back.

I turn again, ready to scream in frustration, only to find Wallace standing between me and Travis, the sketchbook in one hand. He must have caught it out of the air. I didn't think he could move that fast. Travis looks both stunned and vaguely impressed. Wallace turns and stares him down. Travis is about my height, so when they're both standing Wallace is half a head taller than him, and a hell of a lot wider. Travis looks like a sapling standing next to an oak.

Wallace steps toward him, whole body tense, and Travis holds up his hands and backs away. "Yo. Okay. Chill, dude. Damn." He looks at Deshawn, jerks his head toward the parking lot, and the two go loping off. On the way, Travis scoops up one of my fallen pictures, then stares me in the face as he folds it and slips it in his pocket.

Wallace is already walking across the front sidewalk to pick up the other loose sheets. I scramble for the few near me—

Amity using her crystals to launch herself into the sky, Damien surrounded by a cloud of fog and a flock of dread crows—and wipe my eyes.

Wallace lumbers back, holding my sketchbook as a hard surface so he can scribble on one of his loose papers. He stuffs that inside the sketchbook along with all the pictures he grabbed, then holds it out for me. Instead of looking at me like I should be invisible, he doesn't look at me at all; his eyes rove left, then right, then down, until I take the sketchbook from him. I almost drop it and have to catch it against my leg.

He stands there. Am I supposed to say something? Does he want me to say something? He scratches the back of his head, lets his hand fall to his neck, and takes a deep breath.

I dig in my pocket for my phone, but Emmy and Max probably aren't even around right now. Emmy's in class and Max is at work. My fingers hover over the keys with nowhere to go. Wallace is still standing there, but now he has his phone out too.

He has his phone out. He's not paying attention.

I turn and march away before he has the chance to look up again. I'm pretty sure he does, but it doesn't matter because I'm already halfway across the parking lot and I don't care if he thinks I'm weird, because I'm never ever going to speak in front of him again. When I reach my car, I dive inside and slam the door shut behind me. The parking lot is still too full to leave. I should probably take off my backpack before I try to drive, anyway.

I move my backpack into the passenger seat, buckle my seat belt, and rest my forehead on the steering wheel. Breathe in. Breathe out. I'm light-headed. This isn't good. The heat in my face fills the car, and I bathe in gross sweaty embarrassment. Why did Travis and Deshawn have to pick today to mess with Wallace? Why couldn't Wallace take care of them himself? Why did he have to maybe be writing *Monstrous Sea* fanfiction?

I lift my head and glance at my sketchbook. If not *Monstrous Sea* fanfiction, he was definitely writing something. I reach over, flip the sketchbook open, and grab the paper he stuffed inside.

A normal piece of college-ruled notebook paper. On it, in handwriting surprisingly precise and neat for how quickly he wrote them, the words:

Thanks.

The drawings are really good.

IF YOU HAD TO CHOOSE, WHICH WOULD IT BE—
-DYING IN A YEAR, OR LIVING FOREVER?
NEITHER. A YEAR IS TOO SHORT AND FOREVER IS TOO LONG.
THAT'S THE POINT OF THE QUESTION. IT'S DIFFICULT.
THEN WHICH WOULD YOU CHOOSE?
LIVING FOREVER.
I WANT TO SEE THE STARS DIE.

emmersmacks: Hold on

emmersmacks: Wait

emmersmacks: So you stood up for him?

MirkerLurker: Yeah.

emmersmacks: . . . Im failing to see the issue here E

emmersmacks: Did they hurt you??

MirkerLurker: No . . . not really. Just took my sketchbook and threw it around a little.

MirkerLurker: Okay look I know it doesn't sound that bad

MirkerLurker: But, like, you don't understand the way this guy looks at me. He's one of those where it's like, "Why are you even standing in front of me, you're uglier than the stuff I crap out after eating too much Chipotle."

3:19 p.m. (Apocalypse_Cow has joined the message)

Apocalypse_Cow: i feel like i came in at a bad time. i'll go.

emmersmacks: E is having a crisis

Apocalypse_Cow: crisis over what?

MirkerLurker: Just this stupid new kid at school who may or may not be a fanfic writer for Monstrous Sea and who definitely thinks I am the scum of the earth.

emmersmacks: Why would he think that?? You stood up for him

MirkerLurker: I don't know! Because I emasculated him, probably. Or something. Max, I need advice from someone who's felt emasculated.

Apocalypse_Cow: why would you immediately assume i've felt emasculated before?

MirkerLurker: Because you're the only male here.

Apocalypse_Cow: if you want to know if some guys feel emasculated when a girl stands up to a bully for them, then unfortunately i must say that yes, that does happen.

Apocalypse_Cow: BUT NOT ME.

Apocalypse_Cow: LET IT BE KNOWN THAT MAX CHOPRA HAS NEVER FELT EMASCULATED.

Apocalypse_Cow: but really, did this guy say something to you? why feel so bad about it?

MirkerLurker: He didn't say ANYTHING. That's the problem!

MirkerLurker: He just stood there and wouldn't even look at me.

emmersmacks: Did you say anything

MirkerLurker: . . . No.

emmersmacks: Well

emmersmacks: E

emmersmacks: There you might have a problem

Apocalypse_Cow: you're getting schooled in social skills by a twelve-year-old in college. how does that feel

emmersmacks: Im fourteen not twelve

emmersmacks: Asshole

Apocalypse_Cow: wait, he left a note in your sketchbook? what did it say?

MirkerLurker: It said thanks, and that the pictures were good.

emmersmacks: OH MY GOD

emmersmacks: THATS WHY HE DIDNT TALK

MirkerLurker: What?

emmersmacks: HE WAS TOO NERVOUS

emmersmacks: AW HE LIKES YOU E

MirkerLurker: I really really doubt that.

MirkerLurker: Like, I mean, REALLY doubt it.

MirkerLurker: He's not exactly the kind of guy that's usually interested in me.

Apocalypse_Cow: what kind of guy is usually interested in you?

MirkerLurker: The kind I make up in my head.

Apocalypse_Cow: wooooooooooooooooooooooooooow

Apocalypse_Cow: wooooooooooooooooooooooooooooooooooo ooooooooooooooooooooow

Apocalypse_Cow: wooow

Apocalypse_Cow: do you want me to go ahead and fill your house with cats right now, or do you want to put that off for a few years?

MirkerLurker: Har har

MirkerLurker: I have to sit next to this guy in homeroom on Monday. What am I going to say to him?

emmersmacks: What have you been saying to him

MirkerLurker: Nothing. I thought that was clear.

emmersmacks: Then continue doing that

emmersmacks: If he wants to say something to you he will

MirkerLurker: Why does a twelve-year-old know more about boys than I do?

emmersmacks: IM FOURTEEN

CHAPTER 6

On Monday I walk into homeroom—past victorious homecoming banners that say WILDCATS ARE THE CHAMPS—and Wallace is already there in the seat next to mine. But Mrs. Grier is there too, and she catches me by the door. Today it's earrings shaped like shamrocks and a green dress shirt with black slacks.

"How are you this morning, Eliza?" she asks, smiling. It's seven in the morning, how is she already smiling? I wait for her to continue, but she stands there staring at me like she actually wants to know the answer to that question.

"Um. Okay?" I say. She frowns and leans in. I raise my voice. "Okay."

"Great! I just wanted to check and make sure everything was going good."

Just wanted to check? Why? Did she hear about the Travis and Deshawn thing Friday? Wallace wouldn't have told her about that, would he? When she again doesn't continue, I shrug and edge my way past her. It's bad enough that I have to deal with Wallace; I don't want to deal with teachers worried about bullied students too.

I slide into my seat as quietly as I can, but Wallace looks up from his phone anyway. He lowers his head again, scratches at his neck, looks away. I hold my backpack in my lap and stare at the back of Shelby Lewis's ginger head. Then, after a few seconds of frozen anxiety, I take out my phone and start going through last night's long chat with Emmy and Max. I'd text them now, but Emmy's asleep and Max is at work. They won't respond anyway, and by the time they do I'll be out of this situation.

I switch over to the MS forums. I don't normally read forum posts on my phone, but, well, desperate situations. There are a few noticeable people online, among them rainmaker and Fire_Served_Cold, who are playing a game of tag in the General Topics threads. As I refresh the page, more and more people join in. Where rainmaker goes, the fans follow.

After a few minutes, the hairs on my neck rise. I stare at the phone screen and pretend I don't notice Mrs. Grier looking at me from her spot by the door.

The bell rings. Mrs. Grier closes the door and goes to her desk for her attendance list. Per school rules, I shove my phone into my pocket and look like I'm paying attention to what's actually going on instead of thinking about the next time I can take the phone out again.

Then I find a paper on my desk that wasn't there when I sat down.

On it, in handwriting so neat and precise it looks like it was printed out by a machine, the words:

Do you like Monstrous Sea?

The handwriting is nicer and less hurried. I don't know anyone else who writes with such blocky, printer-neat words like that. I glance at Wallace and he's bent over his desk, head turned slightly away so he can massage the tip of his right ear. His hair sticks up on the back of his head where he scratched at it.

Great. He really does like *Monstrous Sea*. I don't know if that should be flattering or terrifying. With the sheer number of people that go to my school, I figured at least one of them would be a *Monstrous Sea* fan, but I also figured I'd never end up talking to them. Ever. Ever in my life. Why now? I only had to survive another seven months without something like this happening. *Why now, O cruel universe?*

Wallace turns back, and he looks *at my freaking desk.* God, he's waiting for an answer. Great. What could this hurt, really? He doesn't know who I am. All he knows is that I draw *Monstrous Sea* pictures. It's fan art. That's all it has to be. And this paper—this paper is a chat window. I don't have to look at his face while I write. Just put the words down and hand it back.

I take out a pen. The tip hovers over the paper. *Do you like Monstrous Sea?*

Yes, I do. *Monstrous Sea* is my favorite thing in the whole entire world. I like it more than any person. I like it more than I like myself. I like it more than food, and sleep, and hot showers. I like it more than I like being alone. It is everything to me.

I write *Yes.*

Then I shove the paper back at him.

If Mrs. Grier sees this from the front of the room, she doesn't say anything. Wallace rights the paper on his desk, stares at my one word, then slowly reaches for his pen and begins carefully printing. He goes so *slow.* It feels like the tectonic plates move faster than he does. I look away while he writes, until I feel the gentle nudge of paper against my hand.

Who's your favorite character?

My favorite? All of the characters are my favorite. I've known them all for so long even the ones I used to hate are my favorites. They're more real to me than most of the real people I know. I love all of them. But I suppose I love some more than others. And LadyConstellation loves asking her fans which ones are their favorites.

I write *Izarian Silas.*

When I get the paper back, he's written, *Izzy's a good one. Mine's Dallas. He has the best power of any of the Angels. Favorite location?*

Orcus itself is my favorite location. If I could live there instead of on Earth, I would do it in a heartbeat. I would build an airship and fly over the monster-filled oceans, and I'd visit all the places I've only ever seen in my head. Dark and isolated Nocturne Island, where Amity grew up; the vast and beautiful Great Continent, where the ancestors of the Earthens laid their roots; the clockwork city, Risht, where Amity and Damien learn to be friends, and realize they're stronger when they work together.

I write Risht. In Risht, no one fears monsters. In Risht, monsters are a memory of a bygone age, and the people who vanquished them are revered as gods.

He writes faster this time. *Same. For the fusion power, the clock palace, and the music. Also because of that giant antlered phoenix statue they made out of food for Rory's birthday. I want a giant edible phoenix statue.*

No question this time. I sit with the paper on my desk for several minutes, staring at the back of Shelby Lewis's head and her retro 90s butterfly clips. The tip of the pen presses into the paper until there's just a large blue dot beside Wallace's neat "palace."

Finally, I put down *Were you writing MS fanfiction?*

But when I push it back on his desk, the bell rings for first period. I grab my bag and run, and hesitate for only a second at the door. It's not even first period yet, and I've killed my deodorant. It's not even first period yet, and the new kid is a *Monstrous Sea* fan. The first one I've ever met in real life.

I rush into the hallway before Wallace can catch up.

✦ ✦ ✦

Between first and second period I message Emmy and Max, even though they won't see it until later.

MirkerLurker: New Kid update—he actually does like Monstrous Sea, and now he knows I do too. Not sure what to do about this. Please advise.

By fourth period, my body temperature has returned to normal. Thankfully. Just in time for me to get my lunch and find my seat in the courtyard. The grass is curled and brown. Dead leaves skitter over concrete in the stiff breeze. When I sit at my usual picnic table in the corner, the bench freezes my butt through my jeans. This seems too cold for October in Indiana, but maybe I'm not as acclimated to temperature changes as I used to be. I don't spend much time outside anymore.

I'll take the cold if it means I'm alone out here, though. I check my phone to find one response from Emmy—IN LOVE WITH YOU E—probably when she was between classes. I roll my eyes, then pull my headphones and sketchbook out of my bag. The headphones go in the phone to put on some music—Pendulum, of course, the only music for *Monstrous Sea* action scenes—and the sketchbook falls open to a fresh page. Finally, some uninterrupted drawing time. I jam a few french fries in my mouth and start sketching out a rough idea of the next page.

Last week wasn't quite a full chapter week; I only made four pages, but they were an awesome four pages. I got to introduce the giant animal-headed mechas that the Haigans, the desert dwellers, use to fight in the Battle of Sands. I love the mechas, but they take forever to draw, and if I put less detail into them I'd feel like I'm letting down the great anime mecha artists. The battle's going to go on for at least two more chapters, max four, and that means a lot of panels involving giant fighting robots.

I want to roll in pictures of highly detailed mechas.

I feel around for my lunch tray to grab another handful of fries and instead touch the edge of a paper hanging in the air.

Reflexively, I snap the sketchbook shut and rip my headphones out in the same motion. Wallace stands in front of me, holding the same piece of paper. My heart races in my chest; my neck twinges from how fast my head whipped up to look at him. He's frozen, eyes wide, like I caught him in the middle of something. He withdraws the paper a little, then holds it out again. In his other hand is a lunch tray.

The only noise comes from the leaves tap dancing across the ground and "Propane Nightmares" blasting from my headphones.

I take the paper. There's the last thing I wrote earlier—*Were you writing MS fanfiction?*—and below that, his response—*Yes.* Then on the next line, in pencil instead of pen, *Can I sit here?*

I'm sweating again. Dammit. Also I just realized I ripped the paper out of his hands, and now it shakes because I'm shaking. He doesn't think we're friends because I told Travis and Deshawn to stop picking on him, does he? Because we're definitely not. Does he think he owes me something?

I use my drawing pencil and write. *Can you talk?*

He takes the paper back, reads it, then puts it on the empty half of his tray to write. He hands it back.

Yes. Sometimes. Is this weird?

Weird? Yes. Bad? Depends.

You can sit down.

I move my sketchbook, backpack, and phone so he can set his tray down across from me. He really does look like he should be a football player—he has to fold his legs into the little picnic table bench, his shoulders hunched so his elbows reach the table—and he eats like a football player too. Two hamburgers, two french fries, two cartons of milk, and a Drumstick. His nose is crooked like it's been broken, and his cheeks are red from the cold.

When our eyes meet, he smiles a little. Just a little. He holds the paper down with one huge hand and curls the other around his pencil to carefully spell out something new. His lips move as he writes, like he's sounding out the words as he puts them down.

Thanks. I know Mrs. Grier already introduced us, but I'm Wallace. I write fanfiction about Monstrous Sea. It's kind of hard to make friends when you switch schools partway through senior year.

Probably also hard when you don't talk, I write back. *I'm Eliza.*

He eats with one hand and writes with the other.

Hi, Eliza. Yes, also the talking.

What kind of fanfiction were you working on?

He looks up after he reads that, then looks back down, then taps his pencil on the paper. *Right now I'm working on transcribing the comic into prose form. Into books.*

Books? I've thought of doing that myself—and I would, if I had any skill writing long form—but comics don't translate perfectly into books. The best I've been able to do so far is to compile all the comic pages into graphic novels available for purchase in the Monstrous Sea store.

That's a tall order, I write. *There's a lot of comic.*

He puts on that little smile again. It takes him a good three minutes to write.

The main story could probably fill a trilogy, and that's if I take the backstory out. The backstory—all the stuff with the Orcian Alliance, and Damien's pirates, and the Angels and the Rishtians—all that could fit another two or three prequels.

I take a deep breath. *And you want to write all that? For something you didn't even come up with?*

He shrugs. *I really love Monstrous Sea. And it seems like a challenge.*

I bite my lip to keep in this wash of emotion bubbling up in my chest. He doesn't even realize he's praising me. This is weird. And probably wrong, right? Like, I should tell him who I am. But what if that ruins this? I don't want him to know who I am because it's not who I am all the time. I'm not LadyConstellation right now. I can't be.

When I don't immediately answer, he carefully touches the tips of his fingers to the edge of the paper and reclaims it. He writes more and slides it back.

I actually need a new beta reader for it—would you want to read it? I saw some of your pictures the other day, and it seems like you know a lot about the world.

My hand hesitates before I answer.

I'm not much of a fanfiction reader. I don't know how much help I would be.

This is true; I try to stay away from the fanfiction because I don't want it to accidentally bleed into the story, and then have one of the fans say I plagiarized off them. I would be interested in seeing a prose transcription of the comic, but I don't actually know how good of a writer Wallace is, and I don't want to read it and have it be horrible and then I have to pretend to like it so I don't hurt his feelings. Though Wallace doesn't look like the type of person to have his feelings hurt easily—or at least he might not show it when he does.

He reads my note, then holds up a finger and puts down the second hamburger to reach into his bag. He pulls out a sheet of paper, covered in writing on both sides. Then he adds to our conversation, and hands both papers back to me.

Read the first page. If you don't like it, you don't have to read the rest.

I'm not sure if he understands that reading *any* of it will make it hard to say no to reading the rest, but I take the page from him anyway and flatten it out on the table in front of me. The breeze nips at the corner of the paper. Spelled out across the top of the page is the title *Monstrous Sea: A Transcription of the Comic by LadyConstellation.*

And below that, in his printer-precise handwriting:

Amity had two birth days.

This is my story. This is my story in words, something I could never do.

I don't need to finish the page. I already know I want to read the rest.

Wallace writes, *Is it that bad?*

"No!" My voice shocks both of us, a sudden sound in the quiet courtyard. Wallace stops with his Drumstick halfway unwrapped. I scramble for the paper and write down, *No, it's really good! How much of this have you done so far?*

Just one chapter, he writes.

Are you sure you want to let me read it?

I already typed this chapter up, so it isn't my only copy. You can mark on it too, if you want.

That wasn't really what I was asking him, but whatever. He fishes a sheaf of papers out of his bag and hands them over. They're covered front and back with his handwriting, and small, neat page numbers decorate the top right-hand corners. I slide them inside the front cover of my sketchbook, the safest place I know.

I can have them back to you tomorrow, I write. *Is that okay?*

He reads that and nods, smiling again.

Just a little.

CHAPTER 7

How I look has never seemed that important. Not the clothes I wear or the poor hairstyle choices I make, but my actual body. I'm not especially tall or short. No rampant acne or unfortunate placement of facial features. I'm not fat—Mom says my BMI is probably below what it should be, whatever that means. People don't point out how I look, but I've never been more aware of it than when I'm next to Wallace.

We walk back to the cafeteria together at the end of lunch. His legs are longer than mine, but he moves so slow we walk at the same speed. It's a weird kind of slowness; a lot of people move slow because they meander, like they don't know where they're going, or don't want to get there. Wallace moves slow the way those giant mechas move slow: there's so much to move it takes a while to get it going. But he knows exactly where he wants to be.

We walk, and I am acutely aware of my arms and legs, and what direction my feet point on the floor, and all the hair on my body. I wish there was something strange about the way I look so I could focus on that, assume *he's* focused on that, but there's just me.

We don't speak. Wallace folded up our conversation paper and put it in the pocket of his jeans, along with his pencil. We get a few looks from the tables we pass as we go to dump the trash from our trays. I imagine the looks are more for him than me, but maybe new-kid strangeness has worn off already. When he turns around, I notice for the first time the words in neat handwritten Sharpie along the bottom of his backpack:

THERE ARE MONSTERS IN THE SEA.

It's a fan-favorite *Monstrous Sea* quote. Dallas Rainer. He did say Dallas was his favorite character, but I always find it interesting when fans send me pictures of which quotes or pictures they put on their walls or their clothes, or even what they get tattooed on their skin. Though usually people do it because they think it sounds cool, sometimes it means something.

I don't get a chance to say good-bye to Wallace. We leave the cafeteria with the tide of students and get separated at a hallway, and he disappears.

◆ ◆ ◆

I see him again later, waiting outside on the bench. Travis and Deshawn are nowhere in sight. I hesitate by the doors, then creep toward him. He has headphones in, and he's writing something. Always writing something.

I tap him on the shoulder. This time, he's the one who jumps and rips out his headphones. I clench my fists tight around my backpack straps and press them into my stomach to stop them from shaking.

"Do you . . . do you need a ride?"

He shakes his head and scribbles quickly on the top of his paper. *My sister is coming to get me.*

"Oh. Okay." Of course he didn't need my help, stupid to ask. Not like he wasn't sitting here every day last week and managed to get home fine. "Well . . . see you."

I don't wait to see if he says anything back. I hurry to my Nissan and barricade myself inside. Then, finally, I smile.

I've never met a real live fan before. I didn't think about it until now, and it's a strange thing. All these people who love *Monstrous Sea*—they're numbers on a screen. Comments, views, likes. The bigger the numbers get, the less like people they seem. It's easy to forget they're humans like Wallace. Like me. Finding someone who likes it—who *loves* it—enough to make their own art about it and actually hand it to me themselves, instead of sending it to a P.O. box or emailing it, is surreal to the highest degree.

But he doesn't know I'm me. He doesn't know he handed his

fanfiction to LadyConstellation. That is definitely wrong. It feels wrong. But it's not like I'm going to use it to hurt him. And what was I supposed to do? Maybe if he knew who I was, he'd have shoved it at me and forced me to read it. I've never met fans in real life, I don't know what they'll do if they meet me.

I know, if I had ever met Olivia Kane, author of Children of Hypnos, I would have probably burst into tears and collapsed on the floor at her feet. I doubt Wallace will do that, but I don't want to take the risk.

Interacting with Wallace would be so much easier if he knew who I was. I would control every conversation. Every meeting. Every action and word that passed between us. LadyConstellation is a god who creates currents in her own world. Eliza is a guppy getting tugged along by those currents, unable to even see where they take her.

LadyConstellation will have to wait. For now—with Wallace, at least—I'll have to make do with Eliza Mirk.

CHAPTER 8

Two things wait for me at home.

The first is Emmy's care package, a neat little box taped with hearts and frosted with glitter.

The second is Davy. When I step through the door, his big white body careens around the corner and slams into my legs and hips, knocking me off balance. He never jumps, but stands there, tail wagging, waiting for me to pet him. Which of course I do, because who can resist petting their dog when he offers himself up like that?

I fall on him. Davy holds me up, panting and shedding and being adorable.

"Somebody's back from doggy camp!" Mom comes around

the corner after him, wearing her baby-talk face and making pouty lips at Davy. "You had a fun time with your friends, didn't you, Davy-Dave?"

"You don't have to talk to him like he's a child," I mutter into Davy's fur.

"What was that?" Mom says.

I straighten up. "Nothing."

"He got a nice long week running with the pack, and now he's back with us in time for Halloween. Aren't you, bud? Oh, Eliza, you got a package. I put it on the kitchen counter."

The way she says it, you'd think it had a bomb inside. She only puts things on the kitchen counter when she isn't sure if she wants to keep them or take them out to the garbage cans in the garage.

"It's from Emmy, Mom," I say.

She frowns. "From Emmy. What is it?"

"I don't know yet."

I release Davy; he follows me into the kitchen, Mom trailing not far behind him. I grab a pair of scissors and tear open the box.

Inside is a note from Emmy and a pile of assorted goodies one might expect to receive from a fourteen-year-old college student: hard-lead drawing pencils she probably got at a steep discount from the campus bookstore, or charmed out of some art student; a picture of a man made from a collage of body parts she must've found in magazines and online, who somehow manages to be anatomically correct; and of course a few packages of ramen. Mom makes a face at the man picture and the ramen. I ignore her and open the letter. It's handwritten; Emmy likes to dot her I's with hearts. Ironically, she says.

E!!!

You better like your care package! I know you said you needed some new hard pencils, so I hope you haven't bought any yourself yet. The ramen is for eating, because I know you forget to do that sometimes. But of course we both know the best part of this is the Mr. Greatbody. Yes, he has a name. I have taken everything you've told me about your perfect man over the years and I have created him for you. Marvel at my masterpiece. Feast your eyes on my fantastical creation.

Speaking of eyes . . . if his eyes fall off, it's because I ran out of glue. I'm a civil engineering major, not a craft supply store.

Love you lots!
Emmy

I look at Mr. Greatbody again. Strong jaw, striking eyes, lean muscle—honestly, it's the sort of thing anyone could find attractive.

I've never been picky about what guys look like, and I think Emmy buried a joke about that in here somewhere. I laugh anyway.

"What is that?" Mom asks. I taste the disdain in her voice.

"Nothing," I say, gathering up the box and its contents. "Inside joke."

"Is Emmy . . . Emmy's a girl, right?" Mom follows me again as I leave the kitchen and head up the stairs.

"*Yes*, Emmy's a girl. When have you heard of someone named Emmy *not* being a girl?"

"I don't know, but with these internet people, I thought I'd ask. . . ."

I clench my teeth to keep my mouth shut. I don't think she means to offend me anymore—she probably never did—but whenever we get into this conversation, one of us ends up too angry to continue. I jog up the stairs, Davy on my heels, and turn down the hall for my room.

"I'm not sure I like that they have our address, either," Mom starts.

"They're my friends. I don't give our address to people who aren't my friends." I step inside my room. Davy scoots in after me, and I close and lock the door. Mom's footsteps stop outside. Then comes her huff at the closed door.

"You should take Davy for a walk later!" she calls.

"Sully and Church take him for walks," I yell back. "They love it."

"What kind of homework do you have?"

"I don't know. Math. Physics."

"Make sure you get it done. We got a call from your homeroom teacher again, she's worried you aren't doing as much as you should be—"

"It's not like I'm applying to Ivy League colleges, I'm going to get in. Why does it matter?"

She doesn't answer, but I know what she'd say. First, that I should aim higher and not settle for any school less than the best—but right now, I don't care about learning, I care about drawing. And second, even non-Ivy League schools can be hard to get into, or I could lose scholarships, or whatever. It can't be that hard to get into college, because all kinds of people do it all the time. And I already don't have anything in the way of scholarships, and I plan on paying for college with the money I'm making off my *Monstrous Sea* merchandise. When Emmy made monstroussea.com, she also set up a store page where we could sell official gear—bags, notebooks, binders, pencils, shirts, buttons, wallets, phone cases, anything we could brand with designs and logos from MS. It's how I bought my computer, and the newest version of Photoshop, and most importantly, my pen display.

My parents don't know the extent of this. They know I bought the stuff, but when this all started, they helped me set up a bank account and gave me their tax man's phone number and told me if I wanted to make a little money off my hobby, I'd have to learn how to take care of that money myself, that it would be educational for me.

The comic didn't really start making me money until earlier this year, and as soon as I realized what was happening, I plucked up my meager reserve of courage and marched down to the bank to set up my own account, one they couldn't see online. I funnel money from it into my other account sometimes, so when Mom looks at it she still sees that I have income, but she and Dad don't know the actual amount. They don't know I could pay for college and make a living off of it.

I don't want them to know. I don't want them to become as involved in my online life as they try to be in my offline one.

Mom stomps away from the door. I'll hear about this when Dad gets back from . . . wherever he is today. Probably at some meeting about high-tech sporting gear. He'll say I should do my homework because it'll make me a well-rounded person regardless of what it does for my college options; he'll also say I should go walk Davy because it's good exercise. "Good exercise," aka the actual worst phrase in the English language next to "wake up" and "all the eggs are gone."

I drop my backpack on the floor, put Emmy's box on the desk—removing Mr. Greatbody to tack him up on the wall between two *Monstrous Sea* posters—and flop over on the bed with my sketchbook. The books in the headboard bookcase slump over on themselves. They're all different editions of the four published Children of Hypnos books, the series forever incomplete. Davy climbs up beside me.

For a minute, I lie on my side and bury my face in his ruff of white fur. The world becomes the quiet hum of the heater kicking on and the smell of dog dandruff. No one is watching me, or judging me, or even thinking about me. No one else is in the room. Davy sighs and lays his head across my arm.

After a minute I sit up and reach for my sketchbook. First my sidewalk-dirtied drawings fall out, then Wallace's papers. He actually gave me these to critique. To write on. And we only talked for the first time today. I don't know many writers, but I don't think that happens very often. Maybe he was just happy to have another *Monstrous Sea* fan to talk to. I hold the papers out to Davy; he sniffs them, nudges them with his nose, then lays his head on his paws and stares at me with big dark eyes.

"Good?" I ask. "I'll say that's good."

I flip through the pages. They have such a nice crinkly feeling, and they don't sit quite flat on each other because Wallace's pen strokes have warped the paper. I trace my fingers over the words without reading them. So clean and precise—one benefit of moving slowly, I guess. He could be an artist with this kind of dexterity.

I hold my excitement in check.

Amity had two birth days.

I read fast, flipping through pages like it's my job. It is kind of my job. Whatever. The story unfolds slowly but smoothly, moving through parts of the narrative I wasn't able to explore until later in the comic. I didn't expect Wallace to get the feelings right—Amity's feelings about Faren, the atmosphere of their home island, the scope of the story—but he did.

There were pictures of all this in the comic, one or two panels for atmosphere and sense of place, but he brings it alive in words. Maybe this is only because I know what it looks like. It's too good. This is like eating cake you didn't know you could have.

I made *Monstrous Sea* because it's the story I wanted. I wanted a story like it, and I couldn't find one, so I created it myself. And now someone else has remade it for me in a different medium—a medium I couldn't do myself—and he's letting me experience it. I am finally seeing the story I wanted, and even though I know how it unfolds, and I know exactly how all of these things look, it is new again.

This is more than I deserve. It's perfect.

Chills course the length of my spine. Too late I realize I'm crying, and a few tears drip on the paper. I curse, push the papers away from me, and pull my sweatshirt up to quickly wipe my eyes. Davy moves his head to rest it on my thigh.

"I'm okay," I say, but my voice shakes. I dab my sleeve on

the page to try to dry the tears. Wallace will probably see those tomorrow.

I am laugh-crying alone in my bedroom. Wonderful.

Wallace has read my mind. He has divined the things I thought while drawing this comic and put them down on paper. I don't understand it, and I don't know how this chain of events happened. But Wallace Warland can do magic. Actual, real magic. With words.

And it's not just that he read my mind. It's that he knows the material. Wallace knows the constellation Faren drew on the ceiling above their bed is called Gyurhei. He knows its mythology—or close, anyway. I could correct him on the page, but it seems like a shame to mark up such careful writing when I can't find anything else wrong, so I'll tell him tomorrow. None of that—the name, the mythology—was laid out in the comics. It was one of those things I had to explain when someone asked on the forums.

There's more. I flip the last page over.

It's a quote from *Doctor Faustus*.

"This word 'damnation' terrifies not me,

For I confound Hell in Elysium."

He remembers. Once, and I don't know if this was on the forums or in chat, I said *Monstrous Sea* was a combination of the Final Fantasy video games and the Faust legend. Most of the fans didn't know what Faust even was, they just knew it was Damien's last name. That was so long ago. Back at the beginning of the website, the forums. That post is long buried now.

But Wallace remembers.

CHAPTER 9

I spend a careful ten minutes sketching a stylized Orcus and its three moons around Wallace's *Doctor Faustus* quote. Then a serpentine sunset riser lifting out of the ocean on one side and a dread crow with wings spread on the other. I hope he doesn't mind.

I grab the gifts I've been meaning to send Max and Emmy—a copy each of the newest *Monstrous Sea* graphic novel compilation and a pack of Twizzlers for Max and Starburst for Emmy—and pack them up. Max lives in Canada; Emmy goes to school in California. Max's shipping is usually a killer, but whatever, I can write it off as business expense.

Then it's on to finishing a page of *Monstrous Sea* and starting another. I know the colors are on a computer and they're the same colors I always use, but today they seem brighter. The lines are darker, stronger. I already drew the character expressions in detail, but they look better too.

The forums are alive tonight. Rainmaker has posted another chapter of his latest *Monstrous Sea* fanfiction, *Auburn Blue*. I only know this because ninety percent of the people on the boards are looking at his fanfiction thread, and he's nowhere in sight. I don't think he ever sticks around to see what people say about his writing. A man after my own heart.

I ignore the thread. The only fanfiction I ever plan to read is what Wallace gives me. There's a purity to it, in knowing that it's so good and that I'm the only one who's seen it, that I'll never get from something published online. This is just for me. At least for now.

I stop and reread the chapter he wrote two more times. Then I check my messages.

Emmy and Max have advised. To put it lightly.

> *2:00 p.m. (emmersmacks has joined the message)*
> **emmersmacks:** Wait
>
> **emmersmacks:** So what happened with New Kid
>
> *2:30 p.m.*
> **emmersmacks:** But seriously
>
> *3:01 p.m.*
> **emmersmacks:** E!!

3:33 p.m.

emmersmacks: E I swear to God

3:59 p.m. (Apocalypse_Cow has joined the message)

Apocalypse_Cow: e's dealing with new kid again?

emmersmacks: Well I think so

emmersmacks: She isnt responding

emmersmacks: And Ive only been texting her every HALF-HOUR

emmersmacks: EEEEEEEE

Apocalypse_Cow: somehow I don't think yelling will make her look at her phone faster.

Apocalypse_Cow: why were you messaging her at 2:30? Isn't that like 11:30 your time? I thought you had that architecture class.

emmersmacks: Dropped it

emmersmacks: Architecture is stupid

Apocalypse_Cow: but you're a civil engineering major . . .

emmersmacks: Whats your point

Apocalypse_Cow: never mind.

Apocalypse_Cow: ELIZA. WHAT IS UP WITH NEW KID.

4:12 p.m.

emmersmacks: Let me just go die and rot in my dorm room

4:40 p.m.

emmersmacks: ughhhh

Apocalypse_Cow: *prepares funeral rites*

4:46 p.m. (MirkerLurker has joined the message)

MirkerLurker: Whoa, okay.

MirkerLurker: Obviously I should have checked this sooner.

emmersmacks: -_-

MirkerLurker: I got your package! I really like Mr. Greatbody.

emmersmacks: NEW KID

emmersmacks: NOW

MirkerLurker: What if it had gone horribly and I didn't want to talk about it? What if I found out he was a serial killer?

emmersmacks: For godsakes at least tell me what he looks like

MirkerLurker: Max probably doesn't want to hear about this stuff.

Apocalypse_Cow: actually, emmy built it up a lot and now i kind of want to know too.

MirkerLurker: Fine! Fine.

MirkerLurker: Dark hair, dark eyes. Taller than me. Built like a football player.

Apocalypse_Cow: a football player is writing fanfiction? remind me what world we live in.

emmersmacks: Im sure there are plenty of football players who also partake of the occasional fanfiction

emmersmacks: Go on E

MirkerLurker: He found me in the courtyard during lunch and came out to eat with me. It's kind of weird though—he only talks sometimes, I guess, so we wrote everything down.

MirkerLurker: He showed me this thing he's working on.

I stop. I could tell them exactly what it is, but Wallace didn't give it to me so I could go blab about it to people. Especially not Emmy and Max—I love them, but if they know someone is trying to transcribe *Monstrous Sea*, and if they know I think it's really good, they're going to want to read it too.

I don't want them to read it. Not only would it be without Wallace's knowledge or permission, it would kind of ruin this happy little bubble I'm in right now. It's a secret between me and Wallace, and I like it. I like being the only one who knows.

emmersmacks: What thing

MirkerLurker: Just some fanfiction. Haven't read it yet though.

Apocalypse_Cow: is he on the forums? what's his username?

MirkerLurker: Don't know. We didn't really get to that point.

I don't even know if Wallace is on the forums, though I feel like it's difficult not to know about the forums if you're a *Monstrous Sea* fan. Maybe Wallace doesn't post his work online.

Davy whines. I glance at the clock; it's dinnertime. He's standing at the door; I let him out so he can run to the kitchen, where Mom is already pouring his food. Church and Sully come pounding up the stairs as Davy goes down, and I shut my door before they can force their way into my room.

emmersmacks: Is that all you talked about?? Fanfiction??

emmersmacks: Boring

MirkerLurker: You've been watching too much Dog Days.

MirkerLurker: I'm pretty sure you don't have to suddenly have some super-deep relationship with someone as soon as you meet them.

Apocalypse_Cow: are you saying we didn't have a super-deep relationship as soon as we met?

Apocalypse_Cow: offended.

MirkerLurker: >.>

MirkerLurker: I don't know how to tell you this, Max, but uhhhh . . .

Apocalypse_Cow: no. the time has passed for all that. i am in a happy, committed relationship, and neither of you can talk me out of it.

MirkerLurker: How is Heather, anyway?

Apocalypse_Cow: well, she got a job with that modeling agency . . .

emmersmacks: -_-

Apocalypse_Cow: she's teaching sixth grade.

Apocalypse_Cow: but she could be a model if she wanted!

Oh, thank god. A conversation shift.

MirkerLurker: Haven't you been dating for like five years? Are you going to marry her?

Apocalypse_Cow: dunno

Apocalypse_Cow: if she says yes.

emmersmacks: ASK HER!!

emmersmacks: What are you waiting for???

Apocalypse_Cow: um

MirkerLurker: Leave him alone, Emmy. If he doesn't want to ask yet, he doesn't have to ask yet.

emmersmacks: Boo

Apocalypse_Cow: thank you, eliza.

Apocalypse_Cow: now, about that gentleman you spent the afternoon with . . .

MirkerLurker: We just ate lunch together!

Apocalypse_Cow: as you've said. however, i intend to get to the truth.

emmersmacks: Whats his name??

MirkerLurker: Wallace.

Apocalypse_Cow: . . .

emmersmacks: . . .

Apocalypse_Cow: . . .

emmersmacks: . . .

Apocalypse_Cow: . . .

emmersmacks: . . .

MirkerLurker: What's wrong with the name Wallace?

Apocalypse_Cow: it's, uh.

emmersmacks: Its silly as hell

MirkerLurker: Wallace isn't a silly name!

Apocalypse_Cow: it makes me think of a cartoon character.

emmersmacks: There are hardcore potheads on campus named Wallace

MirkerLurker: Why do you know the names of hardcore potheads on campus?

emmersmacks: Because theyre friendly

MirkerLurker: I am now concerned about your acquaintanceship with the potheads, but I'm not sure what you want me to do about Wallace's name.

Apocalypse_Cow: he doesn't go by Wally or something, does he?

MirkerLurker: He told me Wallace. So that's what I'm going to call him.

emmersmacks: Are you hanging out with him again

MirkerLurker: I don't know. Probably. I have to give him his stuff back.

emmersmacks: You better keep us updated

MirkerLurker: On what?

Apocalypse_Cow: I second that.

MirkerLurker: Updated on what?

emmersmacks: I have homework to do

emmersmacks: but when we talk tomorrow there better be some GOOD NEWS

MirkerLurker: GOOD NEWS ON WHAT?!

CHAPTER 10

There is a small monster in my brain that controls my doubt.

The doubt itself is a stupid thing, without sense or feeling, blind and straining at the end of a long chain. The monster, though, is smart. It's always watching, and when I am completely sure of myself, it unchains the doubt and lets it run wild. Even when I know it's coming, I can't stop it.

For example:

I know, when I walk into homeroom and return Wallace's chapter, that he will probably say thank you—written, of course—and maybe smile a little, and that may be the end of it.

But I feel, standing outside the door, that I will walk in and give Wallace the papers and his eyes will skim over me in indifference because he's realized he shouldn't have wasted his time on me. He shouldn't have asked me to read his work, because we don't even know each other. Yesterday was a fluke, a bad move on his part. He knows that now. He must. Eliza Mirk is no one, to nobody. They should make that the headline of the Westcliff Star every day. ELIZA MIRK: NO ONE TO NOBODY.

I use my sweatshirt sleeve to wipe my forehead. My freaking eyebrows are sweating, and I can't even tell Emmy or Max about it. A few people go in the room before me, and I creep inside in their shadows.

Wallace isn't there yet. I put the pages on his seat and curl up with my sketchbook. I trace the lines on an old drawing, making them too dark and too thick. Wallace arrives a minute later, lumbers in, and grabs the papers before sitting down. He flips through them, stares at the drawing I did in the back over the *Doctor Faustus* quote. My sketchbook slips out of my hands, and I have to catch it between my legs.

Then Wallace pulls out a new piece of paper. He writes something, then slides it onto my desk.

This picture is really awesome. No comments though?

I close the sketchbook and stop pretending. My writing comes out shaky against the paper.

Just one, but I didn't want to mess up your nice writing. Gyurhei comes out of the sea to swallow the sun every thousand years, not every hundred.

When he reads this, he covers his face with a hand and shakes his head. I shouldn't have corrected him. Why did I correct him?

He sends the paper back.

Wow. You are completely right.

Then, below that:

My usual betas wouldn't have caught that.

Because your usual betas aren't the creator of the world.

I hesitate for a minute, then write, It was really really good. And shove the paper back at him before my fingers spasm and rip it to pieces.

Thanks! Are you feeling okay? You look pale.

I'm fine—I always look like this.

Like a drowned rat in sweatpants.

Mrs. Grier gets up and starts taking attendance.

Okay then. Lunch again today?

It's going to be too cold in the courtyard. Wind.

I'll punch someone for a seat in the cafeteria. I'm good at stuff like that.

After I read this, he makes a show of placing his elbow on his desk and flexing his arm like he's stretching. His bicep bulges against his shirt sleeve. Then his elbow slips off the desk and he catches himself, glancing around. A laugh escapes me.

Mrs. Grier pauses, looking back with her onion earrings swinging in her ears, and says nothing. She never calls out students for things like this. I clamp my lips shut until she continues reading. Then I write:

I don't have anything to top that. Sorry.

He smiles and replies, Can't top genius.

✦ ✦ ✦

Wallace does find us a table at lunch, but it's because he gets there early, not because he punches anyone.

The table is at the end of the lunch lines, so after I get my food he's sitting right there, smiling like he's proud of what he's done. His lunch is the same as yesterday: two hamburgers, two orders of fries, two milks. One Drumstick. There are papers on the table across from him, with a note stuck to the front.

Only if you want.

The top page says *Chapter Two.*

"Really?" I notice too late, again, that I've said it out loud. Wallace doesn't seem to mind, though—he grabs another piece of paper to write on.

New beta?

I don't have a pen handy. "Yeah. Yes. Definitely." I know my voice is too quiet now. When he doesn't speak, it feels like I shouldn't either, like I'm ruining the atmosphere. I dig in my bag for my pencil, then reach for his paper. He gladly hands it over.

Sorry I keep forgetting to write. You think I'd remember, considering how much time I spend online.

It's okay. You don't have to if you'd rather talk.

I don't know if I would.

He smiles a little. *So you're online. On the MS forums?*

Yes. Sometimes.

Username?

I give him the only one I can, the only other username I have.

MirkerLurker.

Let me guess—you don't post much.

Not if I can help it. What about you?

Do you read the MS fanfiction?

Sometimes.

You know rainmaker?

Everyone knows rainmaker.

Hi.

No fucking way. I look up and he's looking down, putting ketchup on his french fries like he said nothing of significance. There is no fucking way this kid sitting in front of me is THE rainmaker. The head honcho of *Monstrous Sea* fanfiction, the most popular person on the forums behind LadyConstellation, shepherd of a million fans. This is NOT the guy who winky faced at me last week.

I write:

NO FUCKING WAY.

and I hold it right under his nose.

He gingerly takes the paper from me.

I'll message you later to prove it.

I almost believe you right now because people don't lie about being RAINMAKER. Is this why you like Dallas so much?!

I became rainmaker because I liked Dallas, not the other way around.

I scan the cafeteria. Someone else must be witnessing this

right now. Someone else must be in on this monumental revelation, because this doesn't happen in everyday life. Rainmaker does not just wander into my school and drop a transcription of *Monstrous Sea* into my lap.

But he has. And no one around us understands what has just happened. No one at the nearby tables knows who we are or what we're sharing.

Right now, it's only us.

Here.

Wallace takes the paper back and writes, *What are you doing for Halloween on Friday?*

Probably going to be dead in my grave because rainmaker goes to my school and I didn't know it until just now.

He purses his lips together to hold back a smile. *But really.*

He wants to change the subject like that? Fine, whatever. *Probably hiding in my room and watching the Dog Days Halloween special.*

That DOES sound like the holiday of a lifetime.

Why, what are you doing?

There's a bookstore my friends and I hang out in that throws a Halloween party every year. We're going to dress up as MS characters.

I've seen tons of pictures of *Monstrous Sea* cosplay online—and it's all pretty great cosplay, if I do say so myself. But I've never seen it in real life.

Let me guess. You go as Dallas.

Very astute. Anyway, I was thinking, if you didn't have anything else to do, maybe you'd want to go. It's a bookstore, so it's not like the party gets wild, and everyone there is nerdy book people. If you don't want to, that's fine.

He wants me to go to a party. I haven't been to a party since Kenny Smith from next door invited me to his birthday when we were eight, and that ended with me getting pushed into his pool and laughed at all the way home.

Can I think about it?

Yeah, of course.

I'm not going. I like to tell myself I might go—I like to tell myself I might do a lot of things—but I and my brain and everyone else know that I'm going to chicken out in the end and barricade myself in my bedroom with a plate of pizza rolls and my Netflix subscription.

I feel bad writing it down on the paper, that I'm going to think about it.

Monstrous Sea Private Message

2:54 p.m. 28 - Oct -16

rainmaker: Hey, it's Wallace. Please tell me I blew your mind again. You make the best face when your mind is being blown.

MirkerLurker: Whoa that sounded dirty.

rainmaker: Too much?

MirkerLurker: Ummmmmmmmmm

rainmaker: Too much. Noted.

MONSTROUS SEA FORUMS

rainmaker *

Fanfiction Moderator

AGE: Not telling you

LOCATION: NO

INTERESTS: MS. Writing things. Campfires. Sweaters. Sleeping in. Dogs.

Followers 1,350,199 | Following 54 | Posts 9,112

[Unique Works 144]

UPDATES

View earlier updates

Oct 20 2016

> The next chapter of the Auburn Blue fanfic will probably be a little late. Just started at the new school. So, that's fun.

Oct 21 2016

> Thanks to @joojooboogee for my new avatar!
> #DallasRainerForever

Oct 23 2016

> If math homework were a real person, I'd be doing 25 to life. #Mathslaughter

Oct 24 2016

> There might actually be other MS fans at this school. THANK JESUS I'M SAVED.

Oct 26 2016

> Life is destroying me today. No time to write. Stupid math. #Mathslaughter

Oct 27 2016

> Definitely another MS fan at this school.
> Pros: Awesome; Not alone; Pretty girl.
> Cons: Pretty girl. #Fuuuuuuuuck

Oct 28 2016

> Heyyyy let's not talk about the pretty girl anymore okay she's probably looking at this.

CHAPTER
11

Wallace thinks I'm pretty.

Wallace thinks I'm pretty?

Did he put that there because he knew I'd see it later? Is he trying to lure me into some kind of trap? Wallace doesn't seem that conniving, but I don't know, I'm not a teenage boy.

Wallace thinks I'm pretty.

This is weird.

I have on a sweatshirt two sizes too big and jeans worn so often you can't see the shape of my legs inside them. My hair's okay, I guess, when it's not covered in glitter. It's not that I think I'm ugly, I just don't think about what I look like. I don't live *out there*. If I had my way, I wouldn't *look* like anything at all. I would be a free-floating consciousness that can also somehow draw. I don't care how I look. I don't want to care.

It is weird for him to point it out. No one points out how I look. I am not a "point out how she looks" kind of girl.

I really want to bring this up with Emmy and Max to see what they think, but I can't, because I don't want them to know Wallace is rainmaker. Like telling them about the transcription, it seems like a betrayal of trust. I could say he said that to my face, but I know for a fact Emmy skims through the Angels' update feeds at least once a week, and she'll definitely see it on rainmaker's page. It doesn't take an engineering prodigy to put those two things together.

But Wallace gave me another chapter of *Monstrous Sea*, so he can't be kidding. He put time and thought into this. He cares about *Monstrous Sea*—he wouldn't use it to hurt someone. Right?

CHAPTER 12

On Wednesday, Wallace and I hang out at school like nothing different has happened. And by "hang out," I mean we pass notes in homeroom and sit together at lunch. I try not to gush too much over the second chapter of his transcription of *Monstrous Sea*. When I pass him on the bench outside school at the end of the day, he looks up and waves good-bye, and I don't feel the need to sprint to my car and lock myself inside.

Thursday's the same, but when I get home that day and check my messages to see if Emmy and Max have gotten their packages yet, I find a new message thread from Wallace.

2:47 p.m.

rainmaker: So, how about that Halloween party? :D

rainmaker: If you don't have a costume, I bet you could put a sign on your shirt that says "lurker." I know my friends would think that was the best thing ever.

rainmaker: btw they're all huge MS fans. Don't know if I mentioned that.

rainmaker: Also I'm driving, so don't worry about getting there.

Well. I suppose he really wants me to go. That must be a good sign. I thought he was as quiet and weird as me, but he's not at all. He's not exactly the center of social life at Westcliff, but this is way more forward than I'd be with anyone. If I invited someone somewhere—unlikely—and they told me they'd think about it, I'd end up barricading myself in my room and never speaking to them again.

Here's what I know about this party so far:

- Wallace wants me to go
- Wallace's friends will be there
- There will be *Monstrous Sea* cosplay
- I will miss the *Dog Days* Halloween special
- It will be at a bookstore, which is not particularly partyish

It doesn't sound completely terrible. And I'm sure if I don't like it, I can find some excuse to leave. But I'll miss doing my live commentary on *Dog Days*.

Wait. I get up from the computer and stick my head out my bedroom door, looking over the balcony railing.

"Hey!"

"What is it, Eggers?" Dad walks out of the kitchen in his windbreaker and running shorts and looks up the stairs.

"Do I have to walk around with Church and Sully for Halloween this year?"

Dad frowns. "Church and Sully are doing Halloween this year? Are they too old for that yet?"

He asks it honestly, because he really doesn't remember. He knows they're in the same grade, and that they're under fourteen because they play on all U-14 sports teams, but anything beyond that is details. Sully is fourteen, Church is thirteen; born eleven months apart exactly, and most people think they're twins.

"They're kind of too old for it, yeah," I say.

"Oh. Well, ask your mom."

"Is she home right now?"

"No, she took Davy for her quick 10K with her marathon students."

"What? Davy can't run a 10K!"

He holds his hands up in surrender. "They're jogging, and the slow students always take care of him anyway. He's fine."

Mom teaches classes for people who want to get in shape to run marathons, which means by definition everyone who signs up is out of their minds. The idea of them pulling my old dog around does not put me at ease.

The front door opens behind him, and Church and Sully barge in, shoving each other over the threshold. They nearly crash into Dad, who steps out of the way just before they reach him.

"Hi, boys," he says genially, smiling again and following them into the kitchen. Their conversation floats up the stairs to me. "How was school today?"

"Macy Garrison stole Church's calculator and wouldn't give it back until he promised to buy her a candy gram on Valentine's Day," Sully says. The refrigerator door bangs against the counter and the shelves rattle as they pull food out.

"I'm not going to do it, though," Church says, quieter.

"Were you two going out for Halloween?" Dad asks. I creep down the stairs to hear them better.

"No," Sully says. "Halloween is for little kids."

"I thought we were . . . ," Church says, his voice tapering off at the end.

"Eliza wanted to know if she had to take you guys out again."

"Eliza hates doing stuff with us," Sully says.

It's not true—I don't hate doing stuff with them, it's just that most of the stuff they like doing is stuff that makes me uncomfortable or angry. Like throwing balls, or moving faster than a quick walk.

Sully yells, "NO, ELIZA, YOU DON'T HAVE TO TAKE US TRICK-OR-TREATING!"

I slink back up the stairs and catch the tail end of Church muttering, "Geez, kill my eardrums."

Well, great. Now I don't even have the excuse of having to take Sully and Church out for Halloween. I could lie, though, and say I do . . . Wallace wouldn't be able to see through that, right? He doesn't know where I live, or how old my brothers are, or even how serious we are about Halloween, which is not at all.

But I don't *want* to lie to him. I'm already lying to him about the LadyConstellation thing, though that's more omission than anything else.

Normally I don't have any problem lying my way out of things. Of course, normally the only people I have to lie to are my parents and brothers, and all I have to say then is I'm sick, or have too much work. My family is easy like that. I don't have friends from school who ask me to do things. Not until now.

I return to my computer, sit, and scratch at the edge of my pen display for a moment. A *Monstrous Sea* page is still pulled up on its screen—Amity fending off hordes of enemies with the Watcher's orange crystals. Amity wouldn't lie to someone to get out of something. If she didn't want to do it, she'd say it right to their face. And if she was unsure, she'd go do it anyway to test the waters. She's a quiet, keeps-to-herself kind of person, but she's not scared of doing things and going places.

I'm not normally one to take advice from my own fictional characters, but there comes a point in every girl's life where she reaches a crossroads: a night alone with her sweatpants and her favorite television show, or a party with real, live, breathing people.

I know what I *should* do. Call it guilt, my parents' voices permanently embedded in the back of my head. *What are your plans this weekend, Eliza? Going out with anyone? Any friends from school? No hot parties?* Hot parties. Only my parents would say "hot parties," and they're not even that old. I'm allowed to say no to their ideas for sports and physical exercise, but so far I haven't found a good way to deflect their questions about my nonexistent school friends and social life. I say "social life" because anything that happens on a computer isn't social to them. If I told them I was hanging out in a Halloween chat room with a bunch of people on the *Monstrous Sea* forums, they'd ask if I actually knew any of these people, and then they'd hover around my door, trying to peek inside all night.

If nothing else, going to this party would get them off my back.

I bring up Wallace's message on my computer and fend off doubt with a gnawed-on lion tamer's chair.

2:47 p.m.

rainmaker: So, how about that Halloween party? :D

rainmaker: If you don't have a costume, I bet you could just put a sign on your shirt that says "lurker." I know my friends would think that was the best thing ever.

rainmaker: btw they're all huge MS fans. Don't know if I mentioned that.

rainmaker: Also I'm driving, so don't worry about getting there.

3:11 p.m.

MirkerLurker: Okay, sure. :)

CHAPTER 13

I don't need the lurker sign.

Last year, a *Monstrous Sea* fan cosplayed one of the characters, Kite Waters, at a con, and posted pictures of it on the forums. When I said—as LadyConstellation, of course—that it was the best Kite Waters cosplay I'd ever seen, she mailed me the costume. Well, she mailed Emmy the costume, and Emmy mailed it to me. It's Orcian Alliance military dress, a white suit with green trim and gold buttons, devoid of any markings of rank because Kite has none. It even includes Kite's boots and her black saber (made of some kind of foam or packing material or something).

The good news is, the costume looks so different on me, Wallace will never recognize where it's from. Everything is too baggy. I slip the belt to its last hole and it's still not enough. I pull the jacket tight to myself and feel my ribs hard against the material. I guess it's fine—it wasn't made for me, anyway.

I stand in front of the mirror and feel only slightly ridiculous dressing up as one of my own characters, even though it doesn't look half bad. It feels like real clothes and looks like real clothes. The girl (I should call her a genius, really, some kind of sewing savant) who made it and wore it first was an islander—Filipina, I think—like Kite, so it looked right on her, made her actually look like Kite, whereas on me it just looks like a costume.

"YOUR BOYFRIEND IS HERE," Sully yells from the foot of the stairs, and a minute later Dad's voice follows, saying, "Eliza, your friend is in the driveway."

When I told them where I was going, Mom and Dad both lit up like the mini marathon had come early. I told them they were not allowed to ask questions, and somehow, magically, they resisted. I told them I was going with a kid from school. I was very careful not to say "boy from school," but Sully has single-handedly rendered that a moot point.

I grab the black saber, the pair of crisp twenties I pulled out of the bank earlier, and my phone, and creep out of my room. Mom and Dad are both standing at the door, looking outside and speaking quietly to each other. I make my way down the stairs.

"What are you supposed to be?"

Church stands in the doorway to the living room, munching

on a granola bar, looking way too lanky in his basketball shorts and T-shirt. Sully appears behind him a minute later, wearing almost exactly the same thing, just a touch taller.

"Is that something from your comic?" Sully says.

Mom and Dad have turned around. Great, let's just get the whole Mirk clan in on this Make Fun of Eliza fest. Bereft of my stealth, I stomp down the stairs, past my parents, and yank open the door.

"I'll be back later," I grunt. "I have my phone."

I close the door behind me and hurry down the driveway. Wallace waits at the end in a swamp-green Taurus, but it's dark and I can't see his costume. My heart juts out a staccato rhythm in my chest and my stomach sloshes around like the great foaming tides of Orcus. I slide into the passenger seat.

"Hi," I say as I buckle my seat belt.

"Hi," he says back.

I stop. His head is turned toward me, but he looks away, at the dashboard, out the windshield. His voice is so much softer than I expected. I imagined he'd be extra loud, maybe to compensate for all the time he spends quiet, but no. It's deep and soft, like a fat fleece blanket in the middle of winter.

"You only talk sometimes?" I say.

He nods. "Alone in my car is okay. School is . . . too much. With my friends, yeah, and sometimes with strangers. Still not weird?"

"No, not weird."

He looks me in the eye and smiles the little smile.

"You make an *awesome* Kite Waters," he says.

My body heats up a few degrees. I remembered deodorant. "Thanks," I say, then look him up and down. "I thought you were going as Dallas?"

"I am," he says. "The wig and the scarf are in the trunk. They're kind of dangerous to wear while driving."

"Ah. Good point."

"You ready?"

"Ready enough."

"So where did you move from?"

We round the corner and continue down the long road that connects my neighborhood to the rest of Westcliff. Wallace's headlights blink on in the growing darkness.

"Illinois," he says. His voice sits comfortably above a whisper.

"Why?"

"Family got new jobs." He pauses. "And my mom likes it better here. I have a few friends here too, so it's not so bad."

"To each their own, I guess."

"You don't like it?"

I shrug. "Maybe, maybe not. I've never been anywhere else, so I don't know if I'd like it better somewhere else, but I'm tired of Westcliff. I'm tired of that high school. And small-town nonsense.

Everyone knowing everything about everyone. Have you read the *Westcliff Star*?"

"Yeah."

"It's stuff like that. All the stories they run—you know how they've had the story about Wellhouse Turn for the past few weeks? That's all they cover this time of year. So little goes on that they have to focus on the killer road. It's kind of . . . disturbing."

"Disturbing?"

"They just get so focused on one or two things. They should leave people alone."

He glances over at me. Smiles. "Got something to hide?"

"No," I shoot back. "I'm just saying, I'd rather be somewhere where no one looks twice at you, no matter what you are."

"I get that."

We climb a hill, drive through a patch of trees, and start over Wellhouse Bridge. On the far side of Wellhouse Bridge, illuminated by Wallace's headlights and the fading sun, is Wellhouse Turn: a sharp jackknife in the road where the ground falls away.

The flowers and other decorations from the picture in the *Star* are still there, some old and wilting, others fresh. There's a bent and mangled metal barrier that gets put back up every time someone drives through it and goes over the side. The steep incline leads to the river below where, some say, you can find old car parts embedded in the ground.

I wonder if death comes quickly for those who go off the

turn, or if the long tumble to the bottom takes years.

Wallace slows nearly to a stop at the turn. Most people slow down here, but never this slow. And never with unblinking rigidity. I get a glimpse of the drop. Even walking down the incline seems like a terrible idea. I bet it would hurt if you slipped, even a little.

Wallace's face looks pale while we're in the turn, but then we pull out of it and beneath the next yellow streetlight, and he's fine again. As if nothing was wrong to begin with.

"Bet you don't have places like that in Illinois," I say.

The used bookstore Wallace's friends told him about is called Murphy's. I've heard of it in passing but never been here; post-Children of Hypnos, I didn't read much, and after that I bought all my books online. Wallace jokes that the store's full name is Murphy's Law. I pray it isn't, because a lot of things could go wrong tonight, and it would be great if they didn't.

Murphy's is a tiny little brick shop sandwiched between two other tiny little brick shops, with a big happy MURPHY'S BOOKS sign in the tall windows and lights on and bodies moving inside. The tiny parking lot is full when we get there, so Wallace squeezes his car into a spot on the street.

Before we go in, he pops his trunk and uses his phone as a flashlight to get out what he needs, because the trunk light doesn't work anymore. He pulls out a lump of what looks like seaweed and a long blue-and-white striped scarf. He winds the scarf around his neck twice, leaving one end hanging down his chest and the other down his back. Then he pulls the lump of seaweed on over his head and shakes it a little so the strands fall in the right places across his face.

"How does it look?" He holds out his arms. Beneath the scarf he wears a ratty button-down shirt and a pair of pants that have been striped vertically, dark blue and green, with fabric paint. Strictly speaking, he's not tall or narrow enough to be Dallas, but damn, he makes it look good.

"Wow."

He spins for me, and the scarf even moves like it should, the ends swishing at his ankles. "Where did you get that?"

"My sister crocheted it for me."

"Kind of sad you have to wear shoes, though."

"Yeah, had to ditch Dallas's bare-feet-as-pacifism metaphor in favor of foot safety."

"You look awesome."

"*We* look awesome."

I strap the saber around my waist before we enter Murphy's.

I think if I had to pick a party to come to, it would be this one. The walls are lined with books, and short bookcases separate different sections of the room. A refreshments table is set up beside the checkout counter. "Monster Mash" plays over the store speakers. A flock of Hogwarts students in black robes and house scarves take up most of the middle of the room. A couple of faeries, a vampire, and a witch chill against the back wall. Fixing the pumpkin decorations around the cash register is a girl dressed as a sushi roll.

"I would kill for sushi right now," I say.

Wallace pulls out his phone. I get a text.

Oh, god, me too. We should get some after this.

Leaving a party for sushi? Yes, please.

Wallace leads me to a dark corner where probably the second-largest group of people has congregated. I almost trip over my feet. They're all dressed in *Monstrous Sea* cosplay. Some have Amity's white hair, or Damien's silverware necklace. Some have the white lines of Nocturnian constellation tattoos drawn on their faces or arms. A large portion of them wear the high collars and red/gold/black color scheme of the Rishtians.

When they see us, several cries of "Dallas!" and "Kite!" welcome us. Wallace smiles, his ears turning pink, and reaches back for my hand to pull me through the crowd. I let him take it. His palm is rougher than I expected from a writer, but warm. We hold on to each other tentatively, and when we reach the table at the heart of the group, Wallace lets my hand slip out of his.

Seated at the small table is a young woman with a toddler in her lap, and a boy our age, smiling at the screen of a laptop. The woman is dressed up with the wild brown hair—wig—and layered desert clothing of Imi, another of the Angels; and the toddler, a little girl, is dressed in a tiny outfit to make her look like Imi's daughter. The boy wears an Under Armour shirt with a high collar—no doubt supposed to be the precise, temperature-regulating thermatrol suits the Rishtians wear—and a jacket made to replicate the one worn by Rishtian aeronauts. Food from the refreshments table litters the space between them.

The boy and the woman glance up at the same time and say, "Wallace!"

The boy turns the laptop toward us, where two more girls sit in one video chatroom.

Wallace starts texting again. Another message pops up on my phone; this time a group message with four numbers I don't recognize.

Hi, guys, Wallace writes. I brought a friend. He steps to the side so I can't hide behind him. This is Eliza. Eliza, this is my friend Cole and his cousin Megan. He motions to the boy and the young woman. And Leece and Chandra. The girls on the computer. They each say various versions of hello, giving me enough time to swallow past the knot in my throat and say it back.

"Wallace said you're on the forums," says Cole. I'm glad he dressed like a Rishtian; he has the sharp, shrewd look many of them wear.

"Um. Yeah. I just don't talk much." Only for Dog Days, which I am currently missing. I left a message on my LadyConstellation page saying I was sick and wouldn't be able to watch, so hopefully no one gets upset. "Are all of you?"

My phone pings.

Oh, right. I forgot to tell you. They're the other Angels. Sorry—I guess it wouldn't be obvious that we're friends in real life too.

I look around at them. These are the Angels on my forums? The next rung down on the popularity ladder from me? And all in one place?

My head feels light. One hand goes for my phone and the other searches at my side for something to hold on to, but there's only open air.

Wallace goes on. *Cole is Fire Served Cold, Megan is Quake, Leece is Tree Chimes, and Chandra is Dark Switch.*

It doesn't mean much until I put the formatting with the names. I see them all the time in different parts of the forums:

Fire_Served_Cold, rainmaker's friend, who hangs around the live chats.

QUaKE, who supervises the roleplaying boards.

~*treechimes*~, who can be found fangirling over the *Monstrous Sea* custom merch threads.

And darkSwitch, who draws probably the best fan art I've ever seen in my life.

With Wallace as rainmaker, together they make the Angels, the guardian clans of Orcus. In the story, the Angels are the ones who keep the planet in balance. When something—like the corrupted hand of the Alliance—threatens that balance, they intervene. These Angels keep the balance on my forums, as moderators.

I feel like I stepped into Power Rangers. They wait for me to say something.

"Um" is all that comes out.

"You make a *great* Kite Waters," says Cole. "Too short, though."

"*Cole*," Megan warns. She bounces the little girl on her lap, who giggles. "You look great, Eliza, don't listen to him. Now sit down, both of you. Eat something!"

It's half invitation and half demand. I slide onto the seat next to Wallace. The saber gets stuck in the chair legs.

"Turn me toward, Wallace!" cries the girl on the computer, Chandra. Cole swivels the laptop around until Wallace and I appear in the webcam. I sink down farther, face hot. "Wallace," Chandra says, "what is this nonsense about the new *Auburn Blue* chapters not going up soon? Izzy and Ana are the only canon ship I like, you *cannot* disappoint me with this."

Sorry. Wallace shrugs. *Soon. I have the rest of the story outlined, I just have to find time to write it. School's been killing me lately. And with the transcription . . .*

"Oh, yes, the transcription you won't let anyone see yet."

You can see it when more is finished!

"Don't worry about it, Wally," says the other girl, Leece. Leece and Chandra sit in two very different rooms; Chandra's walls are blank and dark brown, while Leece's are bright and covered in *Monstrous Sea* posters. A huge stuffed seacreeper rests beside a pillow behind her. "If you have the inspiration to work on the transcription, do that. Besides, Chan doesn't know what relationships are good for her."

"Excuse you!" Chandra barks. "Were you there when Izzy and Ana were forced into their arranged marriage? Were you there when they formed a relationship of mutual trust over the inner workings of airship engines? What about all the times they saved each other while fighting the Alliance? They never even knew if they romantically loved each other—they just grew together. And that is perfect and beautiful and no one can take it from me!"

"Excuse me, everyone?" A voice comes over the speakers. The girl dressed as a sushi roll at the cash register holds a microphone. "It's almost time for the costume contest. If you'd like to be entered, please come fill out an entry card and put it in here." She holds up a jar shaped like a grinning skull.

"Oh, *yes*." Cole pushes himself out of his seat. "Anyone else entering? Wallace and Eliza, don't answer. I'm putting your names in anyway."

Before I can say no, Cole is gone.

Wallace's shoulder bumps mine. *He's always like this*, he texts only to me. *We won't do it if you don't want to.*

I dig my fingers into the edge of the seat and stare at the tabletop, deepening my breaths so it doesn't feel so much like my lungs are being crushed. Stand in front of all these people, in this costume that isn't even mine, and expect them to, what, applaud? I'll fall on my face.

"Eliza?"

I look up. Wallace, Megan, Leece, and Chandra all stare at me.

"Um, what? Sorry?"

"Oh, honey, don't look so worried!" Megan says. "I just asked how long you've liked *Monstrous Sea.*"

"Maybe three years?" I say.

"Wow, so you liked it pre-Masterminds," Leece says.

I liked it pre-everything.

"Is Kite your favorite character?" Chandra asks.

"Uh, no . . . Izzy is."

"Mine too!" Chandra jumps in her seat, her squeal loud enough to crackle the computer speakers. "No one understands the greatness that is Izarian Silas! That idiot Cole dresses up like Rory as if *he's* the best Silas, but the only reason Rory Silas is any good is because Izzy is his father!"

On the other side of the screen, Leece gasps.

"Take that back, you whore!"

Chandra cackles. Megan belatedly covers the toddler's ears, but the toddler isn't paying attention anyway. Wallace shakes his head and smiles.

CHAPTER 14

Cole marches back, chest puffed out in pride, with three cups of punch for him, me, and Wallace. Megan has a no-spill water bottle that the toddler knocks over every ten seconds. I nurse the punch close against my chest and hunker down in my seat while the five of them talk. I am better this way, unseen and unheard, hidden in Wallace's bulky shadow. Some of the other *Monstrous Sea* fans have migrated away from our table, so I turn my face to the empty space beside me whenever I need to breathe.

I learned years ago that it's okay to do this. To seek out small spaces for myself, to stop and imagine myself alone. People are too much sometimes. Friends, acquaintances, enemies, strangers. It doesn't matter; they all crowd. Even if they're all the way across the room, they crowd. I take a moment of silence and think:

I am here. I am okay.

Then I let myself listen in on the conversation again, and slowly slip back into it.

It is amazing how much you can learn when you keep your mouth shut. In half an hour, I know that Cole is a high-school sophomore, a rising baseball star who keeps his love of *Monstrous Sea* a secret to ward off any unwanted questions about his potency on the diamond; Leece is the biggest collector of *Monstrous Sea* merchandise probably anywhere, and is a world-class gymnast living in Colorado who uses the comic as her go-to relaxation therapy; Chandra's across the Atlantic, in India, and though her parents don't entirely approve of the subject matter of her drawings—most of which involve different *Monstrous Sea* characters embracing in one fashion or another—she sees it as a way of life; and Megan lives a few towns away and is a single mother to the toddler, Hazel, and she works one job as an office assistant during the day and the graveyard shift at the Blue Lane Bowling Alley at night.

Megan was into Monstrous Sea *first,* Wallace tells me, *and she got Cole into it, and that was how he and I met. Then we found Leece and Chandra and took our Angel personas, and the rest is history.*

Every once in a while they ask something about me. Friendly questions. How old am I? How did I meet Wallace? What do I do for fun besides read *Monstrous Sea*? I do my best to answer them, not just for Wallace's sake, but a little bit for my own too.

These are not enemies. They're not going to make fun of me for what I like or how I spend my time. They may not be my friends, but they are my people, and just because they're not behind a screen doesn't mean they're not worth talking to.

Still. I miss my quiet bedroom and Davy and my computer. What's going on with *Dog Days* right now? Are people missing LadyConstellation in the chat?

When sushi-suit girl calls up entrants to show off their costumes, Cole manages to pull Wallace out of his seat to stand awkwardly out there, but I refuse when my name is called.

"It's just for a second," Cole says, motioning me out with his hands. "Come on. Just a second."

"I don't . . . I don't really want to."

Wallace gently pushes Cole out of the way so he can get back to his seat and grab his phone.

If she doesn't want to, don't make her do it.

Cole sighs so overdramatically he must be joking, then turns to tell sushi girl I won't be participating after all. A few more people from other groups around the room go up. There's a panel of teenaged judges stationed behind one short bookcase like it's a desk, and at the very end they get together to deliberate before they announce one of the Hogwarts students as the winner.

"Oh, come on!" Cole cries. "The Harry Potter people always win! They've had like twelve years to put their costumes together!"

"I've done my waiting," Megan says to Hazel, pulling up the

little girl's arms. "Twelve years of it! In Azkaban!"

Cole and Wallace tear through most of the food on the table, which I guess means we're not going to get sushi after all. By nine thirty, Leece and Chandra have both signed off and Cole has packed up his computer, and Hazel is fast asleep against Megan's shoulder.

"Time for us to go, I think," Megan says. "It was nice seeing all of you again. We'll have to get together soon. We could plan a *Monstrous Sea* meet-up."

Wallace gives Megan an awkward side-armed hug good-bye. When she pushes her way through the bookshop doors, she lets in a blast of chilly October air.

"I should probably go too," Cole says, scrubbing at his hair and disheveling it even more.

I thought your curfew was eleven? Wallace texts.

"Nah, Mom moved it back to ten when I broke it two weeks ago. What's that look for? I just forgot how late I was out! You know how it is when you're at a girl's house!"

Wallace rolls his eyes.

"Look," Cole says, leaning on the edge of the table so he can stare Wallace in the eye. "That new school has got to be better than the old one. It *has* to be. Right? Things have died down, but you're better off there."

Wallace shrugs. Cole claps him on the shoulder. Then it's me and Wallace in a rapidly emptying bookstore. Why would Westcliff be better than his last school? I don't dare ask, at least not right now. All I want right now is to get out of here.

You up for that sushi?

"You still want to get it?" I ask. "You just ate all this food."

He smiles. *You obviously haven't been paying attention to my lunches. If you say eat, I shall eat. And I can eat a ton right now. So, sushi?*

"Yes, *please* sushi."

We push through the door, and the cold air tears through my costume. We hurry to Wallace's car; I jump into the passenger seat while he throws his wig and scarf in the back, cranks the heater, and sets off for the sushi place he knows.

"Why do you know so many more places to go around here than I do?" I say. "You haven't been here that long."

He shrugs, still smiling. When we get to the restaurant, the glowing sign above the door says SUSHI.

"Is this minimalist, or could they not think of a name?"

"I . . . don't know," Wallace admits. It's nice to hear his voice again. "Honestly, it could be either one."

It's late enough that the dinner crowd is dying down, and the post-trick-or-treating stoner crowd hasn't shown up yet. The inside of this vaguely named place is actually very clean and chic. The hostess seats Wallace and me in a booth, and the walls behind the seats rise up to hide us from our neighbors.

"Fridays are half-price night too," he says, looking eagerly through the menu. "What do you usually get?"

"Um." I hate telling things like this to people. "Just California and Philadelphia rolls." I know exactly what people think about stuff like this: "Do you even like sushi?" "You just get the boring rolls. You're not even eating the good stuff." "Wow, you're boring. What is even the point of you?" "Be more interesting."

"Oh, that's an awesome idea," Wallace says, still looking at the menu. "Keep it simple. I could eat a whole table of Philly rolls right now."

We order as soon as the waiter brings our hot towels. I wrap mine around my cold hands and melt into my seat. My family always says I have cold hands, but I don't notice until something warms them up.

"Was the party okay?" Wallace asks. "I'm glad you were able to go."

"Able to go," meaning "barely beat doubt back into its corner," so I guess he's right with that.

"Yeah. It was . . . it was fun."

Wallace, who has been staring at his hands, glances up. "Really? You didn't say much."

"I usually don't."

"You talk a lot at school."

I smile. "I write a lot at school. And I didn't do that, either, before you showed up."

He hesitates. "How come?"

"I don't know. I just don't like it."

"You're not super into school, are you?"

"Not really, no."

"I'm not, either." He looks down at the table again. "It feels like I already know what I want to do, and school is wasting my time. Like they assume we don't know what we want to do, so they make us keep doing everything. I can't wait to leave."

"*Right?*" The force of my voice shocks even me. Wallace looks up again. "I . . . I mean—*yes*, it's exhausting. I keep telling my parents that. I just want to focus on art, and I'll probably get into college, so why does the rest of senior year even matter?"

"It's stupid, right?"

"*So* stupid."

He leans back in his seat. "Thank god. I thought I had cabin fever or something."

"High school fever."

"High school fever: like *The Shining*, but with teenagers."

I laugh. Wallace smiles. The waiter brings us our sushi, and happiness trickles from the crown of my head to the soles of my feet. Part of me knows it's silly to be happy that someone finally *gets* it. My parents *get* it. They know I don't like school and I don't want to be here anymore. I'm sure most of my teachers know that too. They know I care about my art more than any homework, or sporting event, or dance. They might even get that it's easier to be online, though I doubt that one.

But Wallace is the first person I've met who gets all of it.

Sometimes, when Amity woke from her rebirth dreams, in the long minutes she spent watching Faren sleep, she imagined what it would be like if she had never accepted the Watcher's offer.

Faren would be dead.

Maybe she would be too.

The Watcher would have no host, and the Nocturnians would wait patiently until it did.

CHAPTER 15

Wallace *gets* a lot of things.

He gets that the stuffed crust pizza at lunch should be eaten up to the crust, then the crust should be peeled back and eaten, and the cheese inside should be balled up and consumed last as the crowning jewel of the meal. He gets that sweatpants and sweatshirts are infinitely better than any other types of clothing. He gets that talking is easier when there's a screen or even a piece of paper between you and the person you're talking to.

The first half of November has passed before I notice it going. Every day I wake up and experience the strange sensation of *wanting* to go to school. Now I linger at my locker in the mornings, not because it's too difficult to get my feet to move and start the day, but because Wallace waits for me there, and I like standing in the hallway with him better than sitting in homeroom. Sometimes I go to his locker instead, and we linger there for a while. We don't talk, because there are too many people around and Wallace doesn't like writing on vertical surfaces.

In my classes I throw myself into *Monstrous Sea* sketch pages, cranking them out in the hours before and after lunch, hiding them in the bottom of my backpack so Wallace won't find them. Not that I think he'd look through my stuff. I don't. But my sketchbook might fall open, or a wayward Travis Stone might show up and take them and spread them around for the whole school to see. At lunch, Wallace and I sit together—in the courtyard, if it's warm enough, but usually at one of the tables in the cafeteria—and he forks over new transcribed *Monstrous Sea* chapters when he finishes them, and I devour them like the hungry beast I am, and he kind of smiles. Wallace *gets* it.

Wallace gets the feeling of creating things.

"Do you ever have an idea for a story, or a character, or even a line of dialogue or something, and suddenly it seems like the whole world is brighter? Like everything opens up, and everything makes sense?" He looks down at his sheaf of papers—the latest *Monstrous Sea* transcribed chapter—as he says it. We sit outside the tennis courts behind the middle school. Leaves dance over the empty courts in the chilled breeze. I told Mom I'd pick up Sully and Church after school so I had an excuse to hang out with

Wallace. We're on opposite sides of our bench, turned to face each other.

"I think that's why they call it a breakthrough. It cracks you open and lets light in."

He looks up and smiles. "Yeah. Exactly."

He has dimples. Sweet Jesus, dimples. I want to stick my fingers in them. He looks very cozy in his sweater and coat and knitted hat with the strings hanging down and the little puffball on top. I'm not cold, but I could be warmer.

"Do you ever write your own stuff?" I ask. "Instead of fanfiction?"

"Sometimes," he says, "but I don't think it's as good as my fanfiction. It's easier with fanfiction. Fanfiction is just playing with someone else's characters and settings and themes. I don't worry if it's any good because it's fun. But when I try to write something of my own, it's just . . . constant worry. It never seems good enough." He picks at his papers. "Do you ever draw anything besides MS fan-art?"

"Sometimes," I say, and we share another small smile. "*Monstrous Sea* is all I'm really interested in right now."

"Could I see some of your pictures? The *Monstrous Sea* ones, I mean. I glanced at them that one day, but I didn't get a chance to look."

I've read his fanfiction; it seems unfair not to let him see some of my drawings. The front of my sketchbook, held safely under my hands on my lap, is stuffed with loose-leaf sketches of Monstrous Sea characters and places. It's concept art, but to Wallace it would look like practice and interpretations. I slide a few of them out, check to make sure none of them are sketches for actual comic pages, and hand them over.

Wallace takes his time. Like everything, his examination is slow and methodical. He scans the picture, lingering on some spots; he slides a finger between that page and the next to separate them, then lifts the top one off; he replaces it carefully on the bottom of the stack, and when all the papers are lined up again, looks at the next one.

"I'm thinking about putting the transcription up on the forums," he says. "To see what people think."

"They'd love it." It won't be just for me anymore if he does that, but maybe that's good. Maybe I'll stop feeling so guilty for not telling him who I am.

He glances up. "You should post these online. You've gotten closer to LadyConstellation's style than anyone I've ever seen before. These are amazing." He turns to the next page. "Oh, wow. I really like this one."

I sit up on my knees to see over the edge of the paper. It's a sketch of Kite Waters I did in class the other day because I couldn't stop thinking about Halloween. Kite wears a torn Alliance uniform, bloodied from battle, holding her saber defiantly at her side.

"You can keep it, if you want," I say.

"Are you sure?"

"I'm not going to do anything with it."

"Put it up online."

I ball my hands in my sleeves. "I don't think that's a good idea."

"Why not?"

"I don't want to. It makes me nervous."

"You shouldn't have anything to be nervous about—they're amazing. Everyone will love them."

I shake my head. He can't know, of course, that I'm not nervous about people rejecting them, but about someone linking anything I post as MirkerLurker to LadyConstellation. Plus, I don't know, these pictures are for me. They're concepts, half-formed thoughts. They're not polished and ready for the world, and I don't want anyone to see them. I'm half convinced the only reason *Monstrous Sea* has done so well is because I'm a stickler for perfect pages. Plot, lines, colors, characters. My fans deserve the best-quality work I can give them. I know that's not the whole reason, but it's got to be at least part.

"Okay." He hands the other pictures back to me and keeps the one of Kite Waters. Smiles at it again. "Thank you. Do you mind if I show this to Cole and Megan and the others? They won't share it if I ask them not to, but this is just *so* cool—I have to show it to someone who gets it."

"Sure, I guess." If Wallace says they won't share it, then I believe him. They're nice people, anyway. Even I can tell that much.

The buses begin pulling around the middle school to line up for the end of the day.

"Guess I should go back to my car so my brothers can find me."

"I'll walk with you."

We head toward my car, parked at the far end of the tennis courts.

"Doesn't your sister usually pick you up?"

"Yeah, my stepsister," he says. "But I have a younger sister who goes here, and my stepsister picks her up too. So Bren said she'd get me when she gets Lucy."

"Bren and Lucy?"

"Yeah. Yours?"

"Sully and Church."

"Those are short for . . . ?"

"Sullivan and Churchill. Ed Sullivan, Winston Churchill. Never asked my parents why, never going to ask them why. Just glad I got a normal name."

"Huh."

"What?"

"I never asked why my parents named me Wallace."

"Why don't you ask them when you get home?"

He looks down, picks at his ear. "I can't."

"Why?"

His voice gets quieter. "Both my parents are, uh . . . are gone."

Gone? Does that mean dead? Or absent? Not knowing exactly what "gone" means makes a strange hollow in my stomach, reminding me I don't know as much about him as I thought.

"Oh." Heat floods my face. "Oh, sorry."

He shakes his head. "It's okay. My family is kind of weird. Two stepparents, one stepsister, one half sister. They're all really nice, though. I guess I shouldn't call Vee my stepmom anymore; she was technically my legal guardian. But I'm eighteen, so maybe it doesn't matter. . . ."

I've never known anyone in real life with stepparents. The fact hits me after several seconds' delay, followed immediately by a hot wash of shame. I complain about my family all the time—in my head, to Max and Emmy, even a few times to Wallace, in little messages through the forums, or in quick, throwaway sentences in our paper conversations at school. I assumed his family was the same way. I never thought about the fact that while my family bugs the shit out of me, they are my family, my flesh and blood, still working as a whole unit.

Not that his isn't. He could love his family as much as I love mine. Maybe more, because he never complains about them.

God, I don't know anything.

We reach my car. The doors of the school fly open and thirteen- and fourteen-year-olds spill out, speed-walking to their buses. Wallace waits by my car with me in semi-awkward silence until we see the brown-haired heads of my two brothers charging toward us.

"I'll see you tomorrow," he says.

"See you," I say.

He heads off toward the front of the school, where his younger sister no doubt waits. Sully and Church reach me, backs bent with the weight of their bags, their sports gear already in hand. They're talking about some fight that broke out in the cafeteria today, not paying attention to me as they jump into the car and buckle themselves in. I wait at least a full minute to see if they notice they're not moving, then get into the driver's seat.

"What took you so long?" Sully says.

I shrug, and turn on the car.

Monstrous Sea Private Message

MirkerLurker: Why is Dallas your favorite Monstrous Sea character?

rainmaker: Because he never gives up, even after all the bad things that have happened to him.

MirkerLurker: You don't think he's broken? Most people think he's broken.

rainmaker: I think he's strange, but anyone would be after years of torture and exile. He's doing the best he can. People literally hunt him down, and he still tries to help Amity and Damien understand what the Scarecrow and the Watcher are, where they came from, and why they exist. He becomes Amity's best friend, even though everyone thinks he's incapable of friendship. He's arguably the most powerful character in the series, but he would never use that for revenge or personal gain.

rainmaker: Plus he's funny. He's technically older than most of the other characters, but as soon as he gets to Risht he starts dismantling metal trees like a little kid with a new toy.

MirkerLurker: Aw, I like him for that too.

rainmaker: Izzy's your favorite, right?

MirkerLurker: Yeah, most of the time.

rainmaker: Most of the time?

MirkerLurker: I like all the characters, but usually Izzy is the one I like the most.

rainmaker: Why?

MirkerLurker: Because he was a scaredy-cat. Or . . . because his character arc wasn't that he stopped being a scaredy-cat, but that he learned to act in spite of his fear. He had to. He had to overcome his fear of being married to Ana, his fear of being a ruler, his fear of raising children, his fear of the Alliance, and the idea that he had no power. He never stops being scared, but he doesn't let it stop him from doing what he has to do.

rainmaker: Very good, very good. However, I see you have forgotten to mention a silly reason for liking him.

MirkerLurker: Haha it's his glasses, obviously! The irony that the king of the city of advanced technology won't get ocular implants because he's terrified to put things in his eyes.

rainmaker: Weird, I didn't know you had such a thing for timid guys.

MirkerLurker: Really does it for me when a guy is paralyzed with fear on a regular basis.

rainmaker: Aw. Sad.

MirkerLurker: What's sad?

rainmaker: That it would never work between us. I'm too courageous.

Izzy, Dallas, + Davy

CHAPTER 16

If there's one thing my parents like more than sports, it's family togetherness. Board games, movie nights, vacations. The rest of the year is off-season training; the holidays are in-season, practice every day, games twice a week.

My parents are so into family togetherness that Thanksgiving is like the tournament playoffs. How much can Dad get Eliza and Church and Sully to help him cook? How great can our conversations be at dinner? How easy will it be to get Eliza and Church and Sully to wash the dishes afterward? How many board games can we play? How long can we keep Eliza away from her phone and computer?

Normally we spend Thanksgiving with Aunt Carol and the

rest of the extended family. We get to Aunt Carol's house; Uncle Frank calls Sully and Church "tykes" and ruffles their hair, even though last year they were as tall as he is; Mom and Dad plant themselves at the center of the party, helping with prep and food, flitting around to speak to all the aunts and uncles and cousins at least once; and I sit in the corner with my phone, dreading the moment some family member comes up and asks me what I'm "doing these days." This means they want to know about school, and if I've decided to venture back into the heinous world of sports, and what I'm doing for college. I have my stock responses. "Fine." "No, no sports." "I applied to a few different places. Kind of weighing my options right now." They give me some platitudes about how I'll find my place, and how college is great and I'll never want to leave, and how there are lots of places out there looking for smart girls like me to come make the big bucks. Only my immediate family knows about me and *Monstrous Sea*, and they think it's a hobby. Most of my extended family doesn't even know I like to draw.

I wonder what I look like to them. I must be this bland girl who stares at a blank cell-phone screen all day. Every year, by the end of the night, I want to scream. I want to throw my chair, knock over the table, tear down Aunt Carol's dining-room chandelier. I want to rage.

In some ways I've accomplished more than any of them, and I can't tell them. I don't want them to know it, because that would be a catastrophe, but I do want them to know it, because then maybe they'll stop treating me like I'm some empty-headed teenage drone off to serve my life sentence. Maybe then they'd leave me the fuck alone in the corner with my turkey and my mashed potatoes and my phone.

This year, though, Aunt Carol has the flu and the rest of the family is going to Florida, because I guess going to Florida for Thanksgiving is a thing people do. I don't have to field questions from the rest of the family, a miracle tarnished only by the fact that my parents have decided that in exchange, this will be the most Mirk Thanksgiving that ever Mirked.

It's just the five of us. Sully and Church help Mom roll out pie crust in exchange for the crust leftovers, while I hide at the far end of the kitchen table, awaiting whatever terrible job Dad can come up with next. I hold my phone under the table so none of them can see it, even though they'd know I was texting if they looked at me.

emmersmacks: Ugh I wish I had your Thanksgiving

emmersmacks: Stuck at school right now finishing final projects

emmersmacks: Cant go home until winter break :(

MirkerLurker: I'll trade you.

Apocalypse_Cow: all holidays are overrated anyway.

MirkerLurker: Even Christmas? Presents?

Apocalypse_Cow: a. i don't celebrate christmas. b. i'm pretty sure most parents don't get a lot of gifts for their twenty-two-year-old son anyway. c. yes, christmas is the most overrated of all holidays.

MirkerLurker: ?? I thought Heather celebrated Christmas? Or is she too busy with her sixth-grade-teacher modeling to deal with that this year?

Apocalypse_Cow: eh.

MirkerLurker: Is something wrong?

Apocalypse_Cow: nah. heather went home for the holidays.

Max being weird is . . . weird. I wait for more explanation, but none comes. Something must have happened between him and Heather, but if he won't say it here, then he won't say it anywhere. It would be nice, I guess, if he was sitting in front of me—then at least I'd have a facial expression or some body language or something to go off of. Max and Emmy once suggested we video chat, but I vetoed it. It felt wrong, somehow. Like we would ruin what we had by showing each other our faces. Now it seems like it might be helpful.

A text comes from Wallace.

An actual text too, not a message through the forum app. I gave him my number awhile back, before Halloween, but not because I wanted him to call me or anything. I wrote it on the edge of our conversation paper in homeroom and slid it over to him because sometimes I see something and think, *Wallace would laugh at that, I should send him a picture of it,* but the messaging app is terrible with pictures and texting is way better.

So he texts me now, and it's a picture. A regular sweet potato pie. Beneath the picture, he says, *I really like sweet potato pie.*

I text back, *Yeah, so do I.*

Then he sends me a picture of his face, frowning, and says, *No, you don't understand.*

Then another picture, closer, just his eyes. *I REALLY like sweet potato pie.*

A series of pictures comes in several-second intervals. The first is a triangular slice of pie in Wallace's hand. Then Wallace holding that slice up to his face—it's soft enough to start collapsing between his fingers. The next one has him stuffing the slice into his mouth, and in the final one it's all the way in, his cheeks are puffed out like a chipmunk's, and he's letting his eyes roll back like it's the best thing he's ever eaten.

I purse my lips to keep my laugh in, but my parents are fine-tuned to the slightest hint of amusement from me, and they both look up.

"What's so funny, Eggs?" Dad says.

"Nothing," I reply. Nothing makes a joke less funny than someone wanting in on it, especially parents.

Wow, I say to Wallace. *You really like sweet potato pie.*

He sends one more picture, this one with him embracing the pie pan, gazing lovingly at it. *We're to be married in the spring.*

An actual laugh escapes me. I really hope Wallace is having a better Thanksgiving than I am. It seems like he is. I take a picture of myself pouting and send it to him, saying, *Aw, the cutest of cute couples.*

"Stop taking selfies," Sully says from the other side of the room.

"I wasn't taking selfies," I snap back.

"Why were you taking selfies?" Church asks.

"I wasn't taking selfies!"

"Eggs, why don't you go ahead and put that phone away so you can help me with the cranberry sauce?" Dad says, looking chipper. I clamp down on the immediate frustration that bubbles up in my chest, leave my phone on the table, and get up to help.

Dinner begins as it always does, with Mom joking that we'll be spending all of tomorrow working to lose the calories we eat today. For the rest of them, that's a challenge—see how much you can eat now so you get to do more fun exercise tomorrow. Personally, it makes me want to fast.

Then my parents move on to asking me, Sully, and Church the latest updates from school, and how well we think we're going to end our semesters.

"Church is going to ask Macy Garrison out before Christmas," Sully says. Beside him, Church's face turns a mottled crimson.

"No I'm not!"

"You two sure have been talking about this Macy Garrison a lot," Dad says. "When are we going to get to meet her?"

"You're not going to meet her!"

Sully smiles through the mashed potatoes stuffed in his mouth. Swallows, and says, "And Eliza's hanging out behind the middle school with her boyfriend every day. You guys haven't met him, either."

"He's not my boyfriend!" I snap, my face heating. Sully looks between me and Church and laughs.

"Every day?" Mom says, glancing first at me, then at Dad. "Is that why you wanted to pick up Sully and Church from school, Eliza?"

"I—no! I just thought they wouldn't want to ride the bus. Wallace has to pick up his sister from the middle school anyway, so—he's not my boyfriend!"

Dad holds up his hands. "Whoa, whoa there, Eggs. Your mom and I think we should meet Wallace before this goes any further."

I am burning in the deepest pits of familial humiliation. "Nothing is going to go further. There is *nothing* to go further. Can we stop talking about this?"

Now Mom's holding up her hands too. "Honey, your father's just saying that, you know, this is the first time you've really hung out with a boy, and we should think about scheduling a few doctors' appointments—"

"STOP."

Sully has his hands clapped over his mouth to keep in his laughter. Church's forehead rests on the table beside his plate, his ears and the back of his neck bright red. I sink against my chair. My hands and feet have gone numb. I stuff a green bean into my mouth, chew, swallow, nearly barf it up, then stand from the table.

"May I be excused?"

I don't wait for an answer before I march out of the room.

I have never been so happy to spend an hour immersed in *Monstrous Sea*. I'm on the Great Continent, sketching clouds in a pale blue sky and a ravaged battlefield circled by carrion feeders. Hywolves, raptors, the fanged KiriKiri battlefield mice that spring from the earth to rip rotting flesh from corpses and drag it to their underground nests as food for their young. Fans often ask where I get ideas for the monsters of Orcus. I tell them I don't know, but it's easier to come up with monsters when you're angry or upset.

KIRI KIRI

battlefield mouse

I only stop when I hear Church and Sully pound up the stairs and into their room. It must not be board-game time yet. I check my phone.

Another picture from Wallace waits for me. In this one, an empty pie pan littered with crumbs sits on the floor beside a large knife. Wallace kneels next to it with more crumbs on his sweater, expression horrified.

NOOOO

WHAT HAVE I DONE

MY LOVE

OUR MARRIAGE

'TIS ALL FOR NAUGHT

I text back: *Oh no!! Not sweet potato bride!*

Another picture comes: Wallace sprawled on the floor beside the pie pan, one arm thrown over his eyes.

Let me only be accused of loving her too much.

Wallace is definitely having a better Thanksgiving than me. I wonder if his family asks if he has a girlfriend, and how much further things are going to go. I wonder if he says yes. I wonder how much further he wants to go.

I could ask him.

I probably won't.

The Watcher had to have a host.

The pilgrims who visited for Amity's blessing told her so, each and every one of them. The Watcher had to have a host, because its counterpart already had one, and that threw the world out of balance.

"Its counterpart?"

The old woman who had come to see her—the first of many pilgrims to come—nodded slowly. For the Nocturnians, who defied aging, the deep creases in the woman's face spoke of long decades, perhaps even centuries, of life. A cluster of stars was tattooed over her right cheekbone, the same constellation she was named after. Like all the name tattoos, it was white and nearly camouflaged against her skin.

"Across the sea, they call it the Scarecrow. Its host has been gone from the island for many years. He has abandoned his guardianship. If he ever returns here, you must bring him back to order."

"There's—there's another host?"

"His name is Faust," the woman said. "And he eats souls."

emmersmacks: So how was the turkey??

emmersmacks: Seeing as the only turkey I got was the soupy stuff they serve in the student center

Apocalypse_Cow: you could've asked me this in october. you know, when we canadians celebrated our thanksgiving. it was overcooked, thank you.

emmersmacks: Okay sour goose

emmersmacks: Lets hear from the less salty side of this trio

MirkerLurker: Ehhhhh, it could have been worse. It could have been one of my aunts saying I should have a doctor check out my vagina, instead of my mom.

Apocalypse_Cow: um.

emmersmacks: Seconding that um

emmersmacks: What exactly prompted this??

MirkerLurker: Ehhhhhhhhhhhhhhh.

MirkerLurker: You know Wallace? My parents think we're doing stuff together.

Apocalypse_Cow: i thought you already were.

MirkerLurker: No, we aren't.

emmersmacks: Ew

emmersmacks: Not to you and Wallace doing stuff

emmersmacks: To your mom being all like

emmersmacks: VAGINA EXAM

MirkerLurker: She scheduled the appointment for next Wednesday. Kill me now.

Apocalypse_Cow: can't, you have to finish monstrous sea.

Apocalypse_Cow: also you should probably stick around to keep doing commentary for dog days. I was scanning some of the forums for trolls after halloween and people were concerned that you were gone.

Apocalypse_Cow: also also i believe you have a foot to eat.

MirkerLurker: Oh, yeah. I saw those.

emmersmacks: We really did miss you though

emmersmacks: Are you feeling better??

MirkerLurker: Actually, I was never sick. . . . I went to a Halloween party with Wallace.

Apocalypse_Cow: wait. you're telling me . . . hermit eliza mirk . . . went to a PARTY . . . with a BOY?

Apocalypse_Cow: and you expect me to believe the two of you aren't doing anything?

MirkerLurker: We aren't doing anything! I went to the party because I thought it would get my parents off my back.

MirkerLurker: Plus there was some really awesome Monstrous Sea cosplay there.

Apocalypse_Cow: is there anything else we should know about? harbored fugitives? cult of cthulhu in your basement? secret love of greek yogurt?

emmersmacks: Leave her alone Max

emmersmacks: E if you want to go to parties GO TO PARTIES

emmersmacks: Go to parties for those of us surrounded by parties but unable to attend due to our unfortunately young age

emmersmacks: . . .

emmersmacks: Also you should definitely go out with Wallace because I am surrounded by cute older boys and CAN'T GO OUT WITH ANY OF THEM

MirkerLurker: I don't know.

Apocalypse_Cow: don't know what? if he's cute or if you want to go out with him? you could send us a picture and we'll tell you.

emmersmacks: That is true I definitely would

MirkerLurker: Haha I don't need you to tell me if he's cute or not. I know he's cute.

emmersmacks: Then whats the problem

MirkerLurker: I don't know!

Apocalypse_Cow: look, e. lemme give you some advice.

emmersmacks: Yes

emmersmacks: Advice from the guy who keeps calling his girlfriend a model

Apocalypse_Cow: if you like him, you might as well say it to him.

Apocalypse_Cow: if he doesn't like you, you can stop worrying about it.

Apocalypse_Cow: and if he does like you, you're in business.

Apocalypse_Cow: either way, you'll save yourself a lot of time and pain.

CHAPTER 17

Max and I don't agree on everything, but we see eye-to-eye on this particular thing least of all. I didn't think it would be possible, but admitting to Wallace's face—or even to his username on a screen—that I like him seems like as bad an idea as telling him I'm LadyConstellation. Either bit of information could drive him away.

He has another chapter ready for me on Monday. He has started posting them online—to great response from the fandom—but I still get first look at all the chapters as soon as he finishes writing them. Amity is preparing to leave Nocturne Island for the first time in her life, to hunt Damien Faust for the Alliance; she doesn't want to leave Faren behind, because she won't be there to protect him. In it is a scene the whole fandom knows well, a staple of the series.

Wallace nails it.

The early-morning calm while Amity traces the constellation-name tattoos on Faren's back. The melancholy breakfast where neither of them admits she'll be leaving soon on a mission that is very likely to kill her. And finally, before she goes, Faren's gift to her: the discovery that Amity herself was named after a constellation by her birth parents, though Faren doesn't know what the constellation is called. If Amity can figure that out—what the constellation is called and what culture claims it—she might find out where she came from, and where she belongs.

He had found her in a constellation.

In the comic, Amity repeated it to herself often. "He found me in a constellation." The fandom altered it slightly, made it "You found me in a constellation," and put it on posters, shirts, phone cases, bracelets, actual tattoos. One couple even said it in their wedding vows. It wasn't why I called myself LadyConstellation, but most people thought it was.

I didn't understand what it meant when I wrote it, when I drew Amity saying the words. I understood what I wanted it to mean. I understood what the words literally meant. But I didn't understand the truth behind it.

I guess I still don't. At least now I know it.

CHAPTER
18

As it turns out, it's difficult to keep up a high page count when you spend all your time after school texting the boy you like.

At five p.m. every day, I force myself to turn off my phone, cut my internet connection, and draw. I have to have at least one page a week, and between Thanksgiving and winter break, I average two. It's the quality. I could get whole chapters out if I didn't care about the quality, but quality is king. Quality makes this story look on the outside the way I feel about it on the inside. It's big and colorful and beautiful. The characters are alive. When a page doesn't look as good as it could, shame worms its way into the marrow of my bones, because I've let the story down.

On the weekends, I take breaks. First, so I don't burn out, and second, so I can draw pictures for Wallace. I still haven't posted anything online like he said I should—like Cole, Megan, Leece, and Chandra also said I should, after he showed them that picture of Kite Waters. But I like drawing for Wallace because he likes looking at them. I draw him pictures of Dallas: Dallas playing with a seacreeper, Dallas looking into the bioluminescent tide pools in his cave, Dallas walking along the shore beneath the stars. I try not to make them look too much like actual panels of the comic, but every time I hand him one he beams and says how it resembles LadyConstellation's work.

I know I should stop. I know I shouldn't give him any more evidence.

I kind of wish he knew.

I don't tell him what my family said at Thanksgiving, or that my mom took me to see a doctor. Thinking about the birth control has me short of breath and sweating like a pig. I sweated in the doctor's office, and when the doctor found out that I did that on a daily basis, even she thought something was wrong, and that the birth control might regulate it.

The birth control is not regulating it. The birth control is making me sick to my stomach. It's a strange feeling to like someone so much and yet be terrified to have them in your space, touching you. It isn't that I don't like it when we touch—when we brush arms or when he taps me on the shoulder or when I pick a piece of lint off his shirt. I like it too much. My body gets excited without my permission, and it's not okay. It's out of control. I don't like out of control, but I like Wallace.

So I don't know if it's lucky or unlucky that Wallace and I are limited to homeroom, lunch, and a half hour on the bleachers behind the middle school every weekday. We share an English class too, but Wallace sits on the opposite side of the room. On Saturday afternoons we get in his car and head to Murphy's, where we meet up with Cole. Megan comes if she doesn't have to work and if Hazel is behaving. Cole brings his laptop and gets Chandra and Leece on video chat, but only if Leece has a break from gymnastics and if Chandra is awake, since she's ten hours ahead of us.

"Do you ever think it's weird that we come to a bookstore every week and don't buy any books?" Cole asks, paused, yet again, over his unfinished geometry homework. At this rate, he'll be done next July.

"Speak for yourself," Wallace says. The only reason he speaks is because the bookstore is empty except for us and the one employee stocking books on the far side of the shop. Wallace slumps in the seat beside me, boxing me in, the spine of a book balanced against the table and his eyes moving slowly across the words. I feel like he must be able to absorb everything, know everything about a book, because of how slow he reads. If I like a book, I devour it in one sitting, and then I forget a lot. It's fine with me, because I read them over and over again. But Wallace will take weeks to read a book—shortened to days, if he really likes it—and he remembers all of it, and then he doesn't read it again. At least, he said, not for a very long time.

"Have you ever read Children of Hypnos?" I ask. Cole, Wallace, and Chandra all look up. I don't talk much around them—I prefer listening—but I still like them. I like that they don't expect me to talk. They don't mind that I don't.

"I've heard of it," Wallace says, "but never read it."

"Wasn't that the fandom that cannibalized itself after the author went crazy?" Chandra says.

"She didn't go crazy," Cole says. "She ran into the mountains and barricaded herself in a cave."

"Isn't that covered under 'going crazy'?" Chandra asks. "She chases people off her property with a shotgun, screaming bloody murder. I heard she has all booby traps set up."

"She didn't go crazy," I say. "She just . . . couldn't finish."

The truth is, no one knows the reason Olivia Kane stopped writing. She isn't in the mountains, and she doesn't chase people off her property with a shotgun. As far as I know, she just turned into a hermit. Vanished into the countryside of North Carolina one day and never came back. Once she disappeared, reporters couldn't even get a reason out of her. Plenty of people have heard about the fandom, at least. It ripped itself apart through arguments over speculations about a finale that would never come.

"They're my favorite books," I say. "You should read them."

"Books written by a hermit lady in the mountains?" Cole hops up right away. "Let's see if someone has them around here. Hey, Abigail!" He trots to the girl stocking books—sushi girl from Halloween—and starts up a conversation. Abigail nods at something Cole says and takes him over to a corner of the store. He comes back with a stack of all four Children of Hypnos books in the original hardback covers, though a little worn from their previous owner. "Check it out," Cole says. "They had two full shelves of them back there."

Wallace picks up the top one and reads the inside flap.

"Nightmare hunters, huh?" he says. He closes it again and looks at the front cover. A decorative illustration of a war hammer inlaid with the symbol of Hypnos, a closed eye.

I pick up the second book. On the cover is a great sword. "Yes! So the premise is like, strong dreams and nightmares can cross over into the real world, and we need these people, dreamhunters, to send them back to the dream world. It's an alternate-universe Earth where this whole nightmare hunting system is embedded in society; there's a Hypnos government, and the dreamhunters are like special agents, and they're stronger and faster than normal people but they don't live as long, and they rarely sleep. They have these cool weapons too, like on the covers—weapons they grow from the dream world, that match their personalities. Oh, and my favorite character—okay, I have a lot of favorites, but the main favorite—he never sleeps, and his dream world is this Frankenstein lab, and his nightmares are huge poisonous monstrosities."

Wallace cracks open the first book and starts reading. Cole and Chandra stare at me.

"That is the most I have ever heard you say at once," Chandra says.

I slide a little in my seat, yanking the front of my sweatshirt to get air. I only ever spoke about Children of Hypnos with other fans online. Never anyone in real life. I didn't know all that would come out.

"I'm buying these," Wallace announces, and takes the stack of books up to the counter with his wallet.

While he's paying, Cole asks Chandra what she's working on and she shows us a picture of Damien and Rory from *Monstrous Sea* vigorously making out. Cole scowls.

"Why do you have to put my favorite character in gay situations?" he asks.

Chandra rolls her eyes and proceeds to list off all the times in the comic there were very canon undertones to legitimize Damien and Rory's very fanon gay relationship.

"Damien's already bisexual, my Damien-Amity ship sank back in August when LadyConstellation said it was never going to happen, and Damien makes eyes at Rory ALL THE TIME. And even if there *weren't* legitimate reasons," she goes on, "being gay doesn't make them different people. They're still the same characters. Stop whining."

I love it when they get in arguments like this. Canon vs. fanon, how they think the story should go, how they think it should end, which characters are the best, which places they'd want to live in. It's like reading the comments without ever seeing the trolls—instant reader feedback from people who actually like the comic and are active in its fandom.

Wallace comes back with the books and boxes me in again. I put my back to the wall and sink down, pulling my feet up onto the seat. My toes brush Wallace's thigh. I start to scoot them back when his hand comes down and rests over my shoelaces. The heat from his palm shoots up my ankle, my leg, makes my stomach turn to water. He doesn't look at my foot when he does it, just like he didn't look back at me when he took my hand at Halloween. When he releases my foot a moment later, it's like touching it wasn't even a big deal in the first place. He's already back to reading the Children of Hypnos book. Cole and Chandra don't realize anything has happened. No one else realizes anything has happened. Wallace doesn't even act like he does.

Just me. This tight feeling in my chest is only me.

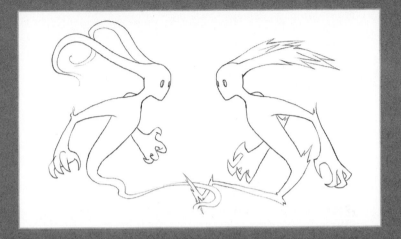

Sato stood behind her. He held out his hand, as always, and as always, Amity didn't shake it. Nocturnians didn't shake hands; meeting someone's eye was considered a more than adequate greeting. Sato knew this, of course, and smiled as he lowered his hand.

"Is there someone like me out there?" she asked.

Sato sat across from her, back straight, hands on his legs. He wore Alliance white and green, with the colonel's gold sword pinned to either shoulder. "I'm honestly surprised it took you so long to ask."

"Are the stories true? Is he out there murdering and enslaving people with the Scarecrow's power, and I'm the only one who can stop him?"

Sato took another second to collect himself, then said, "As far as we know, there are no other creatures like the Scarecrow and the Watcher on Orcus. You and Faust are two of a kind. You've seen the Watcher's healing capabilities. It's an unconscious thing, like breathing, and in the years we've been studying Faust, we haven't found a limit to it. Our best theory, gathered from the Nocturnian stories and from an informant of ours, says only the hosts can mortally wound each other."

Monstrous Sea Private Message

10:11 p.m. 9 - Dec - 16

rainmaker: I never knew these books were about depression.

MirkerLurker: ??

rainmaker: Children of Hypnos. I just started the second one.

MirkerLurker: They're about depression? I guess it's been longer than I thought since the last time I read them.

rainmaker: The whole thing is about Emery dealing with her depression. All the dreamhunters are depressed— they live short lives and they don't sleep and they spend all their time killing other people's nightmares because their dedication to their job is all they have. Klaus is your favorite character, right? He's the most depressed of them all.

MirkerLurker: Oh. Yeah, wow, I never realized. Is that a bad thing? I'm sorry, I didn't mean to recommend a bunch of books about depression to you.

rainmaker: I like them a lot, actually. All the other books I've read about depression take place in present day, and they end with the main character deciding whether or not to commit suicide. I like these. It's like with Monstrous Sea. That's about feeling like you're in the wrong place, and fighting forces you can't stop, and how there are monsters out in the world, but usually the worst monsters live inside us. I like stories like that because they're not so obvious. There's more to like about them than what they have to teach you. You know?

rainmaker: Sorry. I didn't mean to get all deep right there.

MirkerLurker: No, it's okay! You think way harder about stories than I do.

rainmaker: What do you read them for?

MirkerLurker: The characters, I guess. I thought the characters were the reason anyone read Monstrous Sea.

rainmaker: You mean like, shipping?

MirkerLurker: No, not shipping—shipping's great, and I do it all the time, but I mean . . . the characters themselves. The struggles they have to go through, and when you really love them, how much they affect you. When the characters are good, they make you care about everything else. That's why I draw them. It probably sounds dumb, but they're like real people to me. And this will probably sound worse, but sometimes I like them better than real people. I can empathize with characters. Real people are harder.

rainmaker: Real people don't have concise character arcs.

MirkerLurker: Yes, exactly.

rainmaker: I like the characters, but I like what the

story means too. I like how everything comes together. Characters and meaning.

MirkerLurker: You must be a pretty big fan of endings, then. Everything getting wrapped up together.

rainmaker: Haha, good ones, sure. Please tell me Children of Hypnos has a good ending.

MirkerLurker: Um.

CHAPTER 19

Wallace finishes reading the Children of Hypnos series on the second day of winter break. I know, because I get this text:

I NEED TO SPEAK TO YOU RIGHT AWAY ARE YOU BUSY

I am lying on my bed holding Davy like a body pillow and watching reruns of *Dog Days*. So I say no, I'm not doing anything right now, but wow, it's too cold to go outside and my bedroom is too warm. Wallace says that's fine, he'll come to me.

Which means he's coming to my house.

He's coming to my house right now.

I fall off my bed, startling Davy bad enough that he falls off too. Then I scramble up to begin detaching my pen display from my computer. It's too expensive for a normal high-school student, and way too advanced a piece of technology for someone who supposedly just does fan art she never posts online. Unfortunately, it's also too big to hide in a drawer, and beneath my bed is a war zone of childhood toys. I put it carefully in the corner of my closet and toss some old sweatshirts over the top of it.

Then I scan through my desktop and make sure there aren't any *Monstrous Sea* comic pages sitting out in the open. I sign out of my LadyConstellation account on the forums and into the MirkerLurker account. Tear down all the sticky notes on my monitor relating to what pages I need to get done and what plot points I need to work into the story, and I throw those in the closet with the pen display. Davy climbs back up on the bed and watches me like when am I going to come back and hold him like a stuffed animal again?

I throw the door open and hurry downstairs.

"Mom."

"What, honey?" Mom asks. She's in the living room, simultaneously planking and looking at a catalog of carpet swatches. She calls this "home decor calisthenics," and she is a champion. She once redid the entire kitchen while doing pull-ups on the bar across the door to the front hallway.

"We don't have anything to do today, right?"

"Sully and Church have practice later. Are you still available to take them?"

She says it like I have a choice. "I . . . well . . . what time is that at?"

"Four. Why?" She finally looks up. "Is something else happening today?"

"Um. Is it okay if Wallace comes over?"

She's up and at the door in a second. Excitement fills her eyes, but that could be left over from the plank. "Of course. Does he want lunch? I can make lunch. Will you be spending the time in your room?"

"I—I don't know."

"Is he coming now? Is that what you're wearing?"

I look down. I'm wearing a T-shirt from one of Dad's intramural baseball teams, so it's about five sizes too big; a pair of ragged Harlem Globetrotters sweatpants, rolled up to just below my knees; and my thickest, warmest pair of socks. The socks are made out of Wookiee fur or something.

"And you should probably take a shower, don't you think?" Mom says. "Your hair is a little greasy."

I wish she wouldn't point it out, but also she's right. I rush upstairs, lock myself in the bathroom, and hop into the shower. I don't know where Wallace lives, but it usually takes him fifteen minutes to get here. I've already spent ten of those, and I shower in five, and as I'm wrapping my hair up in a towel and pulling on a slightly better-fitting pair of sweatpants, a T-shirt, and my Wookiee socks, the doorbell rings.

"Eliza! Wallace is here!"

I shove the Wookiee socks back on my feet, and when I get to the top of the stairs, Mom is letting Wallace in through the front door.

"Hi there," she says in her normal voice, holding out her hand for him to shake. "It's so nice to finally meet you! I'm Eliza's mom."

Wallace says something back, but it's so quiet I can't hear it. I'm surprised he said anything to her at all. Mom must be satisfied, because she turns around and smiles at me with her eyebrows raised. "Have fun, you two! I'll get some lunch ready."

She disappears into the kitchen. Wallace glances up at me. He's wearing jeans, a sweater, and a fat brown corduroy jacket. All four Children of Hypnos books are tucked under one thick arm.

I jerk my thumb over my shoulder. "You can come up to my room, if you want."

Wallace climbs the stairs. I remember the towel wrapped around my hair and rip it off, chucking it back into the bathroom. I might as well embrace the drowned-rat look, because that's as good as it's getting today. At least I'll smell nice.

Wallace stops beside me, holds up the fourth Children of Hypnos book—the one with a battle axe on the cover—and says softly, "You are joking."

"Yeah," I say. "I was a little worried about that. Okay, come on. . . ."

I bring him to my room. Inside, Davy sits up on the bed, tail thumping against the wall.

"You have a dog?" Wallace forgets the books and stands by the bed for Davy to sniff him. Half a second later they're cuddling on the bed, and Davy is doing his best to climb into Wallace's lap.

I glance around the room to make sure I didn't miss anything. I have a lot of *Monstrous Sea* stuff lying around, but all of it could've been bought by a fan. I turn down the volume on the television but don't turn it completely off—I can't handle Wallace being in my room without *Dog Days* to back me up. "That's Davy. If he gets annoying, shove him onto the floor."

"Davy?" Wallace lets Davy lick his face. "Like Dallas's sea monster Davy?"

Crap. "Hah, yes, like that. I got to name him." Lies. I named the sea monster Davy after the dog Davy, not the other way around. The dog Davy is big and white and happy. The sea monster Davy could crush most cities, sheds clumps of fur that get mistaken for icebergs, and has a long neck and a tiny head with two little round eyes and a perpetual vacant smile. Sea monster Davy came to life when I was very little, and dog Davy dwarfed me.

Wallace looks around the room at the decorations on my walls. "What is that?"

He motions to Mr. Greatbody, who has made his rounds across the walls of my room and now sits above my computer. One of his paper eyes has fallen off, lost forever to the vent in the floor. "Something one of my online friends made for me. It's her kind of joke."

"I won't ask, then."

"So. Children of Hypnos. I'm guessing this means you finished?"

Wallace levels a stare at me the likes of which I've never seen before. Except in the mirror, every freaking time I read through Children of Hypnos. Here's a big football-looking dude sitting on my bed with a very large, happy dog wiggling into his lap, getting angry about a series of novels.

"How is there no fifth book?" he asks. "How can it end there? How does no one know the real reason she quit writing?"

I settle in my desk chair. "Welcome to the pain of the Children of Hypnos fandom."

"But what happens to all of them? Emery? Wes? Will Klaus and Marcia ever be together again? Does Trevor van der Gelt lose himself to his doppelgänger? Does Ridley come back? *Do they ever find Hypnos?*"

I shrug.

"What about the author, though?" He opens up one of the books to the back flap, the picture of Olivia Kane. "Doesn't she know? Even though she never wrote it, couldn't she tell the fans what happened? She must have said *something*."

"Trust me, I've loved these books since I was like twelve. I've looked. Olivia Kane is one hundred percent hermit, she doesn't talk to anyone. She hasn't made a public appearance in four years."

"But—"

"You heard what Cole and Chandra said. Most people think she's a lunatic. She might be, for all anyone knows. Stress does strange things to people."

Wallace slumps against the wall in defeat. "This is the biggest disappointment I've suffered in my entire life as a fan. Can we, like . . . write her a letter, or something?"

"You're really hung up on this, aren't you?"

Wallace runs his hands over Davy's fur. A deep furrow appears between his eyebrows. "I don't know, I just . . . how can she leave it like that? The fifth book was supposed to explain so many things. Do they all die? Does Hypnos wake up and reset the world? Emery was dealing with all that guilt and her depression—what happens to her?"

I pull my knees up to my chest and watch him. He pets Davy, and Davy happily rolls over onto his back. Wallace glances at the stack of books, then focuses somewhere around my feet.

"There's lots of fanfiction about it," I say. "Or there used to be, before the fans scattered to the winds. People have written their own interpretations of the last book. Some of them are really good."

He shakes his head. "It won't be right. Why did she stop writing them?"

"No one knows. I think it was the pressure."

"I guess I can't really be mad about it, then."

"Why?"

He shrugs. "How can you be mad that something doesn't happen, when it would hurt another person? If she had to quit for her health, then I'm glad she did. You shouldn't have to kill yourself for your art. No matter how many fans you have."

I get the very intense desire to hug him then. And possibly kiss him. Still debating the kissing, though. "I'm not sure how many people would agree with you on that."

"Unfortunately," he says. Then he looks toward my headboard shelves, filled with all my different copies of the Children of Hypnos books, and smiles. "I like your house," he says. "It's bigger and quieter than mine."

"It's not quiet when Church and Sully are home, trust me. Speaking of which—do you have to be home at a certain time? I have to take them to soccer practice at four, if you want to come and hang out."

"Yeah, sure."

Now we're both smiling.

Mom calls us down for lunch. I expect to have to pull Davy off Wallace's lap, but Wallace picks him up and sets him on the floor. Davy's tail wags the whole time. I stare.

"What?" Wallace says.

"Do you play football? You seem like you should play football."

"I like watching football. Does that count?"

"You just lifted a hundred-and-forty-pound Great Pyrenees like he was filled with Styrofoam."

Wallace holds out his arms. "Wanna try?"

"Um. Rain check." Despite being almost thirty pounds lighter than Davy, I haven't let anyone try to lift me since some boys at school made a joke out of it in gym class and pretended like they couldn't get me off the ground. That was freshman year, when I was just Creepy Too-Thin Eliza, not Creepy Don't-Touch-Her-You'll-Get-Rabies Eliza.

The fact that Wallace offered is kind of nice, though.

Mom makes us peanut butter and jelly with apple slices, aka the lunch you send to school with your first grader. I stew in horror until Wallace begins eating and says it's "the best freaking peanut butter and jelly" he's ever had, which makes Mom beam like she's won an award. At this point I believe he must be either the least picky eater on the face of the Earth, or he's always so hungry that everything tastes good all the time.

When we return to my room, he finds his spot on the bed. There is plenty of space beside him and the headboard. It's not like we've never sat that close before. We do it all the time at Murphy's, and on the bench behind the middle school. Sure, those are out in the open and this very much isn't, especially now that my door is closed, but it's the same, right? I do my best to hold my frantic heart still, and cautiously arrange myself in that empty space beside him. He doesn't say a word, but watches me until I'm settled.

"*Dog Days* reruns, huh?" he says.

"Yep. How do you feel about it?"

"There is no higher teen soap opera."

"Good answer."

And thus begins our watching of old *Dog Days* episodes. The great thing about *Dog Days* is that it requires so little energy. You don't have to think, you just have to watch characters making terrible decisions in the height of summer. It surprises me a little that Wallace likes it, considering how much he appreciates deeper meanings in his stories, but I guess we all need something that lets us go a little numb.

I focus on forcing myself to relax, stretching my legs out, trying not to look like I think I might be strangled at any moment. My hair is finally beginning to dry—I pray it doesn't frizz—and so far neither my sweatpants nor my Wookiee socks have been brought up in conversation. All in all I think we're doing pretty good.

At one point Wallace stands up to straighten out his pant legs, and when he sits again, he's close enough I can feel his body heat. We sit shoulder to shoulder. I can see his eyelashes touch his cheek when he blinks. His hair always looks black from a distance, but up close it's really dark brown. He's been letting it grow out. I get the strangest urge to trace the curve of his ear with my finger.

After the fourth episode, he says, "Do you have a piece of paper I could write on?"

I jump up too fast. "Sure. Just one? Do you—of course you

need something to write with. Sorry. Here." I grab him a paper from my desk drawer and one of my myriad pencils, and he uses the first Children of Hypnos book as a flat surface to write on. When I'm sure he's writing something for me to read right now, I say, "I thought you only needed to do that when other people were around?"

He etches one careful line after the next. He frowns, shakes his head. "Sometimes it's . . . tough to say things. Certain things." His voice is hardly a whisper. I sit down beside him again, but his big hand blocks my view of the words. He stops writing, leaves the paper there, and stares.

Then he hands it to me and looks the other direction.

Can I kiss you?

"Um," is a delightfully complex word. "Um" means "I want to say something but don't know what it is," and also "You have caught me off guard," and also "Am I dreaming right now? Someone please slap me."

I say "um," then. Wallace's entire head-neck region is already flushed with color, but the "um" darkens it a few shades, and goddammit, he was nervous about asking me and I made it worse. What good is "um" when I should say "YES PLEASE NOW"? Except there's no way I'm going to say "YES PLEASE NOW" because I feel like my body is one big wired time bomb of organs and if Wallace so much as brushes my hand, I'm going to jump out of my own skin and run screaming from the house.

I'll like it too much. Out of control. No good.

I say, "Can I borrow that pencil?"

He hands me the pencil, again without looking.

Yes, but not right now.

I know it sounds weird. Sorry. I don't think it'll go well if I know it's coming. I will definitely freak out and punch you in the face or scream bloody murder or something like that.

Surprising me with it would probably work better. I am giving you permission to surprise me with a kiss. This is a formal invitation for surprise kisses.

I don't like writing the word "kiss." It makes my skin crawl.

Sorry. It's weird. I'm weird. Sorry.

I hope that doesn't make you regret asking.

I hand the paper and pencil back. He reads it over, then writes:

No regret. I can do surprises.

That's it. That's it?

Shit.

Now he's going to try to surprise me with a kiss. At some point. Later today? Tomorrow? A week from now? What if he never does it and I spend the rest of the time we hang out wondering if he will? What have I done? This was a terrible idea.

I'm going to vomit.

"Be right back," I say, and run to the bathroom to curl up on the floor. Just for like five minutes. Then I go back to my room and sit down beside Wallace. As I'm moving myself into position, his hand falls over mine, and I don't actually jump out of my skin. My control shakes for a moment, but I turn in to it, and everything smooths out. I flip my hand over. He flexes his fingers so I can fit mine in the spaces between. And we sit there, shoulder to shoulder, with our hands resting on the bed between us.

It's not so bad.

CHAPTER 20

By a quarter till four I am holding Wallace's hand unapologetically in my lap and thinking I definitely should have let him kiss me. It's always that first hurdle that proves the problem—talking, hand-holding, whatever—and as soon as I get used to it, as soon as I know it's okay, I need more. Logic says I will have to let go of Wallace's hand at some point after leaving my bedroom, if not to drive my car, then at the very least to hide it from my mom. But logic is not around right now, and I do not care.

I sandwich Wallace's hand against my stomach and put my other hand on his wrist, holding him in place. We lean fully against each other now. I nudge his foot with my Wookiee sock. He nudges back. This is a thing. We are doing a thing. I don't have to wonder if it's okay because it's totally okay. He's going along with it. I take a breath and rest my head on his shoulder. He nuzzles his cheek in my hair. I giggle. He nuzzles harder.

I've never been so aware of my body. The way it moves. The space I fill. It isn't good or bad, just different, forced to venture outside my head and explore the strange and mysterious world of physicality. His fingers twitch against mine, against my stomach, and set off another round of involuntary giggles. Thank God I have his hand secured in mine; I can't trust or predict what my body might do if he touches anywhere else.

"Oh, dang it," I say when I finally look at the clock. "It's almost four. They have to be there by four thirty."

I push myself off the bed to stand, expecting him to move with me or at least let go of my hand. He does neither. His grip jerks me back. He slouches against the wall, smiling that little smile, refusing to let go.

"Come on." I laugh, trying to pull him up. "We have to go."

He lets me use all my body weight to tug on him. I end up almost sitting on the floor, and he hasn't budged. He flexes his arm and yanks me up, back to the bed. Laughing.

"Seriously, though!"

"Okay, okay." He lets go.

"I need to change too."

"I'll wait outside."

He does. I change into my best-fitting pair of jeans and an actual non-logoed shirt. Sweatshirt over the top, of course. Sully and Church are already waiting by the front door with their practice bags in tow. Wallace has ambled to the bottom of the stairs, and they've struck up some kind of conversation. When I head down, Sully raises his arms and glares at me. "Come on, Eggs Benedict! We don't have all day!"

"Shut up."

Sully and Church stuff their gangly selves in the backseat of my car so Wallace can sit in the passenger seat.

"No hanky panky up there," Sully says.

"Yeah," Church adds. "If I see a hand cross those seats, it will get smacked."

"Smacked?" Sully says. "If I see a hand cross those seats, I'll chop it off and burn it."

"Shut up." I pray my hair covers the heat in my cheeks. I am not going to get into an argument with my brothers over their stupid inappropriate mouths while Wallace is in my car. I turn the radio to some of the garbage alt-rock they like so much, and pretty soon they forget about us.

Wallace and I walk the perimeter of the sports complex during the two hours of Sully and Church's practice. It's empty enough that Wallace doesn't have an issue talking, though he does speak softer. We don't hold hands, but his knuckles tap the back of mine like he's trying to send me a message in Morse code.

"My sister comes to this place," he says. "For tennis."

"Younger or older sister?"

"Oh, definitely younger. The only exercise Bren gets is playing with the dogs in her obedience classes. Lucy loves tennis, though. And basketball. And most sports."

"Your family seems nice."

"I like them. They want to meet you."

"Is that a thing we're doing now? Meeting each other's families?"

He shrugs. "Only if you want."

"I don't know. I guess that would be fair. You've been subjected to mine."

"You don't like them?"

Now I shrug. "It's weird. Like, I know they love me, and I know I have nothing to complain about, but they're always trying to get me to do things I don't want to do. Every time we come here, my mom and dad try to convince me to sign up for a new club sport or intramural team. If I have my phone out talking to you or my online friends, they think I'm ignoring them, or being disrespectful, or whatever. And it's like, no, I'm in the middle of a conversation. If you saw two people talking to each other face-to-face, you wouldn't interrupt them and call it disrespectful, would you?"

"No, of course not."

"No. I understand that it's *a teenage thing* to say parents don't get it, but they *don't get* it. It's not their fault they were born two and a half decades before me, but would it kill them to ask me what I'm doing on the phone before they assume it's something pointless?"

"Maybe they're worried you'll snap at them if they ask

what you're doing," Wallace says.

I open my mouth to argue but remember that I have actually done that to my parents before.

"Do yours ever do that to you?" I ask.

"Sometimes. Not as often as they used to. We've . . . moved past that, and into other issues."

Before I can ask what issues, he says, "Why did your brother call you Eggs Benedict?"

"Because I eat hard-boiled eggs for breakfast. Dad calls me Eggs, and Sully and Church just kind of tack on whatever egg type they can think of that day."

"Cute."

"I think my brothers hate me."

It must sound too real, because Wallace actually looks concerned. "Why?"

My gaze fixes on my feet, Mom's worn Nikes scuffing the ground. "I don't know. Because I don't try to hang out with them more, or get invested in what they like doing. According to Dad, they're really good at soccer, but I wouldn't know because I never pay attention when we go to their games."

"So hang out with them more."

"But I don't like doing what they do, because all they do is play soccer. Or video games. I don't like sports. They make fun of me for being bad at them anyway, so what's the point?"

"Of course they're going to make fun of you. They're middle-school boys raised in a highly competitive, testosterone-fueled environment. That's how they psych each other up."

"And you know this how?"

"I watch the sportball on the television. Also I played peewee football when I was younger."

"You *did* play football!"

He laughs. "Yeah, when I was like a quarter the size I am now. They had me as a running back."

"I don't know what that means."

"It means I ran real fast."

"You? Move fast?"

"I know. One of life's great mysteries." His knuckles rap the back of my hand. My resistance meets its end, and I grab his fingers, holding them in mine. He smiles and says, "I don't think your brothers hate you. I think you don't like the same things. It's not a bad thing, it just is what it is. They do sports. You do art."

I do *Monstrous Sea*. That is what I do, and all I need from Sully and Church is their silence about it to their friends at school. We don't have to get along. They just have to keep their mouths shut. They've stayed quiet this long; they must have *some* idea how important it is. So maybe Wallace is right. Maybe they don't hate me.

"So where's your house at?" I ask, swinging our hands between us. "I want to properly Google Maps creeper-stalk you before agreeing to meet your family."

He laughs again.

The walk home that Amity normally found meditative now teemed with her own unquenchable thoughts. Her guilt. If she was the only one who could stop Faust, didn't that mean she had to? Even if it meant danger to her? It was easy to think of him in the abstract when he was only terrorizing faraway places, but what if he came to Nocturne Island?

What if, instead of strangers, he attacked Faren?

MONSTROUS SEA FORUMS

USER PROFILE

rainmaker *

Fanfiction Moderator

AGE: Not telling you

LOCATION: NO

INTERESTS: MS. Writing things. Campfires. Sweaters. Sleeping in. Dogs. CHILDREN OF HYPNOS HOLY SHIT

Followers 1,402,834 | Following 51 | Posts 9,512

[Unique Works - 144]

UPDATES

View earlier updates

Nov 24 2016

> SWEET POTATO PIE DAY.

Nov 28 2016

> I have begun reading the work of human genius that is the Children of Hypnos. Why did no one ever tell me how great this series is? I'm holding you all responsible.

Dec 02 2016

> So glad everyone's loving the transcription! More

chapters on the way. Will try to get some of Auburn Blue up in the meantime, but can't promise anything. Also STOP ASKING ABOUT CUTE GIRL FROM SCHOOL. Gosh.

Dec 13 2016

Going silent for a while. Midterms to study for. Will be around the boards, though. #Mathslaughter

Dec 19 2016

As a reward for surviving midterms, the fourth CoH book. No, I don't care if the author is a nutjob. This had better end well.

Dec 19 2016

Yes, I was introduced to CoH by Cute Girl from School. NO THANKS TO ANY OF YOU.

Dec 21 2016

I am an absolute wreck of a human being, and right now I am completely okay with it.

CHAPTER
21

I agree to meet Wallace's family on the Friday before Christmas. For dinner.

I wash my nice pair of jeans again so they'll start at their tightest fit and stretch out as the night goes on, and I steal one of Mom's lacy shirts. I don't even pretend to care what people at school think of my clothes, but if Wallace is going to look nice coming over to my house, then I'm going to look nice at his.

Before I leave, Mom hands me a bunch of flyers for her exercise group ("If any of his family is looking for a new workout, I'd be happy to have them. Let them know! Or if they work somewhere with a bulletin board, have them put those up!") and Dad reminds me with a smile that whatever they eat for dinner is my cheat food for the week. My parents like to assume that anyone who isn't our family eats terrible, unhealthy food. They also forget that I attend public school and therefore eat French fries five days out of seven.

Sully and Church, thankfully, are attempting to give each other black eyes over a first-person shooter in the living room, and don't notice me leave.

Wallace lives on the other side of town in a one-story ranch home with a light-up Santa in the yard and a driveway that's more mud than gravel. Two cars sit in a row, probably neither of them made after the year 2007; the one in the back is Wallace's, or at least the one he drives everywhere, the same one his sister drives to pick him up from school. I pull in behind it. A warm light comes through the curtains behind the window in the front door.

I take out my phone.

MirkerLurker: So I'm here.

MirkerLurker: At his house.

MirkerLurker: About to go inside.

MirkerLurker: Wanting to puke.

Emmy and Max don't respond. Emmy's home for the holidays and Max is off work, so we're in that relaxed lull where they spend the least time online. I haven't actually talked to them in the past few days—at least I remembered to send their care packages out.

Maybe they'll see the message while I'm in there.

I rest my head on the steering wheel, pretend I'm doing something in case anyone is watching from the house, count to twenty, then force myself out of the car—leaving my mom's flyers on the passenger seat—and march up to the front door.

Wallace answers on the first knock. He's wearing sweatpants and one of his sweaters.

"That is so unfair," I say.

He smiles. "I thought you'd say that."

The inside of his house looks straight out of the seventies. Wood-paneled walls, yellow carpet. But it's warm and cozy as hell, and the smell of sizzling fat drifts out of the kitchen to our right. To our left is a wall that divides the entryway from a living room with a TV on, and a back hallway that must lead to bedrooms.

"So this is La Casa Warland, huh?" I say.

"More like La Casa Keeler," he replies. His voice is louder than I've ever heard it before, almost as loud as Sully and Church, who still haven't learned the term "inside voice." He takes my coat and hangs it on the rack beside the door. I stand awkwardly by the door to the living room until someone behind me says, "Oh, you must be Eliza!"

I jump. A middle-aged black woman strides across the living room toward me, arms outstretched. She's short, plump, and has a smile that looks like it could bludgeon the devil to tears. She gathers me up in a hug. I stare at Wallace.

"Eliza, this is my mom, Vee."

"Oh, hon, really I'm his stepmother. Don't want you to get too confused." Vee releases me and takes my hand instead, pulling me toward the kitchen. Movement in the living room blurs behind us, and then there's a girl Sully and Church's age following Wallace, with skin a few shades lighter than Vee's and about a million thin braids scooped into a thick ponytail that hangs past her shoulders.

"I'm Lucy," the girl says. "You're shorter than I thought you'd be."

Vee sits me down at a small rectangular kitchen table. Wallace sits beside me, and Lucy sits opposite me. Her legs are so long she has to whip her feet back when they accidentally touch mine. The table's set for six. On the other side of the room, something that smells and sounds suspiciously like bacon cooks in a skillet on the stove.

"I hope you like breakfast for dinner, Eliza," Vee says, "because it's Friday night, and you know what Friday night means!"

I don't, but Lucy shouts, "Eggs and bacon!" and whoops a few times for good measure.

"I don't understand how anyone is supposed to get any beauty sleep in this house." Another woman steps into the kitchen, hands on her hips. She has to be in her early twenties, and a thick headband holds a magnificent mane of hair away from her angular face. I think she might burn me alive when her eyes land on me, but after a moment, her features soften and she points at Wallace. "Are you Wally's girlfriend?"

Wallace's face flares red. He glances sideways at me. He's not correcting her.

He's not correcting her.

"Um," I say. "I'm Eliza."

She holds out her hand. Grips like a titan. "I'm Bren. I feel like I've seen you around before—do you have a dog?"

"Yeah. Davy. He's a Great Pyrenees."

She nods sagely. "I work for the Happy Friends Dog Day Care. We have Davy in there every once in a while."

"He was there in October for the week-long pack run!"

"Yes, he was!" Bren moves around the table and sits next to Lucy, who immediately tries to stick her finger in Bren's ear. Bren swats the hand away absentmindedly. "I love those dogs. So does Wally—we pay him to clean the kennels and plays with the dogs at the end of the day." She huffs. "You know, when I'm in charge of that place, I'm going to feed them in the morning *and* in the evening, because once a day isn't enough. Especially not when they're running around playing. I wish we could have a dog here, but Luce is allergic." She tugs on Lucy's braids.

"How do you like your eggs, Eliza?" Vee asks.

"Uh . . . any way. Sunny-side up is fine."

"Sunny-side up it is." She finishes with the bacon and starts cracking eggs in the skillet.

Bren and Lucy—but mostly Bren—go through the usual gamut of questions about me. Where I come from, how old I am, how Wallace and I met. Wallace jumps in for that one, talking so loud it doesn't sound like him at all.

"She had those *Monstrous Sea* pictures. I told you about that, remember?" He doesn't mention Travis Stone or Deshawn Johnson, thankfully. I don't want to have to explain to his sisters how magnificently I failed trying to stand up for him, and I get the feeling he doesn't want to tell them he kind of sat there and took it until I showed up. But they probably already know how nonconfrontational he is.

"Right, right." Bren waves a hand in the air. "So you're into it too, huh? *Monstrous Sea?*"

I shrug. "Yeah."

"Do you write fanfiction too?"

"Oh . . . no."

"She does fan art," Wallace says. "I keep trying to get her to post it online."

"Why don't you?" Lucy asks.

I shrug again. "Never feels right, I guess."

Wallace runs a finger along the outside edge of his plate, smiling a little. "They're really great," he says, voice soft again. "You should post some of them. One or two."

Every time he talks like this, voice quiet and eyes cast down, smiling, I want to do it. I want to get on my computer right now and upload a few drawings, just to see how he reacts. I know he wants me to be in it with everyone else. A contributor. I know he wants to show off my art, because he told me so behind the middle school one day, and whenever I think about it my stomach flips over and my heart shoots into my throat and I want to kiss him all over his beautiful, dimpled face.

Every time he talks like this, my resolve gets a little weaker.

No one will be able to tell I'm LadyConstellation from a few drawings.

"I was . . . I was thinking about it," I say finally, and that draws Wallace's eyes up to mine.

"Really?"

"Yeah. Maybe later."

"*Really?*"

I laugh. "*Yes.* What's wrong with you? Do you feel okay?"

He sits straight in his seat like a two-hundred-pound ball of energy. Before he can say anything else, the front door opens again. "Tim's home!" Lucy shouts. A laugh comes from the entryway, and a moment later a tall bald man steps into the kitchen.

"Breakfast for dinner, my favorite!" Tim sweeps by the stove to plant a kiss on the top of Vee's head, then moves around to the table to plant one on Lucy and Bren too. Then he takes the seat at the end of the table, on Wallace's right side, and gives me a genial smile. "And *you're* Eliza." He reaches across the table to shake my hand; he has Bren's titan grip. "We're so glad to have you for dinner, Eliza."

"Thank you." He is very loud, and very confident, and I am shrinking in my seat every second he focuses on me.

"Lucy, hon," Vee calls, "come help me with the food."

Lucy gets up to bring the bacon, sausage, and toast to the table. Vee brings the eggs—all sunny-side up—and begins sliding them onto our plates. My stomach rumbles. Wallace nudges me with his elbow, and I can't tell if it's on purpose or if it's because his shoulders are so wide he takes up all my arm space.

"So, Keelers and Warlands," Tim says, after Vee sits down at the other end of the table. "What'd we accomplish today?"

Vee shares a story about an old high-school friend she ran into at the grocery store while she looked for ingredients to a new recipe she wanted to try. Lucy regales us with the research she did on tennis racquets, and spends five minutes trying to convince Tim to let her buy a restringing machine, which he declines. Bren complains about a young couple who abandoned a puppy at the day care because they got it as an early Christmas gift but didn't want to keep it. The rest of us eat while the other person talks. Then Tim turns his sights on me.

"Eliza, would you like to share?"

"Oh. Um." What have I done today? I lay in bed and watched Netflix. I opened up yesterday's *Westcliff Star* and read the wrap-up story about the Wellhouse Turn deaths about twelve times. Then I scheduled the single *Monstrous Sea* page going up tonight—the only one I could finish, considering the damage Wallace had done to my productivity. After that, I spent a few hours sweating. Then I showered. And now I'm here.

"Why don't I go?" Wallace says. "I'm done eating." He inhaled his food.

Tim turns to him instead.

"I helped Bren get that retriever that's had the trust issues to let me give it a bath today," Wallace says. Then the corners of his lips creep upward. "And, uh . . . I sold two more commissioned stories."

"Two more?" Vee chirps. "Wally, that's great!"

"You didn't tell me that!" Bren says.

Lucy throws her napkin at him. "Are you going to let me read them?"

Tim smiles. "That's great, Wallace. Are these your fanfiction stories?"

"Yeah. Not *Monstrous Sea*, but something else."

"Have you tried selling any of your own?"

Wallace scratches the back of his neck. "That's not really how it works. People request the stories because they already know the characters, and what they want."

"Hmm." Tim goes back to his eggs. "So is this what you'd be doing with your major next year? Writing fanfiction?"

All amusement has left Wallace's face. "No, they don't do fanfiction in any creative writing major."

"So you'd be writing your own work."

"Yeah."

"What is that going to get for you, if you can't make money off your own work?"

"Timothy," Vee warns. "Not while we have a guest."

I shrink into Wallace's side, but Tim's laser gaze finds me anyway. "Eliza," he says. "You plan on going to college next year, don't you? What do you want to major in?"

Art seems like the obvious answer, but I haven't settled on anything yet because there's no major for drawing *Monstrous Sea*. But saying "art" doesn't seem like it'll get me many points in Tim's book. "Graphic design," I say. "For, like, marketing. And stuff." *Way to stick the landing, Mirk.*

"Graphic design," Tim repeated. "See, Wallace, even that has business appeal. Graphic designers can make good money. I'm not saying you can't do writing, just do some writing that you can build a career on. Creative writing isn't going to get you anywhere."

Wallace clamps his mouth shut and stares at his plate. Lucy shoves a piece of bacon into her mouth, and Bren covers her face with a hand, slowly shaking her head.

"This fanfiction thing is for fun. Your mother and I won't be paying for a college education that supports a hobby. We want you to do something meaningful."

Tim keeps going. Wallace's fist tightens against his thigh. I brush my finger against it, and he grabs my hand. Squeezes hard, like he's in pain. I squeeze back.

"I know you don't like listening to this," Tim says, "but it's the way the world is."

A beat of silence falls over the table as Tim goes back to his eggs. Then Wallace says, "May we be excused?"

Tim looks ready to say no, but his mouth is full. Vee shoots him a venomous look from the other end of the table and says, "Yes, hon, you and Eliza are excused. I'll get your plates."

Wallace stands and pulls me out of the kitchen.

CHAPTER 22

Down the back hallway is a set of stairs that lead to the basement. The basement is brick walled, carpeted, and chillier than the rest of the house. Wallace flicks a light switch at the bottom of the stairs that turns on soft, ambient sconces. The room is divided in half by a wall with a large opening. On this side is a moth-eaten couch and a large, old television. Wallace leads me to the other side of the room, through the opening. The darker side. There's a mattress here on the floor covered with rumpled bedsheets, a lamp plugged into a power strip, and books and papers piled around it, including the Children of Hypnos series and chapters of Wallace's *Monstrous Sea* transcription. A pool table takes up a lot of the space. Just to the left of the lamp on the floor is an old recliner. Behind that is a large poster of Dallas Rainer standing on a beach, looking over the ocean, and the words THERE ARE MONSTERS IN THE SEA sketched into the shadow he casts on the sand. Pinned beside the poster is an old football jersey that says WARLAND and the number 73.

From the opening in the wall, Wallace pulls a heavy, sliding wood door and locks it on the other side of the doorframe. It cuts off any residual noise from upstairs, and even from the rest of the basement. He presses his forehead to the door and closes his eyes.

"I am so sorry," he says. "I didn't think he would do that."

I shift from foot to foot. The room is cold, and my jacket is upstairs. "Does he usually?"

"Sometimes. He's—he's a great guy, and he's a good person, but I hate it when he starts saying things are meaningless." He pulls his head away from the door and starts to pace. "Sorry. Sorry, I don't mean to freak you out. I didn't think he would be like that if you were here."

"It's fine. I get it." I'm just glad I can breathe again.

Wallace balls his hands together at his sides. I've never seen him so angry. Not like this. He looks like he could break something. Maybe the pool table. "What's the point of being alive if you don't do what makes you happy? What good is a career that makes you money if you hate yourself every day you do it? I don't have a family to support, I don't have bills to pay, at least not right now. Sure, I'll have to pay student loans, but we only have enough money for me to go to community college anyway, so I'll pay it off with whatever job I get after that. I don't need to be a doctor, or a lawyer, or whatever *important* job he wants me to get. I just want to write."

I watch him pace and feel myself growing to the floor, feet rooted in place, uncertainty creeping its way through my veins. I've never seen him like this—I don't know what to do with him, so I stand there and stare until he finally looks up at me and says, "I'm really sorry" again.

"Do you need something to scream into?" I ask.

He considers. "That would be nice."

I pluck the pillow off the mattress and toss it to him. He presses it to his face and lets out a muffled scream. Probably the loudest sound that's ever come out of him in my presence, and the pillow makes it no louder than his usual speaking volume.

He throws the pillow back to the bed and follows it. He is much less intimidating while supine. I sit on the edge of the mattress and turn toward him.

"I'm sorry he has to be like that," I say.

Wallace covers his eyes with his hands. How easy it would be to lean over and kiss him now, but it doesn't feel like the time. Maybe it will never be the time. It will never be the time because I'm Eliza Mirk, great avoider of life and all its consequences. How can I want something so badly but become so paralyzed every time I even think about taking it?

"I've already spent twelve years of school doing what other people have told me I have to do," he says. "And I know what happens when someone's forced to do something they hate. Is it too much to ask for a few years of what I want? Do your parents do this to you? Are you really going to major in graphic design?"

"Oh, no. I said that so Tim wouldn't throw me out of the house."

Wallace snorts.

"I don't know what I want to major in. I just don't want to be . . . here. My parents like to remind me that I still have to finish high school to know if I get to go to college, and they think once I go I'll become some dorm hermit who never leaves her room and stares at her computer screen all day. But no, they don't tell me what I should do—not all the time, anyway—and I guess that's better."

But the only reason they aren't trying to whip me into shape anymore is because I've raged against it for so long that I wore them out. They still mention it sometimes, in Mom's little jabs about doing better in school, and Dad's mentions of scholarships, but it's not the same issue. Mom and Dad don't know how much money I make, but I do, and I have at least that peace of mind. Wallace only has fanfiction, and that can't help him.

"I'm sorry," I say again. He lowers his hands, stares at the ceiling, and shrugs. Then he looks at me.

"Are you cold?"

My hands are clamped around my upper arms, my torso curled into my legs to keep the heat in.

"Um."

"Here." Wallace sits up and pulls a thick knitted blanket from beneath the other sheets on his bed. "Insulation layer. Hope it doesn't smell bad." He wraps it around me. It's already warm. Probably warm from him, considering he *sleeps with it touching him every freaking night*.

"Smells like Irish Spring and spicy boy shampoo," I say.

"Is that good or bad?"

"It's great."

I have never been so close to something that smells like Irish Spring and spicy boy shampoo, unless you count anything my dad goes near, and I do not. I'm not entirely sure my brothers shower. I curl up in his blanket but stay turned away from him.

"You didn't correct Bren when she said I was your girlfriend."

Wallace shifts behind me. "Oh. Yeah. Well, I thought—you know, it would bring up more questions than it answered . . . and she's kind of persistent . . . and I didn't want to make the situation awkward. . . ."

"Oh."

"Hmm."

Someone flushes a toilet upstairs; water rushes through the basement pipes. I bury my face in Wallace's blanket. Wallace shifts again behind me.

"Unless you want to be," he says.

I look over my shoulder. "What?"

He sits against the wall with his arms wrapped around his knees, his eyes wide. When I look at him, he looks down at his feet. His voice drops, and his words come out in terse little bunches. "I didn't know if—if you wanted to be my girlfriend, so I didn't want to get into a big thing about it at dinner."

"Do you want me to be?" I choke out.

He glances up. "I mean, yes."

Ball in your court, Mirk.

"Yes," I say.

"Yes?" He frowns.

Aghh. Wrong word.

"I mean, okay."

The little smile appears. "Really?"

"Yes."

It becomes the big smile. He lowers his head and drags both hands through his hair. I throw my arms up over me and hide myself in his blanket. Too much, too much, out of control. A moment later his chest presses against my back and his arms wrap around me and his legs box me in on either side. The weight of his head falls on my shoulder.

A moment of silence passes. The world doesn't fall apart. I lower the blanket and twist in his arms, and he lets me, and then we're facing.

I don't want to be the girl who freezes when confronted with new friends, or the outside world, or the smallest shred of intimacy. I don't want to be alone in a room all the time. I don't want to *feel* alone in a room all the time, even when there are other people around.

I lift the blanket open so Wallace can come inside, and when he's holding me again, I lay my arms over his shoulders and trap us both in the warmth. He lets out a contented sigh.

I become acutely aware of my limbs, how quickly I breathe, and every twitch of my lips and my fingers. It helps me stop thinking about what I'm doing wrong. It's not too much. I'm not out of control.

I'm here. He's here.

CHAPTER 23

I say good-bye to the Keelers—and Lucy, who is technically a Warland—before I leave. They're all grouped in the living room, Lucy tucked under Tim's arm on the couch next to Bren, Vee with reading glasses perched on the end of her nose, squinting at the television as she looks for a channel they can all watch. Wallace walks me out to my car. I think he might pull the surprise kiss then, but he doesn't.

"I'm glad you came," he says, squeezing my hand. Then he tugs me closer, into a hug.

"I'm glad you asked me," I say, locking my arms around him. The muscles along his ribs expand and contract with his breathing. My nose brushes his neck, and he shivers. "I should probably go," I say.

"Okay."

I get in my car. As I pull out of the driveway, Wallace leans against the back bumper of his car with his hands in his pockets, his breath puffing fog in the air, and watches me drive away.

When I get home that night, I try to skirt past the living room where Mom and Dad are bundled up and watching their number one favorite movie of all time, *Miracle*. It's the movie they watch on every date night, birthday, holiday, and anniversary. If it hadn't come out six years after I was born, I would've thought they were watching it while I was conceived. Still, their dedication to this crowning jewel of sports cinema does nothing to hamper their parent senses. The minute I pass the doorframe, Mom whips around.

"How was it?"

"Good," I snap. "Fine. I'm going upstairs."

"Why don't you come in here and tell us about it? We'd like to know about his family. And you can watch *Miracle*!"

"No thanks." I start up the stairs.

"Oh, Eliza, please don't go get on that computer! Stay down here and talk to us."

"I have work to do." I reach the top of the stairs and hurry into my room before either of them can punch holes in my happy bubble. I don't want to watch *Miracle* for the billionth time—spoiler alert, we beat the Russians—and I don't want to talk to them about Wallace. It's bad enough that Mom made me go to that doctor's appointment; who knows what she'll do if I tell her we're actually going out now.

I shut myself in my room, ignoring the music blasting from Church and Sully's bedroom, and check my phone. Neither Emmy nor Max have responded to my texts yet, but that's fine. It's a Friday night—they'll see them in the morning. I pull out my sketchbook and flip through my *Monstrous Sea* drawings. I scan three of them into the computer. One of a sunset riser bursting out of a dark ocean, water pinwheeling off its sharp spines; one of Damien looking up at the sky with stars reflected in his eyes; and one of Amity balancing atop a sharp crystal pillar, framed by the sun. I log in to the forums with my MirkerLurker account, find the fan art subforums, and start a new thread.

All three pictures go up. I close the browser before anyone can respond, and throw myself into bed with my clothes still on.

CHAPTER 24

The next morning, I wake to twenty-two messages from Emmy and Max. Separately. And none of them are about me being nervous over eating dinner at Wallace's house last night.

> **emmersmacks:** Are you feeling okay??
>
> **emmersmacks:** None of the pages went up
>
> **emmersmacks:** E???
>
> **emmersmacks:** Did you just forget or . . . ??
>
> **Apocalypse_Cow:** hey so i know you're having fun with sweet cheeks mcdimples, but people are kinda getting antsy.

Apocalypse_Cow: no pages.

Apocalypse_Cow: you feeling okay?

They go on. I throw off my covers and fall over to the computer. Type my password wrong twice for the computer and once for the forums.

LadyConstellation has thirty new private messages from forum admins asking where the new pages are. And the forums themselves—the top post in almost every subforum is someone asking if there's an issue with the website, or something wrong with LadyConstellation, or if the pages are late.

I skip over to the website itself, where the pages go up. The latest post is still the last page from last week.

But I scheduled the post to go up. I know I did. I check the settings and there it is—in the drafts. Unpublished. I click the post button so hard my mouse flies out from beneath my hand and hits the wall.

In three years, I have never posted late. Reliability is what I sell to my fans, and they are happy to buy it.

I bring up a new forum post.

LadyConstellation:

> Hey everyone—sorry about the missing post last night. Something went wrong and it didn't get scheduled. It's up now!

Replies flood in.

> Yay!

> Only one page?

> Whoo!! Finally!!

> How much can go wrong with post scheduling?

> Just glad you're not dead.

> Fuckin' about time. Man, a lot of work to post one page, huh?

I close the browser and swivel away from the computer, curling up in my chair and holding my head in my hands. It's fine. It was only a few hours. As long as I get the pages in on time from now on, everything is fine.

Don't look at the comments. Never look at the comments.

"You feeling okay, Eggs?"

"Yeah, Dad, I'm fine."

"You haven't come out of your room yet this morning. Your mom and I were getting worried."

"I was asleep."

"Well, Wallace is here. He says you're supposed to go to Murphy's."

"Oh. Um."

"Is it that time of the month? Do you want me to tell him you can't go?"

"I—God, no! I'll be down in a second. Jesus."

Wallace sits in the living room playing video games with my brothers. He's wedged between them, silent and focused on the TV, while Sully and Church yell at each other over his head. Then something happens, and they both groan, and Wallace smiles.

"How long have you been here?" I ask. He looks over and sees me there for the first time and drops the controller.

"A few minutes," he says, coming toward me.

"Play another round!" Sully motions to the TV and then to Wallace with long arcs of his arm, like he can pull Wallace back.

"We have to go," I say. Sully glares at me. I drag Wallace out of the house and to his car.

"Are you okay?" he asks.

"Yeah. Stressed."

"Why?"

I shrug. "Stuff."

We get in the car, lapse into silence. Wallace frowns as he backs out of the driveway and starts toward Murphy's. When we pass over Wellhouse Bridge, he slows nearly to a stop so he can take Wellhouse Turn. Slow and steady, just like always. Too slow. Too steady. He's more afraid he's going to go over the edge than anyone else I've ever met. I look over the side, like I always do, and face the drop below.

It's calm down there. Even if death doesn't come quickly, I bet it's almost worth it for the peace and quiet.

Cole and Megan are already at Murphy's when we arrive, and already talking about the missing pages. The missing pages—*page*, because there was only *one*—that went up this morning, but that apparently people are calling the Missing Pages because it's such a fucking fiasco.

"It's the first time it happened since the comic started," Cole says, scrolling through the forums for more posts about it. "Everyone's talking about it. It's an *event*. Look, there's even fanfiction about the characters temporarily entering a void of no escape between the time the pages were supposed to go up and when they actually did. It's *hilarious*."

He shows it to us. The fanfiction, the forums, the everything. I keep my eyes averted. Wallace scans over it for a second, then shrugs. "I mean, it's funny, but it seems kind of silly for just one missed day of pages."

"Page," Megan corrects, handing toddler Hazel a new picture book to flip through. "Only one page. At least it had some action on it, but those single pages are hard to look past. Nothing happens. I love this comic as much as anyone, but I work fifteen hours a day and take care of this monster"—she grips the top of Hazel's head—"and when I get to the end of the week all I want to do is sit down with some tea and some *Monstrous Sea* pages. Preferably a whole chapter."

Yes, Megan, let me whip up a few dozen pages for you. It's not like LadyConstellation has other things on her mind, either. I don't read the comments, but I know a lot of the fans are like this. I don't blame them. I was like that for a while too, with Children of Hypnos. I was angry at Olivia Kane as much as anyone else.

I don't blame them, but that doesn't stop it from being exhausting.

They talk—and eventually get ahold of Leece and Chandra on Cole's computer, which starts up a whole new round of discussion about the pages—and I rest my head on the table, pretending to sleep. They leave me alone.

A few times Wallace's fingers brush my knee. I let them. I don't move.

I get out my phone to text Emmy and Max and find I don't have the willpower. I put the phone down again.

When Leece and Chandra both have to go, Megan suggests a change of scenery. She's got three free games of bowling at the Blue Lane, thanks to her second job there. Cole jumps on the chance right away, but before he accepts Wallace asks if I want to go.

I start to say no, then stop myself. I have to try. I have to try, because I'm doing it again—I'm shutting everything out because I'm frustrated and tired and because the real world is difficult and

I'd rather live in one of my own making. But I can't. I am here, and I have to try.

Half an hour later I'm standing at the end of a bowling lane, trying to line myself up with the pins. Wallace is at the snack bar. Megan sits at the table behind me, bouncing Hazel in her lap. Cole stands next to me, arms folded over his chest, a look on his face far too intense for a bowling alley.

"Bowling is like any sport," he says, and I think he's mostly talking to himself. "Pros make it look easy, so anyone thinks they can do it. But it's not easy. You think too much and suddenly the ball is shooting out of the gutter and flying three lanes down and you're kicked out of the alley for recklessness."

I press my lips together to hold in my laugh. "I'm not great at bowling, but I don't think I've ever thrown the ball so hard it jumped three lanes over."

Cole stares stoically down the lane. "Well, it happens."

"Have you done that before?"

"Don't worry about it."

I roll the ball. It heads straight for the right gutter, but halfway down the lane it curves back and strikes the first pin. They fall until only the two in the back left are still standing.

"It worked!" I crane my neck to watch a little eight go up next to my name on the screen above our lane.

"Don't sound so shocked," Cole says.

"I've never knocked that many down at once before! At least

not with a real throw." I stopped going bowling with my family as soon as Sully and Church got old enough to make fun of me for my granny rolls. Maybe now I can actually compete with them.

I throw my second ball. It grazes one of the pins, but they both stay standing.

"Watch out." Cole grabs his ball and shoulders past me. "It's time to blow some small fries out of the water."

I return to the table with Megan and Hazel. Wallace returns from the snack bar with three orders of nachos, two hot dogs, a pretzel, and two large sodas. He hands me one of the sodas, sets one of the nachos between me and Megan, one of the hot dogs in front of Cole's empty seat, then arranges the rest of it in front of himself. Then he presses his hands together, looking around at his feast like he isn't sure where he wants to start.

"You better start playing football again soon," Megan says, "or you're going to wake up one day and weigh six hundred pounds."

Wallace smiles at her through a mouthful of pretzel.

We've been here half an hour, and I'm no longer sure why I wanted to say no to coming here. No one's said a word about the missing pages since we left Murphy's, and I feel light, like bubbles fill my limbs.

It's so much better than it would be sitting at home alone, mired in anxiety.

CHAPTER 25

"Eliza, you need to stop sitting at the computer. You'll hurt your eyes."

Mom has her head and shoulders through the doorway. I should have shut and locked the door before I started drawing. I straighten up and look away from the screen. My lower back screams. My eyes water.

"I'm fine." I have four more *Monstrous Sea* pages to finish before this chapter is done. I planned it all out; if I do at least four pages a week, I can finish by graduation. It will keep me sane through this last godforsaken semester of high school, and it'll keep the fans happy after the Missing Pages debacle. I've spent the last three days doing nothing but drawing. "Can you please shut the door?"

"No. You need to get off the computer now." She uses her mom voice. The one that gives me instant heartburn.

"I'm working," I say without looking at her.

"Even hard workers need to take a break sometimes."

"I can't take a break. I have to get this done."

"Eliza."

"Mom, what do you think I'm doing here?" I swivel to face her. "Does it look like I'm taking a jaunty ride through the park? Like I'm having fun? Because I'm not having fun. I have to get this finished. People are expecting it. People who buy merchandise. Those people are going to pay for my college education."

"Eliza Mary Mirk!"

"What do you want me to do once I get off the computer? Go play sports with Sully and Church, even though they hate it when I play because I have no coordination? Watch TV, even though that's about a hundred times more mind-numbing than what I'm doing right now? Play some board games with you and Dad? You know how *that* goes!"

I always end up angry. And if I start it angry, like now, that can't bode well for the rest of the game.

Never one to back down from a challenge, my mother stands her ground. "I want you to go outside! Talk to your friends! Go *do* something! Get into trouble, for heaven's sake!"

"My friends are *on here*!" I hold up my phone, where Max and Emmy have been silent for days. "I talk to them all the time, and you always tell me to stop!"

"What about Wallace? What's he doing?"

"Right now he's working! And later on, guess what—he'll be at his computer, writing something. Probably his transcription of this, which a lot of people are waiting for, just like they're waiting for *this*. And we'll be talking *on the computer*. I don't understand why it's such a difficult concept to grasp."

"Eliza, I can't believe you right now." She shook her head, hands on her hips. She still wears her yoga pants and jacket from her run around the neighborhood. "What is all this about? Do you feel okay? Is something going on at school?"

"No."

"Then what is it?"

I turned away from her, ripping the glove off my right hand to wipe away the sweat. "It's just *Monstrous Sea* stuff. You don't have to worry about it."

She goes quiet. I pull the glove back on and start working on the next panel. The hairs on my neck stand up.

"Your dad and I are really proud of you for that, you know," she says. "I know we don't really get it, but we're proud of you. And we're happy you love to make it. We only annoy you because we're worried about you."

"Okay," I say.

"Will you come down and open your presents, at least?"

I swivel to look at her again. "Presents?"

"Yes, Eliza. It's Christmas."

I stare, sure she must be joking, then glance back at the computer screen and find that no, it really is December twenty-fifth. The realization almost jolts me out of my chair.

"It's Christmas?" My own voice sounds like a dying goat bleat in my ears. I thought it was two days away. Or two days ago. Either way.

She nods. "We went ahead and let your brothers open their gifts, because we weren't sure if you were coming down. Or when."

"Oh."

"So, are you?"

"I . . . yeah, I'll be down in a minute. Sorry."

"That's okay. There are some hard-boiled eggs in the fridge for you when you're ready for them too."

She leaves.

I stare at the clock on my computer.

12/25.

I actually check the messages on my phone, and realize Emmy and Max have been talking to me. Both of them said Merry Christmas, and asked what's been going on, and they've been talking to each other about their breaks. I send a few quick messages to them, then put the phone away and hurry downstairs. Mom and Dad wait for me in the living room, where the tree is set up. Dad has the video camera.

"Sorry," I say again.

"That's okay, Eggsy," Dad says. "Why don't you go open what Santa brought you, and then we can get your brothers back down here for some board games."

I do open what Santa brought me. I know it's from Santa because SANTA is printed on all the tags in my mom's curly handwriting. Most of it is new clothes. Clothes that will actually fit me.

"You were complaining about not having anything to wear last month," Mom says, "so I thought I'd get you some things. We can get some more in the spring, and then you'll have a whole new wardrobe for college. Don't worry, though—I saved the receipts, so if you don't like them we can take them back."

"Thank you," I say, quietly enough so they can't hear my voice break.

It's the first time I've actually been happy to get clothes for Christmas. I didn't ask for anything, because whatever I need I can buy for myself, except clothes. Clothes shopping does not work for me. Mom and I fold them all up in their boxes, and I take them upstairs to my room, where I grab the only Christmas present I could think to get anyone in my family: Monopoly. It takes so long to play, their family togetherness would never have to end.

Dad drags Church and Sully out of their room and forces them to play. They complain at first, until they realize they can bankrupt each other. Mom wins, because she's the only one in the family with any money sense. It takes like four hours. We eat dinner. Then Dad makes cookies, and we all sit down and watch *Miracle* together.

I didn't even know it was Christmas.

Faren turned the book over in his hands. *Earthen Fairy Tales.* The first book Amity had ever liberated from a shop, the one she'd used to learn to read. Faren let the book fall open on its strongest crease and there, on the middle of the right page, was her name.

"Amity and the Sea Monster."

"Sometimes," she said, tracing the letters with one finger, "I think the Earthens lied about this book. I don't think these stories come from Earth at all."

At the end of the story, the fairy-tale Amity killed the seacreeper by outsmarting it and crushing it with a large rock.

Amity's second birth on the beach, years ago, had ended somewhat similarly, but it had been a sunset riser instead of a seacreeper, five times as big and five times as bloodthirsty; it had gone after Faren, not her, because he was closer to the edge of the cliff; and as she stood, horrified, watching the beast swallow him, the Watcher had found her and proposed its deal.

She had accepted, and massacred the monster with the Watcher's help. Afterward, she had cut Faren, unconscious, out of its long throat.

As they sat and looked down at the book, Faren kissed her and said, "If this is what you feel you need to do, then do it. I know you're strong enough. If anyone can stop him, you can."

Then he left her to her reading, and to the feeling that it was not a matter of *need* at all.

She didn't *need* to do it.

She *had* to do it.

CHAPTER
26

Before I go to bed that night, I get an email from Wallace. Not a text or a forum message. An actual email. He doesn't forward things. He doesn't do chain messages. If he wants to tell me something, he either sends it to me live or tells me in person.

But I see his name come up, and I click on it without hesitation.

12/25/16, 11:21 p.m.

To: Eliza Mirk <mirkerlurker@gmail.com>
From: Wallace Warland <wallacewarland@gmail.com>

Subject: You found me in a constellation

I know it's weird for me to email you. I know we're both at our computers, and you're reading this, and I'm sitting in a pool of my own mortification, wishing I could delete emails after I send them. I couldn't give this to you in person, because then you might read it in front of me. I couldn't write it out by hand, because we'd be fifty by the time I finished, and that's not going to work for me.

Normally when I write something, I know how I should begin. I don't know how I should begin this. There are a lot of things I want to tell you, but I don't want to scare you. I cannot explain in words how much I don't want to scare you, and how afraid I am that I will.

So let's start with this: I never lived in Illinois. I've always lived here, in Westcliff. I went to school on the other side of town, with Cole. I'm sorry I lied to you about it. It's not that I didn't want to tell you the truth, but if I told you where I was from, I was worried you would figure out the rest of what I'm going to tell you here, and I wasn't sure I wanted you to know all that.

A while back, you said I looked like a football player. I said I played when I was little. That was only a half lie; I did play when I was little, but I didn't stop until halfway through sophomore year of high school. I was pretty good at it too. Made varsity. I still have that letter somewhere. My teammates called me Warfield Wallace 'cause I fucked shit up.

No, sorry, that's a lie too. They called me Warfield Wallace because it was alliterative, a play on my last name, and more intimidating than Wallace alone. And also because I FUCKED SHIT UP.

Sorry. I am not at the top of my game today.

I loved playing football. I loved hitting people, working in a team, and being with my friends. I loved winning. I loved how proud I made my dad. Not Tim, but my dad Dad, my biological dad. He loved football. He was a big guy, liked grilling out, Fourth of July fireworks, and throwing his kids into swimming pools. You could hear his laugh a mile away. Pretty much an all-around American. He wasn't religious, but he read the Westcliff Star at breakfast every morning like he'd go to hell if he didn't.

A little background about my dad: he never finished college. His family didn't have the money. He got a job in a corporate cubicle, trying to sell things to people over the phone. Long hours, little pay. He was already married to my mom—not Vee—and she was pregnant with me. I don't know if they got married because she was pregnant, or if she got pregnant after they were married. I guess it doesn't matter. Dad didn't like talking about that time, so I don't know much about it. Mom left him before I turned a year old. I don't remember her, so I was never upset about it, but my dad was sometimes.

A year or two later, he met Vee and they had Lucy, and things were good. Dad was the reason Lucy likes sports so much. He always wanted us to challenge ourselves. If something seemed too difficult for us, it was all the more reason to try. Lucy skipped a grade in school because of it. Dad challenged himself too—when he came home from work, he was louder and more colorful, full of energy. Wanted to help us with school projects or practice. Always put himself in the middle of everything.

There were dark parts too. He didn't let us see those, but a few times I walked into the kitchen late at night and found him hunched over the table, head in his hands. When he thought he was alone in the house in the middle of the day, he stared out the front door like the street was some unreachable promised land. When we grilled out, he made extra food for everyone else and ate nothing himself. If he and I were the only ones around, he ranted about his job and forbade me from ever doing anything that made me unhappy, even if that meant going without food or clothes or a roof.

Have you seen it in your parents? That moment when they become people? I think you have. It sneaks up on you, doesn't it? One day they're parents, and the next they say something racist, or get a cut that takes too long to heal, or make a simple mistake driving, and a facade falls away and they become mortals like the rest of us. After the facade is gone, it can never come back.

That darkness made him mortal. I saw it in my dad before the day he died, and I denied it. I shouldn't have. I should have told Vee, I should have told a doctor, I should have told someone. Over winter break of my sophomore year, we were driving home from a Christmas break spent in Tennessee with Vee's family. It was only me and my dad; Vee and Lucy were coming home the next day. Dad was on one of his rants. He'd gotten a little time off from work for the holidays, but not much, and he made me swear I'd never get a job like his. I had never seen him so worked up before. I told him I thought it would be smarter to get a job that paid decently, at least at first. It wouldn't be so bad, as long as I didn't make it my life.

That only made him angrier. I know now that he wasn't in his right mind. At the time, his yelling was incoherent, and when he stopped the car and told me to get out, I thought he was joking. It was almost January, freezing, and there were another few miles to go until home. He kicked me out right before Wellhouse Bridge and kept driving.

The second before he hit the gas, my stomach dropped. Really dropped. Like it wasn't there anymore. Sometimes the premonition of something happening is worse than the actual event, because you know it's coming and you can't do anything to stop it. He was going too fast for Wellhouse Turn, even without the ice on the road.

The Westcliff Star likes to lump my dad's death in with the other accidents that happened there. That band bus. The drunk teenagers. The woman with the kids. They think it was the ice that sent him off the road, but I stood there and watched him and I know that car went straight as an arrow until the moment it disappeared over the hill. I sprinted across the bridge after him, fell on a patch of black ice, smashed my face on the ground, broke my nose. Got back up, kept running. There's no good way to go down the incline at Wellhouse Turn, and I don't remember how I tried it, but I know I broke my leg too before I got to the bottom. They were the kind of breaks you don't feel at the time because of adrenaline and shock and fear. The car was at the bottom, sitting on all four wheels. Only when I got around to the other side of it did I see the smashed front of the car and my dad hanging out the windshield.

He was dead as soon as the car hit the ground. When you go straight off Wellhouse Turn that fast, you pretty much always are. I don't remember calling an ambulance, but I remember my phone smeared with blood after I pulled it away from my face. I don't remember trying to yank my dad the rest of the way through the windshield, but I remember sitting in the snow at the nose of the car, staring at his blank eyes while he lay across the accordion folds of the hood. I don't remember the paramedics getting there and asking if I was in the car with him, but I must have said yes, because that's how the story came out.

That's what the Star does, right? Says "a man and his son" when they list off all the people who've gone over that turn? I only read the Star once after that, two days after, and I never read it again.

My dad didn't hit ice. He wasn't drunk, or falling asleep at the wheel. When they asked me how it happened, I said I couldn't remember. I still say that. I haven't even told Vee, but I think she guessed. My dad didn't want to be here anymore. He was tired of his job, never having enough money, being yelled at by strangers. He was unhappy. Viciously unhappy.

I didn't stop talking on purpose. It just happened. A year ago I couldn't talk to anyone for anything. I'd like to say I tried and nothing came out, but I didn't try. Even trying was terrifying.

I could still write, though. I was into *Monstrous Sea* before Wellhouse Turn happened, but I didn't tell anyone about it, because my friends wouldn't have understood. After Wellhouse Turn, I couldn't do anything because of that broken leg, so I spent all my time writing fanfiction. I love playing football, but writing makes me happy in a way sports don't. We've talked about this before. Having the breakthrough that lets all the light in.

I spent another year and a half in my old school being That Kid Who Survived Wellhouse Turn and Never Spoke Again. I didn't go back to football after my leg healed, so most of my friends floated away. I thought about going to Wellhouse Turn, that maybe being back there would help, but every time I drove past I couldn't bring myself to stop the car. So I never did.

Things got better. Vee married Tim. I started working with Bren and her dogs. I stayed online and practiced my writing. I forced myself to talk at home, and to Cole and Megan and the others when we started hanging out at Murphy's, though I still can't do it when big groups of people are around. I started senior year at my old school, but by then I was the local freak show exhibit, so Vee and Tim let me transfer to Westcliff, where only football players might recognize my name.

The only other person I'd ever met in school who liked *Monstrous Sea* was Cole, and he's the kind of dick who doesn't hang out with you in public if it's not his ideal social situation, so we only talked to each other at Murphy's. And then I met you. You had this whole sketchbook full of Monstrous Sea fan art, and you actually stood up for me. Most people never do that; what kind of two-hundred-pound guy needs someone to stand up for him? I really thought you hated me at first. Or at least thought I was stupid. Most people think I'm stupid because I don't talk and I write slow.

But you wrote back. And you love creating things. And you get what I mean when I say I don't want to spend my life doing something I hate. If you know what you're meant to do, if you know what you love, why not do that? Find a way to do it, find a way to make money doing it. My dad hated what he did, and I think it made him hate himself. I don't want to hate myself. I don't want you to hate yourself.

I know we're both not the most socially adept people. I'm writing this all to you in an email because I'll pass out from stress if I try to say it to you in real time, even with a screen between us. I'm almost passing out from it right now, and we're in different places and I don't have to send it if I don't want to. I should end this before something bad happens.

I like being together. I like feeling like nothing is wrong with me. I like being able to think about something else at night instead of Wellhouse Turn. I know I should see someone about the talking, but for now I'm good with this. I'm happy.

I hope you're happy too.

Wallace

CHAPTER 27

My head is empty and ringing when I scroll back to the top of the email. My fingers feel like jelly. No one has ever told me something this important before. It's like Wallace took off a mask of his own face. The face beneath it is the same, but now I can watch the expression change.

What a whiny, spoiled brat I've been. This whole time.

Then I see the email's subject line.

Monstrous Sea Private Message

12:05 a.m. (MirkerLurker has joined the message)

> **MirkerLurker:** Either of you guys around?

> **MirkerLurker:** I have a question.

> **MirkerLurker:** Really not sure what to do...

12:25 a.m. (emmersmacks has joined the message)

> **emmersmacks:** Sorry

> **emmersmacks:** Been falling asleep way early lately

> **emmersmacks:** Like whats up with that right Im fourteen

> **emmersmacks:** Should be able to crush a Monty D and stay awake

> **emmersmacks:** Anyways

> **emmersmacks:** Whats up

> **MirkerLurker:** I don't know what "crush a Monty D" means, but I'd like to hear about your issues way more than I'd like to talk about mine.

> **emmersmacks:** In college there are these things called projects and if you want a good grade you work hard on them deep into the night for many weeks

> **MirkerLurker:** We have those in high school too.

> **emmersmacks:** Haha no you dont

> **emmersmacks:** Come take mechanical engineering and then tell me you do projects

emmersmacks: If you really want to hear about it I can go on . . .

MirkerLurker: No no, please.

MirkerLurker: I'm having issues of the Wallace kind.

emmersmacks: Oh no

emmersmacks: Bad issues??

MirkerLurker: No. More like the "He pulled the You Found Me in a Constellation card after telling me some very important things and now I don't know what to say to him" kind.

emmersmacks: O.O

emmersmacks: He used the constellation line??

emmersmacks: Wow he must really like you

emmersmacks: So do you not like him back???

MirkerLurker: I do!

MirkerLurker: But what are you supposed to say to someone who says that?

MirkerLurker: And it wasn't even that—he said that and he said all that other stuff too. Like stuff he's never told anyone else before.

emmersmacks: Tell him you love him

MirkerLurker: Gahhh. It's not that kind of conversation. The stuff he told me was . . . sensitive.

emmersmacks: You do love him dont you??

MirkerLurker: I don't know! How are you supposed to love someone when they don't even know who you are? I'm lying to him all the time, and he told me things about himself. Serious things. Things that matter.

emmersmacks: Sounds intimidating

MirkerLurker: It wasn't, not really. Not the way he put it.

MirkerLurker: Where is Max when you need him? He would explain what a guy wants to hear in this situation.

emmersmacks: Max is probably going to be gone a lot

MirkerLurker: What? Why?

emmersmacks: His girlfriend broke up with him a couple days ago

emmersmacks: She said he spent too much time online

emmersmacks: So now hes going to reevaluate his life or something

MirkerLurker: Why didn't he tell me?

emmersmacks: He did

emmersmacks: In a message thread a few days ago

MirkerLurker: Oh.

emmersmacks: But anyway I dont think you really need a guys perspective

emmersmacks: I mean like

emmersmacks: What would you want to hear if you said those things to someone??

CHAPTER 28

I can't even acknowledge that email until we go back to school. What would I say? What *can* you say to that in an email that doesn't sound fake?

Wallace lumbers into homeroom and sits beside me, as usual. He pulls out a paper and a pencil and carefully spells out a message, as usual. He slides it over to my desk, as usual.

Mrs. Grier's earrings look like actual dildos.

My laugh makes a few heads turn, including Mrs. Grier's. Her earrings—which are probably supposed to be eggplants but do indeed look like dildos—shake, and that makes me laugh harder.

It takes me a hot second to regain enough composure to write back.

I'd like to think she knows it and is just sticking it to the school administration by wearing them anyway.

Wallace snorts, then falls silent. It's a heavy, awkward silence, the kind of silence when you know you're both screaming in your heads and wondering why the other person can't read your thoughts.

I'm thinking: *You're the kid I read about in the* Westcliff Star.

And also: *Your dad killed himself and I'm still trying to absorb it, so I can't imagine what it's like for you.*

And finally: *I'm really glad you told me that, but I'm so bad at talking I don't know how to say it.*

Wallace sits quietly with an expression that looks like he must be screaming even louder than I am. He keeps the paper folded under his hands for a minute, gazes around the room, and finally writes, *Email?*

What would I want someone to say to me after all that? If I lost one of my parents that way? If I was afraid of being like that? If I'd been cut off from what I loved doing and the friends I had? If I was happy, and wanted to tell someone?

I write, *Are you okay?*

He writes, *I think so.*

I'm so impossibly out of my depth with this, but damn it, I can learn to keep my head above the water if I try hard enough. I know, then and there, that Wallace needs me to do it. He told me his truth when I couldn't tell him mine; I can at least muster this much for him. I write lines like this all the time. I draw important, character-changing conversations. Maybe I couldn't say these things out loud, but I know how to put them on paper.

I write, *This doesn't change us.*

He takes the paper back, reads it. Then he rests his forehead on his hands. The paper blocks his face. He sniffs, light, dry, and it could be nothing. No one around us pays any attention. When he lowers his hands to write again, he looks normal except for the slight redness beneath his eyes.

His pencil hovers over the paper. He scribbles—actually scribbles, hard and fast—the word *Good*. Then hands it back.

I wait a few minutes before writing,

That had quite the subject line.

I can't not bring it up, and the sooner the better. Wallace's ears turn red.

Super cheese, right?

Maybe a little.

It was all I had.

It is weird to have someone say to me the second most famous line in my own work, and mean it. It is weirder now that I know why his nose is crooked, and why he doesn't speak out loud in public. But he doesn't know who I am. It's not like he's using it to flatter me, or mock me.

I have to tell him that I'm LadyConstellation. Everything is unbalanced now, even if he doesn't feel it. But I have to do it the right way, at the right time.

So I write:

It is kind of a lot to process. Not in a bad way.

He nods.

The first half of the semester quickly becomes an exercise in figuring out how to break it to Wallace that I created *Monstrous Sea*. I cannot begin to fathom what he'll do, or how he'll take it.

Especially after that email. I read it at least once a day.

I know I should stare him straight in the eye and say it, but when I try, my body becomes violently ill. In homeroom, at lunch, on the benches behind the middle school—which has become "in my car behind the middle school," because January in Indiana is like the pregame cold for February in Indiana—at my house, at his house, at Murphy's, wherever.

I don't look at him and see Wellhouse Turn, like I thought I might. I only see Wallace. If he says he's happy, I trust him. The first time we go by Wellhouse Turn on the way to Murphy's, I glance over at him and he shakes his head, smiling a little.

"Don't look at me," he says.

When I look at Wellhouse Turn, all I see is the drop and the wonder.

We dwell on that email as little as possible. When we hang out, we do homework together to try to buffer each other's grades. Wallace checks history, English (of course), and about ninety percent of the elective courses; I cover math, the science courses, and the other ten percent of the electives, which means art class. Wallace only takes art because he hates the prompts in the creative writing class; I don't take art because the art teacher is a notorious snoop who would definitely find the *Monstrous Sea* panels in my sketchbook.

Because of that time around Christmas and the week of New Year's when we didn't hang out in person and I had time to catch up on *Monstrous Sea*, I have a surplus of pages and the momentum to keep going. Reader numbers climb. I post a few more drawings as MirkerLurker, and Wallace tells me how much people love them. I refuse to look at comments. I compile the next graphic novel for the shop, and almost choke at the sheer number of people who buy it in the first three hours after it goes up. I suppose I shouldn't be surprised with the views the pages get online, and the meteoric popularity of Wallace's transcription chapters— which have almost matched the page views of the comic itself— but it still gets me. Just like my alarm clock every morning.

I see Max around the forums every once in a while, banning someone or closing old threads under the Forges_of_Risht account, and Emmy stops by for the *Dog Days* watches, but our messages are few and far between. Usually whenever Emmy has time between classes, and when Max lets himself get online. Sometimes it feels like I see Cole, Megan, Leece, and Chandra more than I talk to Max and Emmy. I like Wallace's friends, but they still feel like *his* friends. I want *my* friends back.

By the time February hits—with some delightful below-zero weather cold enough to give you brain freeze from breathing through your mouth—it feels like I've known Wallace for five years instead of only five months. Neither of us ever brings up his email again, and I hope it's okay, but sometimes trying to read him is like trying to read a brick wall. His neutral expression is flat; when it changes it changes fast, and the change never lasts long.

He said we didn't need to talk about the email, what he said, his dad. We did, kind of, but not out loud. And now I feel like we should. We are both adept at the internet, at molding our text to mean what we want it to mean and what we think it should mean. I can lie on the internet, where people can't hear my voice. But with him, alone, I can't lie—I'm not a good enough actress. I hope he knows that.

"That email," I say one afternoon, while we lie on the mattress in Wallace's basement room. I'm tucked in the curve of his arm. His cheek is pressed to my hair. We both wear sweatpants. Our textbooks are scattered around our legs, and Wallace holds my latest English essay in one hand and a red pen in the other. I am now certain that the old football jersey pinned to his wall, the one that says WARLAND and the number 73, once belonged to his father.

I say nothing else, and after a moment he shifts his head. The essay and the pen sink to rest against my leg.

"That email," he repeats.

"We never really talked about it."

"I didn't know if you wanted to." His voice dwindles away. He can talk about grammatical errors, but not this.

"I wanted to say . . . I'm sorry about your dad. Everything that happened. But I'm happy you're happy. And I'm glad—I'm really glad—you felt like you could tell me all that. I am too. Happy, I mean."

His arm tightens around me.

"I thought it might have been . . . too much."

"It wasn't. What I said—wrote—in class was true. I mean, I'm . . ." I tap a finger on his rib cage without really thinking about where I'm touching. "I'm still here."

The essay disappears first, then the thick arm I was using as a pillow. Wallace pushes me onto my back and buries his head in the crook of my neck. I giggle because I can't help it. My hands find his shoulders. He does this sometimes: one slow, careful kiss gets pressed to my collarbone; another against my neck. The neck one wrecks me. Instant ball of nerves. He can't know how that one feels, or else he wouldn't stop. He pushes himself up so we're eye to eye. Our noses nearly touch. His eyes are downcast. I snap my mouth shut. His fingers run up my sides and I can't breathe, I can't breathe at all.

"Good," he says.

I lock my arms around his neck and pull him down so the weight of his torso rests on mine and his forehead presses to the pillow. His breath hitches. Before I can stop myself I run a hand up through his hair. The short, sharp bristles along the base of his skull and the back of his head. The smoother, longer strands on the top. He turns his face toward me, and I trace a finger along the hair that's fallen over his forehead.

Water rushes through the pipes overhead. A clock ticks in the darkness. One of Wallace's eyes turns amber in the yellow light of his lamp. *Want* rises up in me, sharp and fast, and I know in that instant that I can't hold myself back anymore. I don't want to be the frozen girl, but I can't wait for someone else to thaw me.

I tip my head forward. Wallace meets me halfway. Heat rushes through my face and he must be able to feel it in my lips. He must be able to tell I've never kissed anyone before. I pull away, ducking my chin. Wallace's head follows.

"I thought I was supposed to surprise you," he says.

"You took too long," I say. I turn my face to the pillow so my hair makes a curtain. He brushes it back and kisses my eyebrow. Then my cheek, then my nose, then he leans over me and nuzzles my ear. Warm shocks race down my spine.

It makes no earthly sense how another person can do this. Not even with words, just touches. Just *looks*. He just looks at me and I feel simultaneously like myself and someone else, like I'm here and I'm not, like everything and nothing.

"What are you thinking?" I ask.

He rests on his side, still partially draped over me, and says,

"You know that part in *Monstrous Sea* where Dallas asks Amity to kiss him once before she leaves, because he's afraid he won't live to see her again?"

"Yes."

"And what he says after she does it?"

Of course I do. I wrote it.

"'Like I imagined,'" I say. He nods. I know most people would think it's silly or stupid to explain things this way, in scenes and quotes, but we're both fluent in the language of *Monstrous Sea*. This is the way I understand him best.

"I'm bad at this," I say.

"No you're not," he says.

"I've never kissed anyone before," I say, face still hot.

"Yes you have," he says, with the little smile.

I shove him, which does nothing. "Shut up. You write smutty fanfiction all day."

"Excuse you, I do not write smut. If I choose to include a sex scene, it is both tasteful and classy." He leans in so there's nowhere else to go and nowhere else to look. "Besides, it's not like you have to have actual experience to write smut. Or even kissing."

"Don't pretend like you don't have any kissing experience."

"Okay, I won't."

I shove him again. He catches my wrists and holds my hands against his chest.

He's already so close, all I have to do is stick out my chin.

Again, he meets me halfway. This kiss is deeper, longer than the last one. My face burns, but I keep myself where I am. I've done enough hiding in my life. I hide from my classmates all day long. I hide from my parents, my brothers, even my friends.

I might be hiding LadyConstellation from Wallace under the guise of Eliza Mirk, but it's not LadyConstellation he's kissing right now.

It's Eliza. It's me.

I don't want to hide this part of myself anymore.

The first day Amity met her, Kite stood in the middle of the sparring ring, arms crossed over her chest. Her skin was a darker brown than Amity's.

"Where are you from?" Amity blurted out the moment Kite finished her terse introduction. The older woman turned up her nose and looked vaguely royal.

"The Isles of Light," Kite replied, "and that's all you need to know. Sato tells me you have no formal fighting experience."

"Yes. But I'm fast, and I learn quickly."

The longer Kite inspected her, the more Amity felt as if Kite didn't like her. It didn't come as a surprise. Most people didn't like her upon meeting her, put off by her orange eyes and white hair and the knowledge that the Watcher lived inside her—but it didn't make the idea of spending months training with Kite any easier.

"Are you ready?" Kite asked.

Amity couldn't tell if Kite meant for the sparring, or for hunting Faust. Though, then again, she really only had one answer.

"Yes."

CHAPTER 29

When spring break hits at the beginning of March, my parents decide I've had enough of my bedroom and decline my request to be omitted from this year's family camping trip. Sully and Church find this hilarious. Lazy hermit Eliza trekking through the wilderness with a pack of supplies, reeking of bug repellent.

It's not that I don't like the outdoors. It's that I don't see the point of the outdoors when there's so much I could be doing indoors.

My parents also deny me my sketchbook for this venture, an act that would have had me boiling over in a fit of apoplectic rage had I any less self-control. They've never taken my sketchbook away before, and I don't think Dad felt the shock wave of pure surprise and anger that came off me when he told me to turn around and take the thing back to my room.

Mom and Dad don't say anything about my phone, though. Either they don't think I'll get service, or they didn't realize I had it. I keep it tucked in my pocket.

It burns a hole there the whole way to the Happy Friends Dog Day Care to drop off Davy, then as we drive down a long dirt road between two thick swaths of forest. The camping gear rattles around in the back of the SUV. Sully and Church, on either side of me, sing along with the pop music vibrating from the radio. Mom and Dad politely ignore them. Sully screams all the lyrics correctly but slightly off-key. Church is actually kind of good.

"You should try out for choir," I say when the song ends.

Church's entire head-neck region flares red. "No," he snaps. "Choir is stupid."

I shut my mouth. So much for trying.

"Aw, little Churchy in choir." Sully laughs. "You could hang out with Macy Garrison all day if you were in choir."

"I thought you were going to ask Macy Garrison out before Christmas?" Dad looks at us in the rearview mirror with a twinkle in his eye. "What happened with that?"

"I never said I would," Church grumbles. Then he shoots me a dirty look. "Thanks a lot. Why didn't you stay home with your boyfriend?"

"Mom and Dad wouldn't let her," Sully says, still laughing.

"They think she's going to invite him over for sex."

I am a volcano.

"Oh, Eliza, that's not why we did this," Mom takes her eyes off the road for a second to look back at me. "If you and Wallace decide you want to take that step, it's completely up to you—that's why we had that doctor's appointment."

"Mom, *stop*." My voice drops.

"It's completely healthy for kids your age to be, you know, getting together."

"I'm surprised you haven't yet," Dad chimes in. "Junior year of high school was the first time your mother and I—"

"STOP!" Sully, Church, and I yell it at the same time, clapping our hands over our ears. Mom and Dad look nonplussed and stop speaking.

We drive in silence for three more minutes before Mom pipes up again.

"Just saying. It's how we made all three of you."

"Jesus," Sully groans.

We park at the campgrounds and have to hike like two miles uphill to get to where we're setting up the tents. I knew before coming out here that this would be no walk in the park. My parents and brothers load themselves up with gear and start out with a spring in their steps. I'm carrying my own stuff—two days' worth of clothes, snacks, bug spray, and sunblock—and wearing my old baggy clothes and the hiking shoes Mom got me because she didn't want me twisting my ankles.

Almost as soon as we begin up the path, sweat starts running between my shoulder blades. The sun beats down through the trees. It's chilly late March and yet still terrible. I fall behind instantly. Huffing, puffing, wiping sweat from my eyes. My back is already killing me. My parents soldier on, followed by Sully and Church, whose voices scare birds out of the trees. They don't even look back to see where I am. It's not as if it matters; we're following a defined dirt trail laid out between the trees to a cleared-out campsite up in the woods. I used to come when I was younger, but in recent years I've been able to wriggle out of it by feigning sickness. I tried again this morning, but Dad said I'd feel better once I was out in the fresh air. I know exactly where they're going and how to get there, so I stop to sit on a fallen log by the path and pull out my phone.

My signal's not great out here, but I'm still getting it. I go to my messages. There's nothing from Wallace, but I told him I was going to be out in the woods for two days, so he probably won't send anything until he knows I can read it. There are a few new things from Emmy and Max, though. I open the chat window.

Apocalypse_Cow: you should tell that professor to go stick his head up his ass.

Apocalypse_Cow: but with better words. obviously. can't have a twelve-year-old saying things like that.

emmersmacks: Im fourteen

emmersmacks: I totally could say that if I wanted

emmersmacks: But I wont cause I need a good grade on this test

Apocalypse_Cow: are you going to have him again next semester?

emmersmacks: No this is the last class with him

emmersmacks: But hes the only one who teaches it so if I dont pass I have to take it with him again

Apocalypse_Cow: that's bullshit. you should go to the department head and say he's discriminating against you because of your age.

4:31 p.m. (MirkerLurker has joined the message)

MirkerLurker: What's going on?

Apocalypse_Cow: em's shitty calc teacher keeps singling her out and making fun of her in class because of how young she is.

emmersmacks: Hes not making fun of me

emmersmacks: He calls me a baby every time I point out something wrong with his equations

emmersmacks: Like I was the one who got the answer wrong and Im just upset about it or something

I love that about Max and Emmy. Weeks without a long conversation, and they let me back into the fold like nothing has changed.

> **MirkerLurker:** That sounds like he's making fun of you.

> **MirkerLurker:** Actually, it sounds like he's an asshole. Teachers who call their students babies are assholes, no matter what the ages of the parties involved. You should tell the department head.

> **emmersmacks:** Yeah

> **emmersmacks:** Maybe

> **emmersmacks:** Like I said, I just have to get through the rest of this semester and pass and then I dont have to see him again

> **Apocalypse_Cow:** we're serious, em. this is not okay. he shouldn't be doing things like that.

> **emmersmacks:** Can we change the topic now??

"Got a little winded, Eggs?"

I jump and look up. Dad trots back down the trail, smiling until he sees the phone in my hands. I try to stuff it back in my pocket, but it's too late.

"I told you I wasn't feeling good," I say, picking myself up and brushing my pants off.

"I thought we said no phones?"

"You must have only said it to Church and Sully. I didn't hear it."

"Eggs."

I climb up the trail past him. "I was talking to my friends."

"But this is family time. I'm sure your friends will understand when we get back in a few days." He catches up to me like he was walking beside me the whole time, and holds out his hand.

I still don't hand it over. "It was important stuff."

"I'm sure it was." His voice is light, appeasing. My skin crawls. The outstretched hand grabs my arm. "Eliza."

I spin on him. He never uses my real name. "It's just a phone! I'm probably going to get crappy reception up there anyway! Why do you guys have to take everything away from me?"

"I think you can survive without your phone for two days," he says in official Dad Voice. "And your mother will agree with me. Now hand it over."

I tear my phone out of my pocket, shove it at him, then start up the trail following the echoes of my brothers' voices. Dad stays behind me, probably to make sure I don't stop again.

I don't plan on stopping. I'm angry enough to walk for days.

Mom, Church, and Sully are already at the campsite. Church and Sully fight over our tent. Mom already has the other one set up.

"Aw, I thought you died back there," Sully said. He looked at Church. "Guess we have to share the tent."

I throw my pack into the dirt. "Shut up, Sully."

Dad's talking to Mom in undertones, holding my phone out for her. Her eyebrows press together. She slides my phone into her pocket.

I scrub my face with my hands. My hair sticks to my cheeks and my skin itches. Hives threaten. I took my allergy medication before we came up here, and I have one EpiPen in my bag and Mom has the other, but if I have an allergic reaction out here and have to be rushed to a hospital, it will be a welcome relief.

I won't have an allergic reaction. I haven't had one since I was ten.

Unfortunately.

The sun's below the trees when the tents are up and Dad's starting on the campfire. I toss my stuff inside the smaller tent and climb in after it.

"Thanks for helping set up, Rotten Eggs," Sully calls from the fireside, flipping me the bird.

"Sullivan!" Mom swats his hand down.

He sticks his tongue out at me instead. I ignore him as I lower the tent flap and spread out my sleeping bag in the middle of the tent. Polyester does nothing to keep out the sounds of the woods, and I don't plan on sleeping near one of the flimsy walls if anything decides to attack us. Probably nothing will attack us, but I'm not taking the chance.

As I'm sliding inside the sleeping bag, Mom sticks her head into the tent.

"Aren't you coming to eat s'mores?"

"No," I say.

"Do you feel okay?"

"Fine."

She pauses. "Is this about your phone?"

"I'm tired."

"We want you to spend more time *here*, in the real world. Your dad didn't mean to make you angry, but we . . ."

Her voice trails off when I turn away from her and pull the sleeping bag up to cover most of my head. She sighs.

"We know you don't want to be here. And maybe . . . maybe we just don't understand it well enough. Any of it. The online friends, the webcomic, even the drawing itself. We've tried to figure it out. We want to understand it, to know why it means so much to you. It scares us, how intense you get, and how little we know about it. We can't get you to explain it, so we're navigating in the dark."

There's a beat of silence where she waits for me to turn over. I don't. Then she sighs again and stands. Her boots crunch across dirt and twigs back to the fireside.

The four of them talk and laugh for another hour or two. My stomach rumbles. They ate dinner too, not just s'mores. Mom finally sends them all to bed. I pretend to be asleep when Church and Sully climb into the tent and spread out on either side of me.

"How is she already asleep?" Sully whispers. "At home she stays up until like two a.m."

"She probably was tired," Church whispers back.

"What, from climbing a hill?"

Church doesn't respond. They get into their sleeping bags and whisper for half an hour about the outdoor soccer season about to start. I hadn't even realized the indoor season was over—Mom and Dad just told me when I needed to take them to practice or pick them up. I didn't know how they'd done. Were there any tournaments? Trophies?

After a long stretch of silence, Sully says, "So did you really try out for the spring musical?"

Church doesn't respond for a second. "Yes. Why?"

"Just wondering. Why didn't you tell me?"

"Because you would have made it about Macy Garrison."

"It—it's not?"

"No."

"Oh. But you're not going to try out for choir?"

"Maybe."

"Why?" Just the smallest bit of mocking enters Sully's tone.

"Because I *like* it," Church snaps back. "We don't have to do all the same things. Try out for mathletes or something. You like math. You'd be good at it."

"Mathletes is for nerds."

"Sull, there's something you should know."

"Don't say it."

"You *are* a nerd."

"I'm not a nerd. *Eliza's* a nerd."

"Actually, I think Eliza's a geek. I've seen her grades. Compared to us, she's horrible at school."

"You're a nerd for knowing the difference."

"That's fine."

Sully makes no sound, but I can feel him fuming in the darkness. I didn't know Church could get under Sully's skin so easily. I didn't know Sully liked math. I didn't know either of them were that good at school. I didn't know Church already knew he was good at singing . . . or that he was interested in musical theater.

I've been living with them their whole lives, but until right now, they've felt like strangers.

I let my eyes flutter open for only a moment. I lie facing Church; he stares back at me. I close my eyes again. Pretend I saw nothing. Pretend I'm still asleep.

Sully brings up soccer again, trying to revive the conversation, but Church stops responding. Then Sully stops too, and rolls over with a grunt. The tent goes quiet. I wish I had a bowl of hard-boiled eggs. My fingers long for my phone, my computer, my pen, my *something*. There is so much nothing out here I can't fathom it. Nothing but dirt and campfire smell and s'mores made with stale graham crackers. Nothing but my brothers, who suddenly look much less like twins.

I don't sleep well that night.

In all likelihood, my phone would've died before the end of the camping trip. That doesn't make tromping through the backwoods any easier. On the first day we hike over some fairly impressive hills, because Indiana couldn't manage a mountain or two. I nearly choke on my own spasming lung. Sully and Church make fun of me. On the morning of the second day we visit a few caves, and at least Mom and Dad let me opt out of those—no way will you get me inside somewhere so tight and dark and confined. I don't care if they're not actually going spelunking, I've seen enough horror movies to know what kind of backward urban legends hang out in caves.

I sit outside the cave and draw Amity and Damien in the dirt with a stick. Neither of them had parents around to tell them what to do or where to go. Someone asked me that once, actually, why so many of the characters don't have parents. Amity was separated from her family. Faren was an orphan of Nocturne Island. Damien's and Rory's parents both died in their early teens. Not all of them were horrible people, either—it wasn't like I was taking out some subconscious aggression on my own parents. They were just absent.

I don't know why. Maybe it *was* something subconscious.

Of course it was. All art is subconscious.

I dig the end of the stick too hard into the dirt, and the tip breaks off. I chuck it across the clearing and find a new one.

I wonder what the fandom is doing. I wonder what Emmy and Max are doing. Emmy's probably dealing with that asshole calculus professor, and Max is no doubt trying to get his girlfriend back. Or maybe they're not—maybe Emmy is eating Starburst and watching *Dog Days* reruns, and Max has dealt with the girlfriend situation and has moved on to more exciting ventures, like rearranging his Power Rangers action figure collection. I'll be able to find out tomorrow, when Mom and Dad give me my freaking phone back.

Amity and Damien face the same direction, attacking some unknown enemy, so across from them I draw a long-necked sunset riser rearing up, jaw open and fangs extended. The scale is wrong at first, so I wipe it out with my shoe and stand up to draw the sea monster to its true size.

I miss Wallace. I miss Max and Emmy and the fandom too, but I would miss Wallace even if I had my phone and could talk to him. I miss sitting next to him at Murphy's, boxed against the wall by his big body. I miss the way he dips both ends of his sushi rolls in soy sauce when we go out to eat. I miss how he brushes hair off his forehead with the end of his pen when he's in the middle of writing—because it's grown out since October, and he actually has to do that now.

God, it hasn't even been four days since I last saw him. This is ridiculous. I go to bed thinking about him; I wake up thinking about him. I want to draw him, but I haven't tried it yet. I used to only feel this way about *Monstrous Sea*. It's not like he's taken that away, either—I still love *Monstrous Sea*. I'm still obsessed with it. And that makes sense, right? Because I created it. Who isn't obsessed with the things they create, they love? Ideas are the asexual reproduction of the mind. You don't have to share them with anyone else.

But Wallace . . . I share Wallace with a lot of people. Wallace isn't mine any more than I'm his, but I *want* him. I want to hold him, I want to be near him, I want to crawl inside his mind and live there until I understand the way he works. I want him to be happy.

I wonder what he'd think of this picture I drew in the dirt. He'd probably say it's good, but I forgot the sunset riser's horns.

I add in the sunset riser's horns.

My family exits the cave. Church and Sully charge into the trees, yelling something about the lake. Dad hurries after them, calling at them not to run in the woods. Mom comes last, and her gaze passes over my drawing before I manage to swipe my foot through the middle. Big, arcing foot swipe. Damn giant sea monster.

"Are you still upset with us for taking your phone?" Mom asks. Softly, like I might bite her face off.

I shrug. I'm not allowed to say no to her, and I'm not going to lie to make her feel better.

"We don't do things like that to punish you, you know."

I've already turned to the trees to follow Dad.

"Eliza, I'm trying to talk to you."

I stop and turn back to face her. She puts her hands on her hips.

"Don't look at me like that," she says.

"Like what?" I say.

"Like I'm wasting your time. I brought you into this world, the least you can do is listen to me for two minutes."

"Fine, I'm listening."

She covers her face with her hands. Smooths back the flyaway strands of her hair. A smear of dirt arcs over her left temple.

"Sometimes . . ." She sighs. Sighing means she wants to launch into what she believes to be a long, heartfelt conversation, and at the end of it, if I don't agree with her, then I'm an ungrateful child.

"Sometimes," she says again, "we don't know what to do with you. Your brothers are easy. They want to play sports and video games and eat a lot of food. They tell us about school and their friends. They're like your dad and I used to be when we were younger. We never had the internet in high school. We didn't have smartphones. Even if we did, I don't think we'd use them as much as you do. Oh—sorry, that sounded terrible. You just spend so much time online, we never know if you're okay or not. We don't know what's going on with you. You're so quiet, and you spend so much time on your own—when Wallace started coming over, it was a real relief.

"What I'm trying to say is that we don't feel like we know you anymore. We don't know what you want."

She stops and stares and waits.

I say, "*Monstrous Sea*," because no other words come to me.

She nods. "And we're proud of you for that. But . . . is that it?"

I shrug.

"There's more to life than stories, Eliza."

She says it like it's simple. She says it like I have a choice.

There's the frustration again, hot and ready, and there's frustration's best friend, anger, and there are my hands balling into fists and my stomach twisting in a knot and my jaw clenching so hard my molars squeal in protest. Mom takes a step back and then a step forward. She might try to hug me. I don't want anyone touching me right now.

"I'm going to the lake," I say, and turn again.

This time she doesn't stop me.

Sully and Church and Dad are already at the edge of the lake with the fishing supplies. It's got to be too cold for fish. They're fishing anyway. Mom goes to join them.

I sit on an outcropping of rock above the lake and try to

be angry, but I can't hold the feeling. I need erupting volcanoes, hurricanes, massive earthquakes. Were I working on *Monstrous Sea* right now, Orcus's monsters would bleed from the page in the search for flesh. I need vindication. I do not need little birds twittering over a wide expanse of shimmering lake and a light wind ruffling my hair.

Nature defies my anger. Nature defies every emotion I have. I can't complain to nature, or appeal to it, or rage at it.

Nature doesn't care about me.

Monstrous Sea Private Message

6:43 p.m. 21 - Mar -17

MirkerLurker: Finally crawled my way out of hell.

rainmaker: Haha come on, camping's not that bad. Dirt! Fresh air! CAMPFIRES!

MirkerLurker: I'm convinced there's something wrong with you. No one should love campfires this much.

rainmaker: Campfires are crackly happiness. So how was it?

MirkerLurker: My parents found out I had my phone and took it away. Wouldn't let me bring my sketchbook or anything. How big of an issue is it if I have a freaking sketchbook with me?

MirkerLurker: Sorry. I know I shouldn't be complaining about this. It was only a few days. But they do this kind of stuff constantly, and I don't understand why they can't let up.

rainmaker: I think they want to spend time with you. You do have a tendency to zone out when you're working.

MirkerLurker: So? So do you.

rainmaker: When I say "zone out" I mean I have to shove you out of your seat to get your attention. It's not exactly normal. I get where they're coming from—didn't you say you almost missed Christmas because you were working on something?

MirkerLurker: Well, yeah, but I had to get stuff done. It was really important.

rainmaker: Maybe they have a point. It's not good to get so intense about things so often. Maybe you should see someone about it.

MirkerLurker: That's cute. You're telling me I should see someone.

rainmaker: Real nice, Eliza. I'm trying to help.

MirkerLurker: I didn't ask for help.

rainmaker: You didn't have to.

6:55 p.m. 21 - Mar -15

rainmaker: Are you ignoring me now?

7:03 p.m. 21 - Mar - 15

rainmaker: Fine.

CHAPTER 30

On Monday, I stand at my locker and imagine the floor shaking as Wallace stalks down the hallway toward me, parting a sea of students who scramble to get out of his way. He doesn't look angry. He never looks angry at school. He just looks impassive. Irish Spring wafts over me when he stops two feet away and thrusts a piece of paper under my nose. On it is a single line of his machine-print handwriting.

Are you done?

"Yes, I'm done," I say.

He nods, shoves the paper in his pocket, and leans against the locker next to mine. His gaze settles somewhere on the other side of the hallway. I know he's right, and I get too intense about my work sometimes. I also know that I wasn't wrong, even if I wasn't very nice when I said he should be seeing someone. Apologizing seems right, but also like if I say I'm sorry that means I don't think there's something wrong and that he should go on never talking to anyone.

By the end of homeroom, he seems to have forgiven me at least a little bit, because he texts me a link to what he says is the best Children of Hypnos fifth-book fanfiction ever. By lunch, he hands over a new chapter of his *Monstrous Sea* transcription. He says he's getting close to the end of what would be the first book in the series, and he would've had it done sooner if so much school stuff hadn't gotten in the way.

I inhale the new chapter. I never get enough of his writing, and I don't know if it's because he's writing something I made or if he's just that good. I like to think he's just that good. He doesn't volunteer to show me any of his original work, and I never ask to see it. I don't know what I'd say to him if I didn't like it.

He never asks to see any of my original work, either. Sometimes I'm sure it's for the same reason, but other times I wonder if he doesn't care. If, like most of the *Monstrous Sea* fans, he doesn't care if I have anything else in me.

Production of *Monstrous Sea* is up. Five pages a week minimum, a whole chapter if I'm really on my game. Max, when he's online, has plenty of trolls to keep him busy on the Forges_of_Risht account.

Emmy has to hang around every Friday night to monitor the website and make sure it doesn't crash. Mondays and Wednesdays at three are reserved for our biweekly mandatory chat sessions, where we don't speak a word about *Monstrous Sea* and instead talk about how Emmy's faring at the end of her freshman year ("Im not dead yet"), and how Max feels about his new boss (actual demon).

Weekends are for Wallace. We spend Saturdays with Cole and Megan, when she can join, and Leece and Chandra on the computer, if they're around. Not always at Murphy's. Sometimes we go to the Blue Lane for bowling. One week we go to the park behind the high school, where Wallace and Cole teach me how to throw a spiral, then take turns running around with Hazel on their shoulders while I show Megan how to sketch a landscape using the long field and the trees of the woods in the distance. After a while I hand over the paper and pencil and give pointers while she tries it.

"You're really good at this," she says, tucking a hair behind her ear and squinting at the tree line. "Teaching, I mean."

"You think so? I tried teaching my brothers to draw a few years ago and they said I was mean."

"No, not mean." Megan laughed. "Just blunt. But that's a good thing."

Hazel squeals. Wallace has hoisted her over his head in an airplane, and Cole is pretending to be the enemy jet she has to shoot down.

I don't call them "Wallace's friends" anymore. They're our friends. His first, and still mostly his, but now also mine. I talk to them on the forums through my MirkerLurker account even when Wallace isn't around. That may not seem like much to some people, but it's a lot to me.

When I'm not with them or talking to Emmy and Max or hanging out with Wallace, I'm watching myself. Making sure I don't get too focused on working. But with five pages a week, that's easier said than done. Especially because the comic is so close to the end. If I space it out right, *Monstrous Sea* will end when I graduate. I may not even go to graduation. I'll sit at my computer and post the final *Monstrous Sea* pages myself, no scheduling required.

I know how this ends. The story. The fan reactions.

It will be glorious.

Then the graduation issue of the *Westcliff Star* shows up at school.

The *Westcliff Star* focuses on only two stories every year. The first, obviously, is the Wellhouse Turn memorial. The second is the graduation of the seniors from Westcliff High. This is the issue where all the parents in the township write short blurbs about their graduating seniors and send them in, and the paper prints them with the ugliest student pictures they can find, and everyone in school reads through them and laughs at the humiliating things everyone else's parents said about them.

My parents have been looking forward to this since we got back from the spring break camping trip. They said I'd love it. Absolutely love it.

There's a whole stack of *Westcliff Stars* in Mrs. Grier's room when I arrive that morning, and everyone is reading. I grab one, dread flooding me, sweat building on my back. Yes, let's see what traumatizing thing my parents said about me, and everyone can read about Creepy Eliza. I head to my seat.

Mrs. Grier's gaze follows me across the room. She sits stick straight at her desk, eyes wide, the newspaper spread open in front of her. She doesn't normally watch me like that, so either I have something on my face or my parents really said something they shouldn't have. God, they put a baby picture of me in here. Or they told the story about the time I tried to kick the ball in soccer and missed so badly the momentum threw me on the ground.

I hurry to my desk, sit without taking my backpack off, and tear the paper open. My hands shake as I flip past picture after picture, paragraphs of stories about childhood, broken arms and baseball games, school plays and birthdays. It's in alphabetical order, and I skip past my name and have to backtrack. There it is, a terrible school picture of me from seventh grade, with greasy hair and braces and an actual turtleneck, did-I-come-out-of-the-fucking-sixties a *turtleneck*. My parents have never been great writers, but they managed a full paragraph for this one.

Eliza Mirk

We're so proud of our Eliza. She's our firstborn, and she's as stubborn and passionate now as she always has been. These eighteen years have been a long road, full of lots of twists and turns, but she's taught us so much about being parents—and about being people. She loves hard-boiled eggs, thick socks, and listening to her music maybe a little too loud (but what teenager doesn't?). Best of all, she's an artist, and what she loves more than anything else is her webcomic, *Monstrous Sea*. She has spent so much of her time working on this story, poured so much of herself into it, and built something for herself from the ground up. We know that no matter where she goes or what she does after this, she'll be successful. Eliza, we love you.

Peter and Anna Mirk

I look up and the room is silent. Not because everyone stopped talking, but because there is a ringing in my ears so loud nothing can penetrate it. The room expands and I shrink, the walls exploding away from me, the light dimming. My heart stutters in my chest.

Mrs. Grier walks down my row, newspaper in hand. She kneels next to my desk. Her voice comes out too slow.

"Eliza. Is this true?" She holds up the paper. It's turned to my paragraph and my stupid face. "Did . . . did you create *Monstrous Sea?*"

My stomach heaves violently. I clap a hand over my mouth.

"Because I—well, I probably shouldn't show you this, but . . ." Mrs. Grier pulls back her sleeve. She always wears long sleeves, cardigans over her sundresses, sweaters, even in the summer, and now I know why: in thick black ink up her arm are the words THERE ARE MONSTERS IN THE SEA.

My most famous quote is tattooed on my homeroom teacher's arm.

Behind Mrs. Grier, Wallace walks into the room. Big, lumbering Wallace. Normally he moves slow, but today, in this slow-motion world, he moves far too fast. He reaches the front table where the newspapers are stacked up. Takes one. Opens it. I know he'll look for my name first because mine comes before his. He'll see it. He reads slow, but not that slow.

I shove myself out of my seat, knock Mrs. Grier over, and reach Wallace in time to rip the newspaper out of his hands.

"Don't read it!"

I hold it to my chest, panting, unable to get enough air. Heads turn. Look up from their papers. Wallace stares at me. Confusion and possibly fear flit over his face.

"Don't—don't read it," I say again. Several people are already flipping through pages at their desks, looking for mine. Wallace looks at them, at me, at the paper. Then he reaches for another one. I try to stop him, but his big hand grabs first one wrist and then the other, holding me off like I'm a child. He spreads the newspaper out on the table and flips it open.

"No—Wallace, don't read it—please, please don't read it—"

I press against his arm, trying to push him away from the table, the papers, but he's so *solid*. I whisper now. The others can't hear me beg like this. Wallace's brow furrows as he finds my picture, my paragraph, and begins reading. True dread squeezes around me like a second, larger hand. I know when he reaches the end because the color drains from his face like someone chopped off his head and let the blood run out. He looks at me. Jabs a finger on the paper hard enough to crinkle the page. Jabs it again. Pointing. *Is it true. Is it true, is it true.*

"I wanted to tell you." I can't even tell if sound is coming out anymore. "I wanted to tell you, I did, but I didn't know how—"

He drops my wrists like they're poisonous, steps back, then turns and walks out of the room. I try to follow him, but Mrs. Grier's hand lands on my shoulder. She says something. I shrug her off. Someone from the back of the room says, "Holy shit, you made *Monstrous Sea*?"

I stumble into the hallway. Wallace is gone. The floor sways back and forth, and blackness creeps on the edges of my vision.

After a moment or two, it passes.

At least, it seems like a moment or two. Maybe a few minutes. Maybe half an hour, because by the time I snap out of it, the bell is ringing and students pour into the hallways.

I wander to first period without my backpack.

With each passing class, more and more stares find me in the hallway. People talk, but I can't hear what they're saying. I don't see Wallace again, which is some kind of feat considering his size. My body is a teacup and all my organs have been stuffed inside. Must be my allergies. It is spring, after all.

Wallace will have to talk to me at lunch. He wouldn't sit without me at lunch.

I hang on the fringes of the herd of students surging for the cafeteria and let them pull me through the doors. On the other side I fall away like a leaf flung out on a stray current. I stand for a moment, unsure of the cafeteria's exact orientation, then stagger toward the lunch lines. If I can get some food and find Wallace, it will be okay.

A body steps in front of me. Tall. Deshawn Johnson. He's holding something out. A folded paper. My hand reaches out to take it like this is some kind of dream and my body is responding without my permission. I unfold the paper.

It's my drawing. The one Travis stole in October.

". . . really sorry," Deshawn says. "Travis was being an asshole . . . meant to give it back sooner, but never got the chance . . . it's really cool that you draw *Monstrous Sea* . . . my brother got me into it—"

I might throw up on his shoes if I stand here any longer, so I stumble past him. Wallace has to be here somewhere. At our table. Obviously. By the windows. I look. He's not there.

I get in line and stare at the purse of the girl in front of me. I don't know what I put on my tray until I get to the end, and the lunch lady rings me up for two bowls of tomato soup, a vegetable tray, a handful of mustard packets, and a Drumstick. The Drumstick is for Wallace. Wallace loves Drumsticks.

I wander out of the lines and look at the table again. He's still not there. I scan the cafeteria. He's not in any of the lines. Not at the tables near the door, or by the wall. Is he in the courtyard? It's too cold for that today.

Heads turn. Eyes watch me. So many eyes. I head toward our table. The world tips again. It's like I'm a mustard packet and some baby's hand is squeezing all the condiment out of me. Squeezing my heart, my lungs, squeezing my eyes so my vision narrows to a little point in front of me. Hair sticks to my face. One of the bowls of tomato soup falls off my tray and splatters the white tile floor.

Someone calls my name. I think.

They might have said LadyConstellation.

I walk through the soup. Where is he? He should be here.

Have I gotten this week's Monstrous Sea pages done? I can't remember. I must have. I'm so ahead.

Mom and Dad really shouldn't have written that about me in the paper.

It is so hot in here. Why is it so hot?

I am going to die if my lungs don't get out of this teacup.

Where is Wallace?

I am one hundred percent going to die.

He's supposed to be here so I can give him this fucking Drumstick.

Jesus, I'm dying.

My tray knocks the edge of the table. Catches it, then catches my stomach. Crunches out of my hands. My legs buckle.

Darkness slams down.

LADYCONSTELLATION REVEALED

*Posted at 11:03 a.m. on 05 - 06 - 2017 by **BlessedJester***

> Ladies and gentlemen, on this day of days I bring you information long awaited by internet-goers. The true identity of LadyConstellation, the artist notorious for holding her anonymity, has been revealed by none other than a local news source. Click through to the picture, and be amazed.
>
> *ElizaMirk.jpg*

+90/-21 | 43 Comments | Reply | Flag

Monstrous Sea Private Message

1:15 p.m. (emmersmacks has joined the message)

emmersmacks: E???

emmersmacks: What happened?!?!

1:16 p.m. (Apocalypse_Cow has joined the message)

Apocalypse_Cow: she's not around, is she?

emmersmacks: No

emmersmacks: Shes in school right now

emmersmacks: Do you think she knows??

Apocalypse_Cow: no clue.

Apocalypse_Cow: eliza, we're doing damage control. as much as we can, anyway. but i think this one may be a lost cause . . . masterminds sunk their teeth into it

Apocalypse_Cow: and once masterminds gets it, they don't let go.

CHAPTER 31

My parents put me in swimming lessons when I was younger. A pool of thirty little kids forced to float on their backs and tread water. I'd tripped over my feet in soccer and routinely gotten bowled over in basketball, so I guess they were hoping I'd have more luck as a swimmer.

Back then, I still wanted to please my parents. I *wanted* to be good at something; I just wasn't. I didn't particularly like swimming, but if I was good at it, I would do it.

I wasn't good at it. When the instructor tried to teach us dead man's float—a move everyone else picked up on instinct—I snorted water up my nose and flailed until they said I could stop. But I kept trying.

On the last day of class, one of the boys dared me to dive to the bottom of the deep end. I did it. Or I tried. My fingers touched the bottom and I started back up, only to realize I was running out of air. Three quarters of the way to the top, oxygen deprivation made my vision black and my arms and legs thrash against the water around me. When I broke the surface, the relief of breathing was spoiled by the intensity of my inhaling and the pain of cold air needling my insides. A headache beat through my skull.

Waking up after the cafeteria is like surfacing from the deep end of the pool. Throbbing head, cold air. A narrow hospital room comes into focus around me. My eyes squeeze shut against the brightness overhead.

"Annie, turn down the light."

The lights dim.

"Hey, Eggs. Can you hear me?"

I crack my eyes open again. Dad sits beside the bed. Mom moves back over to him from the light switch on the other side of the room. I swallow against the sandpaper in my mouth.

"Yeah."

They both smile. Mom passes a hand over her face.

"What happened?" I ask.

"You tripped in the cafeteria at school and hit your head on a table." Dad motions to my forehead. I don't have to reach up and touch it to know there's a bandage there. "Bled all over the place, I guess. How do you feel?"

"Head hurts," I say. "Obviously."

"Were you feeling okay when you left the house this morning?" Mom asks. "Did you eat your breakfast?"

I don't say anything, because the reason I passed out finally comes back to me, and that squeezing hand hovers around me again. It threatens. My lungs seize in anticipation.

They told everyone about LadyConstellation. My whole school knows. The whole *township* knows.

Wallace knows.

"How long has it been?" I ask.

"Since the cafeteria?" Dad looks at his watch. "Maybe an hour and a half? They didn't want to take a chance with a head injury, so they got you in an ambulance and rushed you over here. The doctor should be back to check on you any time now."

"You told them. You put it in the paper." Tears blur my vision. The room spins, but I'm still lying down.

"Told them—what, you mean the graduation issue?" Mom blinks at me, then looks at Dad. "That's only the *Star*, Eliza, no one really reads it. We didn't think it would matter if we mentioned the webcomic. And you love it so much—and we really are proud of you for it. We thought—"

"*Millions* of people read it, though! The comic!" I struggle to sit up, hoping that will alleviate the dizziness. It doesn't. "Millions of people! Some of them live here!"

They're going to find me. They're going to know who I am and they're going to find me.

"Eggs." Dad puts a hand on my shoulder to push me back down, worry etched into his face. I don't think he heard what I just said.

"*Wallace* lives here," I say, shoving his hand off. "Where is he? He didn't come here, did he?" He can't see me like this.

Mom frowns. "He didn't know? I assumed you had already told him."

"Of course Wallace didn't know! No one does!"

I swing my legs over the edge of the bed and feel suddenly light-headed, as if seconds away from fainting.

The door opens and a doctor strides in. The name HARRIS is stitched onto his coat. When he sees me there, he drops his file on the desk and hurries over.

"Eliza, are you feeling okay?" Dr. Harris gently pushes me back onto the bed.

"Can't breathe," I say. "Dizzy."

"You *can* breathe. Breathe deep. In your stomach." He lifts my legs up and pushes my head between them. I breathe the way he says and after a minute the light-headedness goes away and the room stops spinning. "You're okay in here. It's just you and me and your parents. Okay?"

"Yeah."

The white noise machine hums softly in the corner. The grip on my insides loosens.

"You suffered a pretty nasty cut to your forehead," Dr. Harris says, "so you might have a little scar once that heals. Is this the same way you felt in the cafeteria, before you fell?"

"Yes. But that was worse."

"Have you felt like this before today?"

"No."

"Can you tell me exactly what you felt?"

"I, um . . . I couldn't breathe. Dizzy. I got tunnel vision, and it felt like I was being squeezed through a little tube. I thought I was dying. I thought I was going to die in front of everyone."

"She said—well, we put something in the newspaper we probably shouldn't have, and that might have caused some issues at school," Mom says, watching me. "Could that have done this?"

Dr. Harris rests a hand on my back. "Possibly. I believe what you suffered was a panic attack. Now, panic attacks can be triggered by extremely stressful circumstances. Big life changes, death of a loved one, things like that."

I shove my head deeper between my knees. My forehead pulses.

"I can recommend a great therapist who helps a lot of teens with panic and anxiety issues," Dr. Harris says. "One panic attack doesn't make a disorder, but if you have more, consistently, that's what it could become. We want to do our best to avoid that."

Panic disorder? I don't have panic disorder. Panic disorder was a thing that came up in my psychology elective last year. I read like half a paragraph on it.

Dr. Harris tells my parents I'm okay to go home, but I shouldn't go back to school today—not that there'd be enough time—and if I'm not feeling up to it, I shouldn't go tomorrow, either. Then he ships us off, and I shuffle between Mom and Dad out to the car, where I sit in the back seat beside my recovered backpack for the ride home and try not to think about *Monstrous Sea*.

Does the fandom know? Have they already been told? Do they believe whoever told them, or do they think it's another rumor?

Over the years, LadyConstellation has been "found out" many times. Usually someone trying to grab a little popularity before the researchers came and stripped away the fame. But this time it's true, and the truth has a way of holding on. Truth is the worst monster, because it never really goes away.

The house is empty when we get home. Except for Davy, who trundles over to the door and slowly smashes himself against my legs, buckling my knees. Church and Sully are still at school. Mom and Dad try to get me to lie down on the couch in the living room, but I insist I'd feel better if I slept in my own bed. They help me upstairs, and set to work making chicken noodle soup and ginger ale.

I let Davy into my room and close the door behind him. Sidle to the computer and shake the mouse to wake it. The desktop is so serene, so quiet. I open the browser and head to the forums.

It is chaos.

To the untrained eye, an online forum looks like a bunch of

random messages cobbled together. To someone who knows how to navigate them, they tell a story. And the story of the *Monstrous Sea* forums is "Eliza Mirk: Hoax or Reality?" Without clicking on any of the subforums or any of their threads, I know the consensus is *reality*. They found the article in the *Westcliff Star*. They found the MirkerLurker account, and the drawings Wallace wanted me to put up so badly. They found *me*.

I'm logged in to the LadyConstellation account, and my inbox number is so high the page no longer displays the quick-tip number over the inbox icon. Just an ellipsis. Half a minute after I log in, messages attack the right side of my screen. From people I know, from people I don't. From friends and from trolls. They come in a trickle at first, and then, as more people realize I'm online, in a flood. There are so many the page begins to lag. They come so quickly I don't have time to read them.

I log out and log back in under the MirkerLurker account.

This one is even worse. There is another ellipsis next to my inbox, but when I start receiving the messages, I do have time to read them. At least one of them.

> I JUST SAW YOU LOGGED IN TO LADY CONSTELLATION
> YOU LOGGED OUT THERE AND LOGGED IN HERE
> IT WAS TOO FAST TO BE COINCIDENCE
> IS THIS REALLY YOU?

A picture comes up in the message window. It's my yearbook photo from this year. Not even the horrible seventh grade one they included in the graduation article. How did this person get my yearbook photo?

I log out of MirkerLurker and close the browser, my stomach cramping.

I push my chair away from my desk and put my head between my knees again. I'm not light-headed or having trouble breathing like before, but this makes me feel better. Makes the space seem smaller and reminds me that I'm the only one in the room.

I grab my phone and open the messenger on there. All the MirkerLurker messages are still there, but at least the phone app lets me shut them out and look at my conversation with Emmy and Max.

Damage control. They tried running damage control. I let out a short, hysterical laugh. How could anyone run damage control on this? This is it. The fandom won. I lost. Eliza Mirk has been swallowed by the tides of their sea.

I switch to my messages with Wallace. There's nothing new since the last time we used the messenger. I don't have any emails from him, either. Or texts. He hasn't tried to call me.

Why would he? I lied to him for months. For the whole time I knew him. I could say it wasn't really lying, it was leaving out details, but that itself is a lie. If I was him, I'd hate me.

Footsteps start up the stairs. I flip my phone over, turn off the computer monitor, and curl up on the bed beside Davy, who lies still and lets me use him as a body pillow. My legs shake. Mom knocks softly on the door—I know it's her because Dad never knocks softly—and comes in with a tray of soup, crackers, and ginger ale.

"Are you feeling any better?" she asks.

"A little."

She smiles and smooths the hair away from my forehead, being careful of the bandage there. "Good. Try to get some sleep."

I don't. I stare at my computer across the room, silent and unmoving, and I wonder what storms brew over the all-knowing internet.

It was only a matter of time. Since that first day I met Wallace in class. Since I hung out with his friends. Since I told myself I would try.

I forgot there's no air this far down.

CHAPTER 32

It doesn't even take a day for internet gossip to grab the story and run with it. By the following morning, even people far outside the *Monstrous Sea* fandom know who I am and where I'm from. They know I'm in high school. They know I have a dog and two younger brothers. I'm not sure if they have my address and phone number, and if they don't yet, they will soon.

The fact that I was anonymous for so long became the fuel for this fire. My anonymity was like a game, a riddle for people to solve. Anonymity on the internet never lasts, and they all knew it.

LadyConstellation was a pretty piñata that they beat down with sticks, and I was the prize that fell out.

I read the messages. All of them. I know I shouldn't, but I can't help myself, and I don't want to draw or read or even watch *Dog Days*, so the hours drag by. Most of the messages are short. I could chart a timeline with them—they start off questioning, some probing to see if the rumor is true and others outright asking. Then they accept my name and question the details. They get hung up on the fact that I'm a girl, then a teenager. The teenage part I at least kind of understand—but why it should surprise them that I'm female, I have no clue. LadyConstellation was female. It's not as if that changed.

Then there are fans. Some of them say how I inspired them. Some say how alike we are, and how they think we'd be friends. Others just want to thank me. They like having a face to the name. They like having a *name* to the name. They like that I'm visible now.

Of course, there are crude messages. Vile ones. Ones that don't seem like they came from a real human being at all, but some computer program designed to say things no person should say to another person. I read all of those too, like Pringles—they might be terrible for you, but once you pop, you can't stop. This is a roller coaster that only goes down. Near the end I feel like a hollow shell clicking a mouse, scanning words with aching eyes.

"Eliza?" The door opens. A dark-haired head pops in. "Mom said to tell you dinner is ready. I yelled it up the stairs, but she said you wouldn't hear."

"Yeah," I say, not turning away from the computer.

"What are you looking at?" Heavy footsteps pad up behind

me. The smell of unshowered boy fills the air. Sully's a fast little shit—I don't have time to click away from the *Monstrous Sea* messages and the myriad news stories I pulled up in other tabs before his hand comes down on the mouse and he closes out of them for me.

"Don't look at that garbage." He actually sounds angry. "People are stupid, and you don't need to read that stuff. Come on, dinner's ready."

It's too late, but he doesn't know that. I already read them all, and was reading the new ones as they poured in. Both on the LadyConstellation and the MirkerLurker accounts. The comments on the news articles. The replies to the Masterminds thread and on the *Monstrous Sea* forums themselves. Good, bad, ugly.

I get up and shuffle downstairs after Sully.

I plead ill and skip school the next day, too. Friday. The *Monstrous Sea* pages are already scheduled to go up. I can hardly handle touching my keyboard, much less returning to the website to put up pages. I can't be near my pen display, either. Or a pencil and paper. I can't even think about drawing.

I can't even think about *Monstrous Sea*.

A crow's wing, a seacreeper fin, a long scarf, a saber, large bodies of water, clocks, planets, stars. They make me sick to my stomach. I have no interest in plotting out pages and panels. None at all in tying up character threads. The end of the story, so close, flits out of my loosened grip and flies away.

I can't do it. Whatever force kept me going has vanished.

I tear the *Monstrous Sea* posters off the walls. I shove the compendium graphic novels under my bed. All the fan art comes down, everything anyone ever sent me, all the little stuffed toys and stickers and especially the Kite Waters costume. Even Mr. Greatbody and his missing eyes. Anything that can get stuffed in the trash can does.

When Mom comes up to check on me later, I'm lying on my bed hugging Davy again, and she sees the blank walls and the overflowing garbage and asks me if I feel okay. I lie. She leaves.

That afternoon, a reporter from the *Westcliff Star* calls the house and asks if she can interview me for a story. Sully, who answered the phone, tells her to fuck off.

Dad scolds him halfheartedly. That's the first time. When more calls come in—and no one tells me who—Dad stops scolding and starts telling the callers to lose our number.

Mom and Dad move around me like I'm electrified. Few words. Distance unless they want to check the stitches beneath my bandage. I'd like to think they feel bad, but I don't think they fully understand what they've done.

Church and Sully come into my room that night—at the exact time the *Monstrous Sea* pages are supposed to go up, coincidentally— and sit on either side of me on the bed to watch reruns of *Dog Days*. That, at least, I've managed to start doing again. A constantly numbed mind doesn't sound so bad at all. Sully and Church bring a bowl of hard-boiled eggs bigger than Church's head as an offering. We eat. They make fun of the stupid characters. I agree that the characters are stupid.

"Have you talked to Wallace?" Church asks when the third episode is over.

"No," I say, picking at an eggshell.

"We saw his sister at school today," Sully says. "Um, Lucy."

"Okay."

I drop the shell in the extra bowl they brought and bite into the egg carefully, trying not to nick the hardened yolk with my teeth.

"So what'd she say?" I ask.

"She said he was really upset."

"And that we should try to get you to talk to him," Church adds.

I want to say it's not my job to make him happy, but I owe him a better apology than the one I squeezed out in Mrs. Grier's room. Still, every time I think about texting him—just texting him, the two words—I imagine him ignoring me, spitting in my face, taking all the pictures I drew for him and burning them.

"I'll think about it," I say.

I'll think about it. If I can even force myself to go back to school on Monday.

CHAPTER
33

I don't go back to school on Monday. I drive to the parking lot of the nearest grocery store, park in the back forty, and climb into my back seat to nap until the car gets too stuffy and I have to roll the windows down. When school would normally let out, I drive home. The next day, I do the same thing.

When I get home, Mom says, "School called today. They said you've missed two days in a row, unexcused."

I hesitate at the bottom of the stairs. "Oh. Yeah. I just . . . I got there, and I didn't feel good."

"If you need a little more time off, I'll call in for you." She wrings an old pair of jogging shorts in her hands. A pile of exercise clothes bound for Goodwill sits on the living-room floor behind her.

"Okay," I say, and start up the stairs.

"Eliza, wait." She moves after me. "If I call you in sick, will you go see the therapist Dr. Harris recommended? Not tomorrow, but maybe next week? We talked to her already, and she said she'd have some time open to see you."

"Why?" I say, but the word feels hollow.

"Because you're not acting like yourself, and your dad and I are worried."

"I don't really want to."

"Please, will you go? For us?"

I shrug. That seems to be enough answer for her, because she lets me go upstairs.

After a week of no school, of lying in bed all day and watching *Dog Days* until I forget why I ever tried to make anything of my own, everything feels terrible. My stomach, my head, my back. My neck aches. My hair is greasy. That's the only thing that makes me get up and take a shower: when I can feel the oil oozing from my scalp. I'm so tired of being gross. So tired of feeling like my body is this thing I have to lug around with me all day. After the shower I collapse on my bed again. The bare walls make my room feel like a cell, but I don't have the energy to decorate them with anything else.

There will be no *Monstrous Sea* pages at the end of this week. I didn't get online to see what the fandom thought of the last ones. My will is gone. My will to draw, my will to talk, my will to do anything. Where *Monstrous Sea* once wrapped around my heart, there is nothing anymore.

Maybe that's normal. The things you care most about are the ones that leave the biggest holes.

There was something distinctly un-Orcian about General White that Amity couldn't place. Everything about him was sharp, like shards of metal fused into the shape of a man, dressed in an Orcian Alliance military uniform.

"If you kill Faust," he said, "you will be regarded as a hero. Maybe even a legend. It won't end our enemies' attacks, but it *will* even the odds, and that's a greater advantage than we've hoped for in these long decades."

"Even the odds . . . ," Faren said, his stilted cadence melting away. "If she kills Faust, but she's still alive, wouldn't the odds be tipped severely in your favor? As far as they're stacked against you now?"

"I'm afraid I don't follow," White said.

"What happens after?" Faren stared White down. "What happens after she defeats Faust? I assume you won't be able to remove the Watcher from her. She'll still be here, and she'll still feel like she has to save the innocent. What enemies will you send her after then? The Rishtians? The Angels? Those are the enemies you're speaking of, aren't they? The clockwork kings and the demons of Orcus?"

His voice rose on the last word. Amity's skin prickled; she had never considered she might have to fight Orcus's Angels. White, unperturbed, stared back at Faren. "No one said anything about further enemies, Mr. Nox."

"Nox-eys," Faren corrected coldly. He'd never demanded—or even asked—to be addressed with Nocturnian honorifics, and that, more than his attitude toward the general, gave Amity pause. The pretense of his poor Colaarin fled completely. "I don't for a moment believe you'll let her come back here to live in peace once Faust is gone. Your people have spent the last half year turning her into a weapon, and years before that studying her. You know what she's capable of. You've convinced her Faust is her responsibility—where does it end?"

CHAPTER 34

"This is stupid."

Sully stands in the doorway to my bedroom, arms crossed over his chest. I lie on the bed and stare unblinking at my TV.

"No it's not," I say. "It's my favorite episode."

"I'm not talking about *Dog Days*."

I turn my head to look at him.

"I'm talking about you lying here, not telling Mom and Dad exactly what they did."

"They know what they did."

Sully rolls his eyes. "Bullshit. They think they know but they don't, because you won't tell them."

I turn back to the TV. "It doesn't matter. It's done."

He growls. "If you won't tell them, I will." He storms off. I ignore him until I hear the door to Mom and Dad's office downstairs bang open, and Sully yelling out to ask if he can use their laptop.

I spring out of bed and rush downstairs. Church and Sully's homework is spread over the kitchen table, but both of them stand across from Mom and Dad at the island counter, bringing up something on the laptop.

The post on the Masterminds site. The one I used to look at every day.

"What is this?" Mom asks, setting aside her fitness magazine. Neither she nor Dad has noticed I'm in the room.

"This is the post that made *Monstrous Sea* popular," Sully says. "This website, Masterminds, is where people share things. There are a lot of people here, and for a post to get to the top of a forum like this one and to stay at the top for as long as it has is *really* hard."

"And look at all the comments on it. And the likes," says Church. "Those are all real people, and most of them are people who read and liked *Monstrous Sea*."

"But they're only a few of the people who *actually* read it." Sully turns the computer around again and navigates to a new website before turning it back to our parents. The *Monstrous Sea* forums. "This is the website where the fans gather. You would have seen this if you hadn't stopped looking at her website two years ago. Look at the numbers on the posts. Look at just the people who are online right now."

They wait while Mom and Dad scroll through the forum threads, reading usernames, post titles, comment numbers. From the door I can see Dad's brow furrow and Mom put her hand over her mouth. I fist my hands in my sweatshirt and clamp my mouth shut.

"There are millions of these people," Sully says. "Way more than are just online here. They read the comic pages Eliza puts up every week. They pay for them. Do you know how much she makes from this? She keeps herself logged in to her bank account on her computer, and we saw. It's ridiculous."

"It is, actually," Church says.

"Like, you keep hounding her about college scholarships and stuff, but she doesn't need it. Did you guys realize that, or did you stop paying attention after you started making her go to the tax guy by herself?"

"But it's . . . it's just a hobby," Mom says.

"No it's not." Sully puts both hands flat on the counter on either side of the laptop. "I don't know what I can show you to make you understand. This is a thing. Eliza is famous. Not like a movie star, or anything, but a lot of people wanted to know who she was. And now, thanks to you, they do."

"None of these people knew who she was?" Dad says softly.

"No, of course not," Church says. "Why do you think she never wanted to tell anyone?"

"She's always been private. We thought she didn't want the attention."

"She *didn't*," Sully snaps, "but not for—ah, you *don't get* it! You always tell us to be safe and to make good choices, but then you do something like this." He grabs something from Church—the *Westcliff Star* graduation issue. "This was not a good choice. This was a very bad choice. You left her wide open for millions of people, and not all of them are nice. She's never gonna get that safety back again. But you know what the—the most—"

"The most aggravating," Church says.

"The most aggravating thing is?" Sully spreads his arms, encompassing the *Westcliff Star* and the computer and all of them. "We could have avoided this if you'd taken half a minute to Google *Monstrous Sea*. You want to know about every other part of our lives, but you never really cared about this."

I step back, and a floorboard creaks beneath my foot. All four of them turn to face me. Mom is crying. Dad looks pale.

"Why didn't you ever tell us?" Mom says. "We thought it was still small. Your bank account never had that much in it . . . the taxes . . ."

"You told him my taxes were my business and you wanted me to handle them on my own." My voice wobbles.

Dad swallows thickly. "We never would have said what we did in the *Westcliff Star* if we knew. We thought it was a thing you did for fun. We wanted to show you that we were proud of you. And the *Star*—the *Star* is such a small paper, who was going to read it? It would just be for us. Just for us."

I shrug again. They wait for me to say something, but what am I supposed to say? Am I supposed to be angry? Forgiving? My parents have never apologized like this. They've never screwed up so badly. Part of me never thought they would.

Mom starts crying for real. She gets up and leaves through the other door, into the hallway to their office. Church goes after her.

After a moment, I escape back upstairs. I lie curled on my bed, with *Dog Days* muted on the TV, and feel strangely awake. Like everything is sharper in detail than normal. I don't feel light-headed, though.

Ten minutes later, Sully knocks on the door and sticks his head in. "Are you okay?"

"I didn't know you knew so much about *Monstrous Sea*," I say.

He shrugs. "We wanted to know what you were doing all the time. You're our big sister, right? But you're like . . . in a different world. It's weird." He shrugs again. "We read the comic. Me and Church. So do all our friends, but we never told them who you were because we figured something like this might happen. It's really cool. Not that this is happening, but that you made all this. With the way Mom and Dad acted around you, I figured they didn't know how important it was."

"Oh." And all this time, I thought they hated me. "I just . . . thanks. I probably wouldn't have told them."

Sully rolls his eyes. "Mom and Dad are too old to get it. They didn't even have cell phones when they were younger. Maybe Googling it wouldn't have helped them." He rubs his nose. "Anyway, if you need to, like, talk to someone, you know where to find me and Church."

"That's—that would be nice, actually." My voice is small, but Sully's expression opens up. After a moment's hesitation, he slips into the room, shuts the door behind him, and sits with his legs curled up on the opposite end of my bed.

"Thanks," I say.

Sully smiles at me for the first time I can remember.

CHAPTER 35

Very early Tuesday morning, when my parents and Sully and Church are all fast asleep, I get in my car and drive to Wellhouse Turn.

There is no one on the roads this early in the morning, so I park on the shoulder, walk the length of the bridge, and peer down the incline to the flat expanse of grass beside the black river. Moonlight illuminates the world. At the top of the hill are the cross, the decorations, the toys. Flowers, some fresh and some wilting, for the people who went over the turn. I wonder if there will ever come a day when they're not needed, when the turn is no longer the turn but just a hill.

Wallace said in his email that he never came back here. Surely

Vee must have dedicated something to Wallace's father in this pile of offerings, but Wallace himself never did.

I don't have anything except my pajamas and my car keys. I look around. There's a smooth rock on the side of the road not far away. I grab that, polish it up a little with my sleeve, and set it on top of an empty baseball card tin, under the arm of a rain-soaked teddy bear.

"Consider this an IOU," I say. "I'll bring something better later."

Wellhouse Turn is surrounded by woods, so it's a quiet place anyway, but the river blocks out the sounds of any other nearby roads. I sit on my butt beside the flowers and toys and slide myself carefully down the incline. I'll figure out how to get back up later. At the bottom is a wide, grassy clearing. How many cars have gone off that road? Why hasn't anyone fixed it yet, or made it safer? Are they afraid they'll lose their news stories? That the future will somehow be less interesting if there aren't pieces of car permanently embedded in the ground here?

I lower myself onto the cool grass and look up at the sky. Stars puncture the darkness. For all the Nocturnian constellations I know, the only real ones I remember are the Big and Little Dippers. Oh, and Canis Major, of course—headed by Sirius, the Dog Star, the herald of the dog days of summer. It's been brought up so many times on the show *Dog Days* it's now the longest-running title-reference joke. But Sirius isn't even in the sky right now.

Four-year-old Eliza would be so disappointed in me.

Four-year-old Eliza would be disappointed in me for a lot of things. For hiding, for making it most of the way through high school without anyone to sit with at lunch, for letting myself sink to this place. Four-year-old Eliza *tried*, at least. She wanted to be good at things. She did things because she wanted to do them, not because other people made her. She had no masters. I don't think any four-year-olds do.

But I'm not four anymore. I can't be her. I can't be my four-year-old self, I can't be LadyConstellation, I can't even be Wallace's girlfriend. Right now I can only be Eliza Mirk, human being.

I tangle my fingers in the grass. A bat flits by overhead, making stars wink off and on again.

Wallace's dad died here. It seems too calm for a car careening toward a fatal crash. I bet Wellhouse Turn was serene while it was happening too. Wellhouse Turn doesn't kill people; bad weather, poor decisions, and unfortunate accidents kill people. Wellhouse Turn doesn't advertise that people die here; the *Westcliff Star* does that. Because Wellhouse Turn, this little clearing, is nature, and nature doesn't care. Nature doesn't care if we throw ourselves against it and break a few bones. Nature doesn't care if we feel so heavy we might sink into the ground and never be able to pull ourselves out again.

Nature doesn't care who I am, online or off, and it doesn't mind if I need to lie here for a while.

CHAPTER 36

Wednesday, two weeks after my unfortunate incident in the cafeteria, I am lying on the floor of my bedroom, staring at the ceiling and letting my wet hair soak the carpet, when the doorbell rings.

I listen to Dad's steps march down the hallway. The soft crack of the door swinging away from its frame. His muffled voice saying hello, then more I can't make out.

Then footsteps up the stairs. Dad's. My heart picks up. Why's he coming up? I'm the only one upstairs right now.

A knock on my door.

"Eggs? Wallace is here."

Wallace is here.

Why is Wallace here?

"I don't want to talk to him." The answer is immediate and strong. There is no doubt in my mind. I cannot talk to Wallace. I can't see him.

"Are you sure?" Dad still doesn't open the door.

"Yes."

"Okay then." He goes back down the stairs, back to the door. His muffled voice says something that sounds regretful. I don't hear a response, but if Wallace is talking, it might be too soft to hear.

The door closes.

I scramble to my window. It looks down on the front lawn and the driveway where Wallace's car is parked.

Wallace tromps down the front walk. From up here he's a head of dark hair and a Colts jersey. I press my forehead to the screen. How can he not feel me here? How can he not feel how much I want him not to hate me, how sorry I am? I don't care if I never look at *Monstrous Sea* again, but I do care if I never see Wallace again. Right now, I care a lot.

He fumbles with his keys, then stops, like he remembered something. He walks to the end of the driveway and turns to look up at the house.

He finds me right away. I fall back from the window, breath caught in my throat. Of course he knew I was here—he had to know I was here. I peek over the windowsill again. He's pacing.

Every time he passes back, he glances up at my window. One pass, two passes, three passes.

He's psyching himself up.

Psyching himself up? What does he need to psych himself up for? Is he going to charge the front door?

Finally he stops and reaches into his pocket for his phone. Types something. Looks up at my window again.

I grab my phone from my desk, where it has been collecting dust. Message upon message appears when I turn it on, but Wallace's text is at the top.

We need to talk.

He doesn't wait for me to respond before he starts typing again.

We really need to talk and I don't want to text outside your house.

And again:

If you don't let me in today, I'll just come back tomorrow.

My stomach clenches. He wants in here so he can yell at me. So he can tell me how wrong I am, how awful, how badly I've treated him. Maybe then I can yell back at him that I know, that I feel it in the marrow of my bones like someone pumped me full of guilt.

I sit and hold myself for a moment, arms wrapped around my legs, forehead against my knees. Then I force myself off the floor, out of my room, and down the stairs one stiff step at a time. I throw the front door open and fly back upstairs, into my room—

leaving that door open too—and curl up on the bed with my back in the corner and my pillow locked between my arms as a shield.

The front door clicks shut. I drop the pillow. Fling it across the room.

Heavy feet climb the stairs. I stand and put my back to the window. Close my eyes and press my phone into my stomach until I can feel his gaze on me, and I look up to find him framed by the doorway.

He's angry. He's so angry. I've never seen his face like that before, not even the times he's gotten mad about Tim telling him he can't write if it doesn't make him good money. This is more than anger, it's anger and betrayal and confusion all fused together.

"How could you n—" His jaw flexes. He looks at the ceiling. "How could you not—" His teeth clamp together. "How could you not tell me . . ." His voice tapers off to a whisper. He growls and clenches his fists. Tears gather in my eyes. He's so angry.

He pulls out his phone again, exhaling hard through his nose, like an enraged bull. I wipe my eyes so I can see my screen. His texts come in rapid fire.

How could you not tell me? That whole time?

Were you messing with me?

Was I a guinea pig or something?

Were you bored?

I let you read my stuff! I let you read everything!

I brought you to my house!

You met my family!

How could you not tell me who you are?

Did you not want to?

Did you even think about it?

The tears are so thick I can't see through them. Wallace takes a step into the room. I move my thumbs over my phone but can't make them work. I'm sniffling too loud, anyway. Hiccuping. Hiccuping through my sobs.

I curl my phone in one hand and ball the other in my shirt when I really want to hide my face. I can't hide myself from him, not now. There are no words I can say to him to make him understand how sorry I am, and that only makes me cry harder.

His weight makes my bed creak. When I bring myself to look, he sits there, his elbows braced on his knees and his head in his hands. Without him watching, I can bring my phone up again.

No, I type. *I wasn't messing with you.*

I didn't want to tell you at first.

I lower the phone and say, "And then I saw how much *Monstrous Sea* meant to you and I couldn't tell you."

We sit in silence for several long minutes until he says, quietly, "I kind of thought it might be something like that. I hoped it was."

I lift my head.

"I thought, *If this was me, what would I have done?* I think I would have told you, but who knows? Maybe not. Maybe I would have done the same thing."

He runs his hands through his hair, making it stick up.

"I don't understand. How can you be her? How did I not notice?"

He pauses like he wants me to answer, but I don't know how, so I keep my mouth shut.

He looks up again. His gaze roams over my desk, my computer, the pen display that wasn't there before. Then at my blank walls.

"What happened to your room?" he asks.

"I couldn't look at it anymore," I say.

He frowns at me.

"And at school?"

I explain it to him. I don't know if he understands, but he listens.

"I don't want to go back," I say. "I know it'll happen again. Even when I'm alone, I don't feel alone, because it's like people on the internet are watching me. At school it's worse because I can *see* them."

"They don't hate you," he says. "Most of them are fans, actually. Or people who think it's cool that you're kind of famous."

"It doesn't make a difference. I've read all the messages. It's like I can't hold it all inside me at once. Good or bad."

"Have you been on the forums?"

"Not since last week. I don't really want to go near my computer anymore."

"Yeah," he says. "Neither would I."

That confirms it, then. Things have been as awful since I stopped looking at them. Big news tends to blow itself out quickly on the internet; everyone's up in arms about it for a day or three, and then it's on to the next thing. So if the LadyConstellation reveal is still news a week after it became public knowledge, they're not going to let it go.

"What do you think they'll do when the pages don't go up this week?" I ask. "Or next week?"

"You're not putting pages up?"

I shake my head. "I have a few in reserve, but I haven't drawn since last week. Since before. I don't want to anymore. I don't even want to hold a pencil."

"Are you going to put them up eventually?"

"Maybe. I don't know."

There's a hitch in his breathing. He looks at me, at his hands, back at me. There's something about his stillness. A nervousness, an uncertainty. "I have to tell you something." His voice is louder than usual, like he's forcing the words out. "A day before this happened, before the graduation issue, I got an email from a publisher. They found the transcription. They're excited about how big *Monstrous Sea* is, and they want to be the ones to publish it in novel form."

"They want to publish yours?"

He nods. I swipe my sleeve over my eyes. "That's great. That's *awesome*. That's a book deal."

"They said they would need permission to publish it, though. From the creator."

"Of course," I say, scrambling over myself to get the words out. This is the very least I can do for him after all of this garbage. It doesn't matter anymore if my name gets out. "Of course you can have permission. Always. Just tell me where to sign."

But he doesn't look happy. He stares at me like I've missed some great point. "They don't want it until they know how it ends."

"So write the ending," I say.

"They don't want my ending, Eliza. They want yours. It won't be right if it's not yours."

"I could tell you how it ends and you could—"

"They. Want. Yours."

"They aren't going to take it if the comic isn't finished?"

He keeps staring at me. My stomach goes cold. "That's ridiculous," I say. "It's still a good story—people will buy it—"

"You have to finish." There's a sternness to his voice I've never heard before.

"I can't."

"You *have to finish*, Eliza."

"I can't even touch a pencil right now. You've had that before, haven't you? Where you can't do anything because nothing's flowing, nothing's coming out, like your head is empty—"

"You have to finish." His voice is hard. I wish I'd kept my

pillow as a shield. "I'm never going to get a chance like this again. If this doesn't happen, it's going to be four more years of doing what other people tell me to do. Maybe longer than that. I can't anymore. Please, Eliza. It's only a few chapters, just push through and finish it."

He doesn't get it. Or he doesn't want to.

"I can't," I whisper.

"Why not?"

"There's . . . there's nothing there."

"Why not? There doesn't have to be anything there. Artists create when they have no motivation all the time. If I could do it for you, I would—I would kill to write something without motivation if it meant I got to make what I wanted later."

I have never had that problem. I have never been forced to make anything. I don't understand how that works.

"I can't."

He pushes himself off the bed. His hands scrape through his hair, then ball into thick fists at his sides. A muscle jumps in his jaw. He looks around, scanning the empty walls, the empty desk, the silent computer. "You have a perfect life," he says, "and you can't draw a couple of chapters."

"My life isn't perfect," I say.

"You made this awesome thing that millions of people love and adore you for. Everyone knows what you've done. They recognize your talent. You don't have to worry about how you're going to pay for college, or get a real job, or figure out what you're supposed to be doing with your life. You don't have anyone telling you what to do or who to be. All you have to do is draw a few more pages. That's it. It'll take you, what, a week or two at most? So please, Eliza, *draw the pages*."

When I can't come up with any words, I shake my head.

Wallace turns and leaves. His footsteps clomp back down the stairs. The front door shuts gently, with a little *whoosh* of air.

It would've been better if he'd slammed it.

CHAPTER 37

I sit at my desk with a sheet of blank paper and my pencil. The pencil is next to the paper, aligned parallel with the short bottom edge. I stare at the pencil. The pencil stares back.

A few chapters. The end. I don't know the details, but I have a vague idea of what's going to happen. It can't be that hard.

Blank pages are supposed to be an invitation. A challenge, even. Here is your canvas—how creative can you be? What limits can you stretch to bring to life that creature in your head? A blank piece of paper is infinite possibilities.

Now when I look at it, all I see is an abyss. Where ideas and excitement used to spring up inside me, now there's a granite block. Huge, immovable, and so cold it makes my limbs go numb.

Looking at paper only reminds me that I'm not strong enough to shift it.

I have to try. For Wallace, I have to try.

I reach for the pencil. My hand stalls, my fingers curling in, my wrist dropping until it rests on the edge of the desk. It's not going to look right, though. The characters. The scenery.

People will know. They'll know it's wrong. I'll have to put the pages up online because the publisher won't take Wallace's transcription until the story is complete, and all the readers who have been circling the boards all this time will know that the panels aren't as good as they could be. The art isn't as good, and the characters aren't as good, and the story isn't as good.

And when they know that, they'll know where to find me and how to find me and they'll be able to question me directly. Some of them probably at school.

What if they send me mail?

What if they come to my house?

What if they start talking about me the way they talk about Olivia Kane? Hermit Eliza ran to a cave in the mountains and chases people off her property with a shotgun. Sets booby traps for her own fans. She drew so many monsters that she became a monster herself.

I realize I'm gripping the edge of the desk so hard my nails have left shallow grooves in the wood, and I let go. I force myself to breathe, to shove all other thoughts to the back of my mind, and think of Wallace. Wallace will have a book deal. Wallace will be able to use that money to pay for college, and he'll be able to major in what he really likes. Wallace won't have to worry about appeasing Tim, or falling into a job that makes him hate himself.

I *have* to try.

I reach for the pencil again. Pick it up. A shock races up my arm, raising the hairs on my head, sending ripples of disgust through my muscles. I grip the pencil tighter only so I don't toss it away. The first line I draw is lopsided. I don't even know what it was supposed to be. The edge of a panel? A plane in a character's face?

Where in the story am I? I don't remember anymore.

I press my hands to my forehead. My chest tightens and tightens and tightens. This used to come so easily to me. *Monstrous Sea* has never been difficult. Even when I wasn't sure where I wanted the story to go, I could just start drawing and it would eventually spill out. Now there's nothing but aching panic. Panic *because* there's nothing. Because even though I know it's silly to think so, because I know everyone would call me ridiculous for it, I feel like something terrible is going to happen to Wallace if I don't finish.

I don't know exactly what, or how. All I know is dread rising in my throat.

I try to start again. Anything. Faces. Eyes. Clothing. Nothing comes out right. It's too dark, then too light, then skewed to the left. The proportions are off. The lines are shaky. The weight is in all the wrong places.

The pencil ends its life in two halves, one behind my monitor, the other jammed into the space between the desk and the wall. I shove over to the other side of my desk, wake my computer, and Google "Olivia Kane disappearance." The results are all speculation from online news, fan forums, and social media. Cole's cave-and-shotgun theory is near the top. Other people think Olivia Kane went all-purpose insane, as if that's really a thing. Some people say she tried to kill herself. A lot of people. The theory is everywhere. Have I really never seen that one before, or did I ignore it? Was I so naive I thought she'd just hidden somewhere?

Broken people don't hide from their monsters. Broken people let themselves be eaten.

I curl into myself on my chair, head tucked between my knees and my arms banded over me as a barricade. I can't cry anymore. I want the tears to come out because I might feel better if they did, but my parents would hear, or Sully and Church would hear, or someone on the omniscient internet would hear and find me and rip me apart. I can't cry and I can't draw and I can't get online and I can't talk to anyone, so what good am I?

What is the point of me?

CHAPTER 38

School is a terrifying beast.

You spend seven hours a day walking around inside it, and when the day ends it grows small so it can hitch a ride home with you. It burrows into your ear and whispers all the things you can expect for the next day. Your clothes won't fit right. Your hair won't behave. You'll forget your homework. You'll get more homework. You'll have to fight for your lunch table.

Everyone everyone everyone will judge you.

There are only two more weeks until graduation. I have no options.

What I want: to stay home. In my room, specifically, with the shades drawn and the TV on, but the volume low so I can doze to the murmuring, mind-numbing voices of *Dog Days*. I want Davy around to hug, and I don't want to talk to or see any people. Not in real life, and definitely not online. I don't want to think about the pages I haven't finished, and Wallace's face, burned into my memory, when I told him I can't.

What will happen if I get what I want: I stay home for the last two weeks of senior year and my parents make sure I visit that therapist until my brain is scrubbed squeaky-clean and I get popped back out like a plate from a dishwasher. That could take months. Or, heaven forbid, *years*. I don't want to be this way for years. I don't want to feel this way for years. Even going to college won't make this better, because there will be people there too who know who I am. There's no escaping it now.

So I go back to school.

This spring is too hot for sweatshirts. I make do with a technique for shrinking myself I perfected years ago when I got tired of being picked for activities during sport camps. Never make direct eye contact. Dress in drab colors. Move at the same pace as the rest of the crowd. Disappearing is an art form, and I am its queen. Or at least I used to be.

As soon as I step inside the doors, my knees lock and heat rushes in behind my eyes. I control my breathing. When I'm sure I can move again without falling over, I do. One foot in front of the other.

I will not trip and knock myself out.

I will not trip and knock myself out.

I will not trip and knock myself out.

I reach my locker. Forget the combination. Have to pull out my phone for the first time since Wallace came to my house so that I can find it in my notes.

The door swings open and folded papers spill out onto my feet. More perch precariously on the locker shelf below the slats in the door. I scoop one up and unfold it.

Hi, Eliza,

You don't know me, but I'm a big fan of Monstrous Sea. Probably like the biggest fan. I've only been reading for six months, but it's my absolute favorite thing. I love your art, and I hope I can draw like you one day. Get better soon!

Listria_Dreams

P.S. I know you like asking who our favorite characters are—mine's Rory!

This person stuck a note in my fucking locker.

I drop it and bend to shovel the rest back inside before anyone sees. They burn my skin like they're on fire and slip back out. There are too many of them.

A finger taps my shoulder. I jump to get away from the person and slam my head and shoulder against the locker door.

It's Wallace.

He bends down and starts loading notes into one big hand. He doesn't try to put them back in the locker; instead he takes off his backpack and shoves them in there. I bottle my questions, my panic, and my tears, and go back to what I meant to do, which was get my textbooks for the first part of the day. Wallace slings his backpack over his shoulders and walks away, to homeroom.

I haven't talked to him since he came to my house last week. What would I say to him? "I tried and I still can't finish the comic and I'm sorry I ruined your life?"

I don't know how my identity has impacted his involvement in the fandom, but it must've. People on the forums knew rainmaker had a thing with MirkerLurker, though we didn't make it obvious. When it came out that LadyConstellation and MirkerLurker were the same person, did he have to convince them he had no idea who I was? Has anyone linked rainmaker with Wallace himself? My own anonymity stripped away is bad enough—I don't know what I'll do if I have Wallace's on my conscience too.

I can't begin to think about Cole, Leece, Chandra, and Megan. I missed their meet-up at Murphy's last weekend. I couldn't face them. I lied to them like I lied to Wallace, and they're Wallace's friends first. They'll be as angry as he is—maybe angrier.

When I get to homeroom, Wallace's expression is carved in stone. He doesn't look at me.

A few heads do turn to look at me, but most mind their own business. Wallace pulls out a paper and starts writing. Mrs. Grier, at her desk, keeps her head down and her eyes focused on the book between her hands. The very tip of a tattoo pokes out of her right sleeve. If I didn't know to look for it, I wouldn't have seen it there.

I'd hoped it was a nightmare. The tattoo. Some messed-up vision I'd had because everything was so weird that day.

But no, it's not. My homeroom teacher has the most popular phrase of *Monstrous Sea* tattooed on her arm in all capital letters, like a battle cry. THERE ARE MONSTERS IN THE SEA. Yes, Mrs. Grier. Yes, there are. You are one of them. You are one of the ones that was supposed to stay beneath the surface, but you didn't. You came up to the top, and now I can never forget that I saw you. I can never forget that you exist.

I turn my attention to my desk and cup my hands around the back of my neck. Creators shouldn't feel this way about their fans. I shouldn't want them to disappear. They're the reason I have . . . the reason I have *anything*. They're the reason I can pay for college, for my pen display, the reason I can spend so much time doing what I love.

I hope Olivia Kane would never feel this way about me.
Olivia Kane.

I don't know exactly what happened to her, but I know I don't want it to happen to me.

I rip a notebook out of my backpack and open it to a blank page. Before all this I never would've attempted to contact Olivia Kane. My heart would've exploded with the effort, and I would've been too afraid of the answer I might have gotten.

But desperate times.

Mrs. Kane,

My name is Eliza Mirk. I'm not writing to you to talk about Children of Hypnos, though I am a fan of yours. I'm the creator of the webcomic Monstrous Sea, and recently my identity was revealed to my fans. The day this happened, I had a panic attack, tripped, and knocked myself out on a cafeteria table.

I'm pathetic, I know.

Since then, I have been contacted constantly and by any means possible, including online messages, emails, and even notes shoved into my locker at school. Some are very nice, and some are not. I feel like people are always watching me, always aware of me, even if I'm sitting alone in my bedroom. I haven't been eating or sleeping well, and I don't know what to do with myself.

After two weeks home, I'm back in school now, but my skin is constantly crawling and it feels like I'm teetering on the edge of breathless dizziness, like that panic could reach out and grab me at any second. I want to go home. I never want to leave my room.

I know this isn't exactly the same as your situation, but the worst part of it all is I can't finish Monstrous Sea. I was so close to the end, and now the motivation to do it is gone. Like a dried-up well. I don't know how to refill it, and I don't know if I want to, but I have to. There are so many reasons why I have to finish. I shouldn't feel like this, should I? I shouldn't feel so attacked. This is what public figures deal with. I'm afraid something's wrong with me, and I don't know how to fix it. I'm scared I'm going to be like this forever. I'm so scared, all the time.

I don't know if you can help me, or if you even know what I'm talking about, but you were the only person I could think of who might understand.

Thank you for your time.

Eliza Mirk

P.S. Sorry, I know I said I wasn't going to talk about *Children of Hypnos*. You don't have to answer this, and I'm sure you get this question all the time, so if it makes you uncomfortable, please ignore it. Do you know how you would have ended the series? I don't need specifics; I was just curious if you knew and couldn't finish it, like me, or if there was no end.

CHAPTER 39

I get through the rest of the school day with the letter to Olivia Kane folded carefully in thirds and clutched between my hands.

At lunch in the courtyard, Wallace hands his conversation paper to me over his loaded tray of food. At least someone's appetite hasn't been disturbed by all of this.

What is that?

They're the first words he's said to me, spoken or written, since my bedroom. Even after looking at his face, his body language, I have no idea of his tone. Is he upset? Curious? He couldn't be worried, could he? I don't even know why he's sitting with me right now. Habit, probably.

A letter to Olivia Kane, I write back. There are other students in the courtyard today, and I don't feel like speaking aloud.

Wallace frowns. *Can I read it?*

I run the folded letter between my fingers. It wasn't meant for Wallace. He's not waiting with his hand out or anything. It wouldn't do any harm to let him read it. Maybe then he might understand what I was trying to explain to him before. He could even tell me if I could make it better—he's the writer, after all.

No, it's kind of just for her.

He reads this and says nothing else.

When I get home, I find an envelope and a stamp in Mom and Dad's office and take the letter down to the mailbox. A few years back, the Children of Hypnos forums came up with an address for Olivia Kane's publisher, where they were accepting mail on her behalf. I don't know if they're still collecting it for her, or if they send any of it her way. The odds of her reading my letter are slim to none, and the odds of her actually replying even slimmer. But I don't care if she chases people off her property with a shotgun, screaming like a banshee.

I at least have to try this.

CHAPTER 40

"Eliza, why don't you go ahead and take a spot on the couch? Make yourself comfortable."

"Okay."

"Would you like anything to drink?"

"Um, maybe water."

"Water it is. I'm glad you decided to come talk to me."

"I wasn't going to. I mean—my parents wanted me to. I don't really like talking. I just want to get past all of this."

"Of course. I've been reading over the questionnaire you filled out for me, and matching that up with what your parents told me— it seems like you've had quite a roller coaster of a school year."

"Sure, I guess."

"Why is that?"

"Everything's gotten worse. Well, not worse. Kind of worse? I don't know, worse doesn't sound right. More intense?"

"Intense might be a good word for it. Where do you feel like it started going downhill?"

"It went uphill before it went down. I don't know. Maybe October."

"What happened in October?"

"Um. That was when I met Wallace."

"Wallace is your boyfriend, correct?"

"Yes. Or he was. I don't know anymore."

"Okay, so when you met Wallace. How did things change for you then?"

"We started hanging out. I didn't hang out with anyone in school . . . or outside of school. Wallace is a *Monstrous Sea* fan, and it was the first time I'd ever met one in real life. I met his friends too."

"Did you get along with them?"

"Sure."

"Did Wallace meet your friends?"

"Technically, yeah. Max and Emmy are both on the *Monstrous Sea* forums, so he's probably seen them before."

"You don't know Max and Emmy in real life?"

"I know them in real life. It's not like they're pretending to be somebody else just because they're online."

"I mean face-to-face, as in you could reach out and touch them."

"No. One of them lives in Canada and the other's in school in California."

"So you're used to interacting with people mostly on the internet."

"I guess. Before Wallace I mostly only interacted with my family. Is that bad?"

"Not necessarily. Many people, especially teenagers your age, find their closest friends and communities online. I apologize for saying 'in real life'—I didn't intend to sound like I thought they weren't valuable relationships."

"That's okay. You're better than my parents were."

"What do your parents say?"

"Lots of things. They used to say they were okay with the online stuff, but I don't think they were. They were happy when Wallace came around, though. I guess they thought I was breaking out of my shell, or whatever."

"Were you?"

"Maybe. I don't know. I started doing more stuff outside my house, but it still wasn't the same as being online."

"How did you feel online?"

"Like the creator of one of the most popular webcomics in the world. I was invincible. It's so much easier to deal with people when you feel like they can't touch you."

"It's normal to experience those kinds of power differences. Did you feel that way around Wallace all the time?"

"No. Sometimes, but not all the time. I pretended to be a fan too. Wallace is the most popular *Monstrous Sea* fanfiction writer."

"Why don't we talk a little more about *Monstrous Sea*?"

"Like what?"

"Why don't you tell me what it's about?"

"You haven't read it? Ugh—sorry, that sounded bad. I mean like, all of this is about *Monstrous Sea*, I thought you might've gone online to look at it . . . sorry, I'm not pretentious, I swear."

"That's okay. I did look it up, but I wanted to hear you describe it."

"It's . . . hard to explain. There's a boy and a girl and—have you read *Faust*? Or seen it? You know the Faust legend, right?"

"Yes, I know Faust."

"Okay, so the boy and girl have basically sold their souls for great power. Kind of. It's weird. They live on this huge, distant planet called Orcus, and it's mostly ocean. The boy and the girl are the only ones who can kill each other, and they're pitted on opposite sides of a war—I'm not explaining it well."

"You're doing a fine job."

"So the girl finds out she's been misled by her side, and the boy tries to influence her over to his, but he turns out to kind of be the monster everyone always said he was, just in a different way. . . ."

"How long have you been working on this?"

"A long time."

"Do you think about it often?"

"Every day. Sometimes it's all I think about. But I haven't been able to work on it since . . . a few weeks ago."

"When it was revealed that you created it."

"Yes."

"Why?"

"The motivation is gone. It used to be part of me, something I did all the time. I don't even know if I miss it or not."

"Have you been working on anything else?"

"No. I've tried, but then I feel guilty about not working on *Monstrous Sea*."

"Why do you feel guilty?"

"Part of it's the fans, I guess. They've been reading it so long, and it's so close to the end, I feel like I'm letting them down. I *am* letting them down. But the other part is the story itself . . . never mind. It's stupid."

"Nothing's stupid, Eliza. What about the story?"

"I feel like I'm letting the story down. Like I'm not worthy of it because I couldn't finish it."

"Does that bother you often?"

"I've had a few nightmares about it."

"Nightmares?"

"Like . . . 'getting eaten by sea monsters' type nightmares. So that's normal, right?"

"It's normal to have nightmares when you're stressed, yes. I've met artists before who have experienced similar feelings—not feeling worthy of their own work, guilt over an incomplete piece, anxiety about what their fans want and how they might deliver it. It's normal, but that doesn't mean it's always healthy. Eliza, your worth as a person is not dependent on the art you create or what other people think of it."

"Then . . . what is it dependent on? What is there beyond what we create and leave behind?"

"Do you believe the people of highest worth are those who only do excellent work?"

"Well . . ."

"Let me put it this way: your brothers are athletes, aren't they?"

"Yes."

"If they lose a game, don't they risk also losing supporters?"

"I guess."

"Does that make their lives worth less than those of two boys who only win?"

"Of course not. That would be ridiculous. It's just a game."

"They might say the same of Monstrous Sea. It's only a comic."

"It's still different."

"I think you might be surprised how thin the lines between art and sports really are—some artists consider their craft a sport, and some athletes consider their sport an art. My point is, we ascribe value to the things we care most about, but sometimes we don't stop long enough to take a look at the bigger picture. You are able to see who your brothers are, separate from what they do and accomplish, but you have trouble doing the same for yourself."

"I . . . maybe . . ."

"Worth as a person is not based on any tangible evidence. There's no test for it, no scale. Everyone's got their own idea of what it is. But I can tell you that Monstrous Sea is not the measure of your value in life, Eliza. Whether or not you finish it does not determine if you should live or die."

"But . . . Wallace. Wallace was offered a book deal for his transcription of the story, and it would completely change his life, but the publisher doesn't want it unless it's done. If I don't finish, he's going to lose everything."

"Is it a life-or-death situation?"

"No."

"Is he in some sort of danger only this can save him from?"

"I . . . no. But it would make things easier for him. . . ."

"It does sound difficult."

"What am I supposed to do? That's why I'm here, that's why I'm trying to get through all of this and be able to draw. If it weren't for him, I'd never think about the comic again. I *want* to finish the comic for him, but I can't. If he doesn't get this, it's my fault."

"I don't think the important thing here is that you finish the comic. It's that you realize that you can't be held responsible for Wallace's life, or the lives of your fans. The state of your fandom shouldn't dictate your self-worth."

"But it's my fault. I should be able to finish even if I don't feel like it."

"I understand that may not be your first choice of action, and certainly it may not seem like the kindest, but is it more important that you work despite the block, or should you take the time to rest?"

"Shouldn't you be the one telling me that?"

"I think in this case it's more important that you decide for yourself. This issue—your anxiety—may not be a quick fix. I can prescribe medicine for it, but it's vital that you learn how to identify it when it feels like you're being overwhelmed, and to know when you can push through it and when you need to step away."

"Oh."

"Let's explore something else. Did you give any thought to what you would do after Monstrous Sea was finished?"

"I . . . I kind of felt like I'd collapse on the ground. You know, like a puppet with its strings cut."

"You didn't have any other ideas you wanted to explore?"

"No."

"Life doesn't end with the story. Maybe you won't finish

Monstrous Sea. Maybe you will. Maybe you won't draw anything else after *Monstrous Sea.* Maybe you will. The fans will still love it. The haters will find something else to hate. Time will go on, and so will you."

"But . . . how long will that take? I'm tired of feeling like this."

"That's hard to tell."

"I have to go to college in the fall. I can't—I don't want to deal with this and be in a new place too."

"Have you thought of taking time off? A gap year? You don't have to jump into college right away."

"But what would I do with myself? I can't stay in my room all the time, right? Even though I want to."

"If you continue coming to see me, we can talk about this, but it would be a great time to take stock of things. Recenter yourself. It will also give you plenty of breathing room to work on your anxiety."

"That . . . sounds nice."

"Would you like more water? Your ice has melted—it must be warm by now."

"Oh. Yes, thank you."

CHAPTER 41

Graduation couldn't come fast enough.

My grades slipped over the past few weeks, but it was so close to the end of the semester it didn't matter. It wasn't enough for any college to rescind their offer of admission. I accepted at a small local university, and almost immediately wrote a letter to the director of admissions explaining why I wanted to defer for a year.

Last September, Mom and Dad wouldn't have loved the idea of me taking a gap year. After all this, they agreed that it might be for the best. I think part of the reason they did was because of Sully and Church's impromptu intervention on my behalf. Right away Dad began intercepting all phone calls and mail meant for me, and Mom planned a list of activities we could do to get me out of the house more—most of which involved walking Davy around the neighborhood, thankfully—and she hung up a little sign on the fridge with a row of emotion faces so I can mark how I'm feeling every day. I would've called it stupid before, but it's easier, some days, than having to talk.

"What do you mean, you won't have to go to school next year?" Sully roars at the dinner table when Mom and Dad announce the plan. "*We* still have to go to school next year! That's so not fair!"

Church quietly shovels peas into his mouth.

"*Sully!*" Mom hisses. Neither of my brothers is allowed to complain about anything that happens because of my "meltdowns," as Sully calls them, even if they're joking, but I like it that Sully gets so upset. He makes this all feel like some goofy problem in a movie. It'll get resolved with a neat little bow after an hour and a half of family fun.

Sully sinks in his chair with a sour look.

Something buzzes. Church pulls his phone out of his pocket.

"Oh, hey, look." He passes it across the table to me. On it is a message from Lucy Warland.

"Why do you have Lucy Warland's number?" I ask.

"Because she's cool," Church says. "Also because Sully didn't want to ask for her number himself."

Sully's face turns red.

"She told me she'd send pictures from the graduation ceremony," Church goes on.

Ah, graduation. That thing I achieved, and then refused to celebrate. Just knowing I never have to set foot in that high school again has made it easier to breathe. I bring up the picture full screen and find a ceremony hall full of my classmates, seated in neat rows of silky graduation robes. A line has formed on one side of the stage, where the graduates are ascending to take their diplomas from the principal.

Lucy snapped the shot as Wallace went up. I can see it as if the picture's a video: Wallace sets his own deliberate pace up the steps and across the stage. His face is stoic, as always, because there are far too many people in the room and the more overloaded he is, the less expression he makes. He's bigger than the principal. His hand dwarfs the smaller man's. He takes his diploma and lumbers off the stage, and most of the crowd thinks he's stupid, or a dumb jock, or nobody at all.

I know who he is. I know what he can do.

"Can I have my phone back now?"

I hand the phone to Church. Sully glares at me.

"What's wrong with you?" he asks. "You look like you swallowed a tire."

"May I be excused?"

Mom blinks. "Sure. What for?"

"I need to go upstairs. To change. I was supposed to meet Wallace at his house after the ceremony."

Mom and Dad look at each other. "We didn't know about this," Dad says.

"Sorry, I forgot to tell you."

I hurry upstairs and look through my dresser for something nice to wear. Something actually nice, like one of the outfits Mom and Dad got me for Christmas. I fix my hair. Try to put on some makeup, fail, try again. "Warland" is so close to the end of the names they call—the ceremony must be over by now.

Mom and Dad let me leave without much fuss. I think they're shocked to see me looking that nice and wearing makeup.

The Keeler house is empty when I arrive. I park along the curb and walk up to sit on the porch. The late-May night is warm, the sun halfway below the horizon in the distance. It's been too long since I've been here. Wallace and I haven't really spoken since the Olivia Kane letter, though we still eat lunch together at school. It's too much trouble to break routine. I don't know if the publisher's offer to him still stands, and I don't know if he expects me to show up on his doorstep one day—like I'm doing now—with those pages in hand.

I do know that's not why I'm here. I'm here because I have to make him understand this guilt festering inside me.

I wait fifteen minutes before a car pulls down the street and into the driveway.

The Keelers get out. Tim, Bren, and Lucy first. Then Vee. Wallace gets out of the back seat last, which means he must've been sandwiched between Bren and Lucy. How the three of them managed to fit, I'll never know.

"Oh, Eliza! We didn't expect to see you here, hon!" Vee flies over and sweeps me up in a hug.

Lucy comes next, like friendliness is programmed into her DNA. Her million little braids have been replaced with smooth, straight locks. "Did you see the pictures I sent Church? I didn't get very many, but he said he wanted *some*, so . . ."

"Yeah, I got them."

Then Bren and Tim appear, but neither of them are huggers, and that's fine with me. Bren puts a hand on my shoulder. Her hair is held back today with a thick orange headband. "How are you feeling?"

"Not too bad."

She smiles.

"We were sad to miss you at graduation tonight," Tim says, also smiling. I wasn't sure about his opinion of me before, but now that he knows I made *Monstrous Sea*, it must be higher. Surely. "Are you going to be staying for a while?"

"Oh—I don't know. I wanted to talk to Wallace for a few minutes."

Tim looks over his shoulder to where Wallace still stands by the car. "Okay then, we'll leave you kids to it." He herds the rest of the family into the house, and then it's only me and Wallace and the quiet of the street.

"Hey," I say.

"Hey," he says. His quiet voice barely crosses the distance between us. His cap and gown are tucked under one arm; he wore a suit beneath them, without the jacket.

"You look good in a tie," I say.

"I feel like I'm being strangled," he says. "Are you wearing makeup?"

"A little. Does it look stupid?"

"No."

I tuck hair behind my ear. I force my breathing to even out, and my thoughts slow down from there. *My body is not a disgusting thing I have to carry around with me. I am not being squeezed through a narrow tube. I am here. I can do this.*

I repeat these things to myself over and over again, but I don't know that I believe them. Not yet.

"Lucy sent us a picture of you. It made me—it made me really happy."

"Okay."

I take a step closer to him. "I haven't finished the pages. I would have told you if I had. I . . . I did try." He doesn't move. "I want to finish so badly. I hate that I can't. I hate that I'm the one holding you back. And you were right. That I have everything I could ever need. I don't think my life is perfect, but it's pretty great compared to others, and I shouldn't complain about it as much as I do."

He stays silent.

"I'm sorry," I say. "For lying to you about everything, and for not being able to finish."

Still nothing.

Finally I blurt out, "I miss you."

"You miss me," he says. I can't read his face.

"I know things are weird now for a lot of reasons. And I don't blame you if you—if you hate me." My legs start to shake, so I press my knees together. "But I wanted you to know that I miss you, and I don't want things to be like this. If you just want to be friends—or if you don't even want to be that—that's fine, but after this summer we won't be in the same place anymore."

After an unbearable stretch of silence, he says, "I don't know if you understand how angry I am."

My stomach plummets. "What?"

"You lied for so long, even after my email, and then . . . the writing stuff." He shrugs his massive shoulders. "I'm not sure how I'm going to pay for school. Get a lot of jobs, I guess. I'm going to be working most of the summer, so I don't think I can hang out."

"Oh."

"Just. You know."

"Yeah." I focus on the car's front bumper.

He walks past me to go inside. No good-bye. No see you later. He disappears into the house, and I'm left standing alone.

It feels as if the ground is swallowing my feet. Walking down the driveway is like walking through mud, and when I reach the end, I can't move any farther. I kneel, hands cupped around the back of my neck, shoulders between my knees, and my breath comes out in harsh ratcheting gasps.

Wallace won't forgive me. It doesn't matter what I say to myself. It doesn't matter how many times I apologize or explain. In my worst nightmares, I never imagined him not even wanting to be friends with me. But in my worst nightmares, the most terrible thing that happened was he found out who I am.

Wallace won't forgive me.

How can anyone else?

Monstrous Sea Private Message

10:05 p.m. (MirkerLurker has joined the message)
   MirkerLurker: Are you guys around?

10:08 p.m.
   MirkerLurker: I'm just

   MirkerLurker: having some trouble

   MirkerLurker: With everything

10:10 p.m.
   MirkerLurker: Okay

10:21 p.m.
   MirkerLurker: I have to go.

CHAPTER 42

I sit in my car on the far side of Wellhouse Bridge, staring at Wellhouse Turn. Wallace's words pound in my head. They bring to the surface all the forum posts, all the emails, all the messages from the people who want to know who I am and what I am and when I'm going to finish *Monstrous Sea*. I'm alone here in the middle of the road, but it doesn't feel like it.

The weather-worn ribbons tied to the cross at the top of Wellhouse Turn are still. The sky is velvet black, punctured by stars.

Car tires squeal in the distance. I freeze, lightning in my veins and fear coiling in my chest. Anyone who sees a car stopped at Wellhouse Turn will know what I'm doing here.

A minute passes. The night is quiet again.

My body settles and the fear ebbs away, leaving only that tight tension in my stomach that hasn't faded completely since my name was revealed. I am not okay. I know that I am not okay and that there are ways for me to be okay again, but I can't wait that long. It won't be worth it to be okay again, because people will still hate me. I'll always be the letdown, the weird girl, the low-level villain in the sewers.

Everything will work better when I'm gone, anyway; I won't be around to mess up family togetherness time, or bother Max and Emmy with my problems, or remind Wallace of everything he could have had.

I'm so tired. I'm tired of anxiety that twists my stomach so hard I can't move the rest of my body. Tired of constant vigilance. Tired of wanting to do something about myself, but always taking the easy way out.

I thought that's what this would be. I stare at Wellhouse Turn, and Wellhouse Turn ignores me as it ignores everyone. When I drove past an hour ago, it seemed so convenient. Providential, even. So many times I looked at Wellhouse Turn and thought it might be nice to fly. And here it was, right when I needed it. An hour ago, when I stopped, I thought it would be an easy decision to drop my foot on the gas pedal and hold the steering wheel straight. But just thinking about it—the speed, the rush, the drop—no, that's not easy at all. Anyone who thinks that's an easy way out hasn't had to face it.

It'll be okay, I tell myself, then let out a hysterical laugh.

I'm thinking about killing myself. Of course it won't be okay.

I bury my head in my arms. I don't know anymore. I don't know, I don't know, god, I'm so tired. I miss Davy, and my nice quiet room where no one gets hurt, and the perpetual hum of my computer. I want to be there.

So maybe I should go. The idea blunts the edges of my panic. I *could go home*. Just for tonight. I'm more stressed-out sitting here than I would be at home, anyway, and I don't have to rush into this. For now I can sleep, and at least that's a few hours that I don't have to think about anything.

Yes. That is what I'll do.

I lower my legs and search for the gearshift. I never take my eyes off Wellhouse Turn, as if it's a sleeping dragon that might wake and attack me. *Not today,* I think to it and its pretty memorial. *You can't have me today.*

The words send a thrill up my arms. Not today.

Tires crunch on asphalt. Headlights appear ahead, coming around the turn. The lights blind me as I fumble for my seat belt and my keys.

The other car stops in the middle of the turn, near the memorial. The driver's door opens and a bulky, dark figure flies out so fast he trips and has to catch himself before he hits the pavement. He sprints through my headlights—Wallace, moving faster than I've ever seen him move before—and he skids to a stop and almost rips off my sideview mirror.

He scans the interior. Our eyes meet. He pounds on the window.

"GET OUT OF THE CAR!"

He doesn't wait for me. He tears the door open, pushes my half-on seat belt aside, and lifts me out like I'm as heavy as a bag of leaves. He sets me on my feet right outside and immediately lets go.

"You should have been home by now. You didn't answer your phone." His voice rasps with every harsh breath. Eyes wide, face flushed. "Why didn't you answer your phone?"

"I turned it off. I'm going home now." I don't need to tell him the whole truth. He already knows it. I see it in his eyes as they fill with tears.

Then I'm crushed in his arms. He has forgotten how big he is; I bend backward to fit the curve of his torso, the breath squeezed out of me, tingles flushing from the crown of my head to the soles of my feet at how nice it is to be held.

I don't move. I can't, not yet.

"You were angry." My voice doesn't come out much louder than a whisper.

"Jesus, Eliza, no." He doesn't pull back to say it, but his arms tighten. His voice breaks over and over, rapid-fire. His whole body trembles. "No, I don't care about any of that. Did you come here because of me? I was such an asshole. I should've seen—I *did* see what was going on, but I didn't . . . I didn't even try to help, I was so stupid and focused on what I wanted—" He sniffs, hard, his voice broken and high. "Please don't. Please. I can't lose anyone else to this stupid turn."

Then I understand what I was going to do, and what it would have done to Wallace, and I start to cry too.

How terrible it would have been if I'd actually done what I thought about. How terrible it is that he found me here, thinking about it.

"I'm sorry." The words hiccup out of me. "I didn't . . . I didn't mean to . . . I didn't think. I wasn't thinking. I shouldn't have—not here."

"No, no." He grips the back of my neck. His fingers are hard and reassuring, keeping me from putting distance between us. "I'm just glad you're alive. That's all. You're not a bad person. Please don't think that."

"But I lied to you. And the transcription is important." My hands creep up his sides, around his back, to his shoulders. "Writing and college and doing what you love. That's important."

He squeezes me, hard. We fall against my car and sink to the ground.

"Not as important as your life." He sniffs again, loud, then sits back and lets me go. I rock toward him, then force myself to sit back too. Wallace uses his shirt collar to wipe his face. "Dammit, I'm going to poke my eyes out, I'm shaking so hard."

I laugh, just a little, because even though I still feel like a shitty person and an even shittier friend, I'm shaking too. It's a constant tremor from nerves held taut for so long, and it radiates from the base of my skull out through the rest of my body.

"Were you really going home?" he asks.

"Yeah."

"Please don't come back here."

I nod. I don't want to. I won't.

Wallace grabs my hand and holds it with both of his against his stomach. Closes his eyes. His palms are rough where he fell on the pavement. "I was so scared."

"I know. I'm sorry."

"I'm sorry too." Wallace hulks when he sits with his head bowed like this, and his hands dwarf mine. Thick hands, thick wrists, thick arms. Every part of him shivers with guilt, and so does every part of me. There are no rights and wrongs between us anymore. At least, I hope there aren't.

"Wallace."

He looks up.

"I want to be happy," I say.

"Me too," he says.

We sit in silence for several long minutes, until we both stop shaking. I stand and tug him with me, but with his weight it's more like me leaning into air until he picks himself up. He hugs me again, softer this time.

He watches me get in my car and head toward home.

✦ ✦ ✦

I wake up to Sully tossing an envelope at my face.

Sunlight streams through my bedroom window. Davy lies on my feet. Sully leaves the door open, letting in the sounds of Mom and Dad and Church moving around downstairs. On the front of the envelope is my address, and a return address that's just a P.O. Box with no name. The handwriting is flowing script in heavy ink. I pry open the flap and pull out a note written on thick parchment.

I know whose signature will be at the bottom before my eyes ever get there, but it doesn't make it any less unbelievable.

Dear Eliza,

Thank you so much for your letter. I don't often write letters, and it has been some time since I've corresponded with someone outside a five-mile radius of my home, so excuse me if any of this comes off as strange.

I should start by saying you are not pathetic. I don't know you, yet I know that by no stretch of the imagination are you pathetic. Most people aren't, and only think they are. Knocking yourself out on a cafeteria table does not make you pathetic. (Though I'm certain it couldn't have made you feel very well.)

Being exposed to the public is certainly difficult enough without also being in high school. And being a teen girl, no less. I was a teen girl in high school once, and I do not remember it fondly. My sister loved high school. I didn't have her knack for navigating schoolwork, extracurriculars, and social circles, often all at once. I never begrudged her this, though, because I was able to escape into my writing.

I feel this may not have been the case for you. My popularity didn't come until later in life, when I was well settled and hadn't thought about school for many years. Yours has been with you all this time; from what I've gathered in the few news articles I've had relayed to me, you've been working on this story for most of your time in high school. I can't imagine what it must have been like to keep that secret while sharing this part of your heart with so many people.

Creating art is a lonely task, which is why we introverts revel in it, but when we have fans looming over us, it becomes loneliness of a different sort. We become caged animals watched by zoo-goers, expected to perform lest the crowd grow bored or angry. It's not always bad. Sometimes we do well, and the cage feels more like a pedestal.

I hope I haven't scared you off with this zoo metaphor. I didn't expect it to turn as sour as it did. This is part of the reason I never finished Children of Hypnos— at the time I felt as if my writing was going through a shift, and I feared the fifth and final book wouldn't sound like the others. I was afraid my fans would notice and hate it. I was afraid they would never buy another one of my books. That was ultimately what stopped me from continuing: fear. Fear drove away my motivation and love for the story.

I believe what you have to ask yourself, if you truly want to finish what you started, is why did you stop? Was it fear? Pure apathy? Or something else? I'm afraid I can't answer this question for you, but I can tell you that if it's because of something inside you, if there isn't someone *in the physical world holding a knife to your throat and threatening your death if you continue to write, then you can work through it. Whatever this is, it will pass. My fear of the reaction to the fifth Children of Hypnos book has been gone for several years now, and every few weeks my interest in it rekindles. The small flame in my chest flickers for a few hours, waiting for more firewood. If I feed it, the interest continues. If I starve it, the interest wanes.*

If you want the motivation back, you must feed it. Feed it everything. Books, television, movies, paintings, stage plays, real-life experience. Sometimes feeding simply means working, working through nonmotivation, working even when you hate it.

We create art for many reasons—wealth, fame, love, admiration—but I find the one thing that produces the best results is desire. When you want the thing you're creating, the beauty of it will shine through, even if the details aren't all in order. Desire is the fuel of creators, and when we have that, motivation will come in its wake.

I lost the desire to create Children of Hypnos. I could do it still; I could write the final book. But it wouldn't be as good as it once was, my fans wouldn't be happy with it, and I would truly feel that I had let them and myself down. I would rather they speculate ceaselessly on the end than have a poor ending they didn't deserve. More importantly, a poor ending I didn't deserve—the younger me who created this story originally, who had a love for it I'm only starting to recover.

I hope you don't lose your desire to create <u>Monstrous Sea</u>. It sounds like a wonderful story.

Much hope,

Olivia Kane

P.S. Truth be told, I don't mind answering this question. Children of Hypnos may not have an ending that its fans can read, but I did have one in mind while writing it. I think we always do, somewhere in our heads, even if we don't seriously consider them. Like life, what gives a story its meaning is the fact that it ends. Our stories have lives of their own—and it's up to us to make them mean something.

Monstrous Sea Private Message

10:58 a.m. (MurkerLurker has joined the message)

MirkerLurker: So...

MirkerLurker: Anyone home?

10:51 a.m. (Apocalypse_Cow has joined the message)

Apocalypse_Cow: the prodigal daughter returns. sorry we weren't around yesterday—was everything okay? we started to get worried.

Apocalypse_Cow: I mean, who was emmy going to watch Dog Days with?

MirkerLurker: Ha

MirkerLurker: No, I'm okay. I was trying to stay away from the internet.

MirkerLurker: And I wanted to say sorry for disappearing for so long.

MirkerLurker: And also thank you for everything you guys did for me when the news broke.

Apocalypse_Cow: no need to apologize. i would've done the same thing. no one needs that much attention on themselves, especially if they've been anonymous for so long.

Apocalypse_Cow: and you're welcome—i do deserve much praise for my honorable actions in the eliza mirk scandal operation. perhaps a promotion to god overlord of the forums, and a statue of myself made of solid gold.

10:58 a.m. (emmersmacks has joined the message)

emmersmacks: E!!!!!

emmersmacks: YOURE BACK!!!!!!!

MirkerLurker: Hey, Em.

emmersmacks: HOW HAVE YOU BEEN???

emmersmacks: ARE YOU OKAY???

MirkerLurker: Yeah, not bad. Mostly staying away from the internet.

emmersmacks: People have been loving the Monstrous Sea pages

emmersmacks: They say youre not coming back to finish them

Apocalypse_Cow: seriously though, em. keep your mouth shut.

Apocalypse_Cow: you don't have to finish them if you don't want to, e. you don't have to do anything just because those brats on the forums tell you to.

MirkerLurker: They're not brats, though, they're fans. They're the only reason all of this exists. I have to try to finish it for them, right?

Apocalypse_Cow: no.

emmersmacks: I mean I want to see the end

emmersmacks: But if its going to make you sad then I dont want you to do it

MirkerLurker: Whatever, I didn't come here to talk about Monstrous Sea anyway. What have you two been doing? And Max, don't say something stupid like eating Twizzlers. I haven't sent you any Twizzlers lately and I know the only Twizzlers you eat are mine.

MirkerLurker: Em, did you finish school?

emmersmacks: Yes!!

emmersmacks: Got a 92 in that Calc class

emmersmacks: Suck it Professor Teller

Apocalypse_Cow: she actually said that to him too.

MirkerLurker: You didn't.

MirkerLurker: Tell me you did.

emmersmacks: I might have

emmersmacks: What they dont tell you about college is how good it feels to stick it to dickhead teachers

Apocalypse_Cow: i'd give you an a+ just for that alone.

emmersmacks: Thank you

emmersmacks: Ooh ooh!!!

emmersmacks: But Max got back together with Heather!!!

MirkerLurker: Really?

Apocalypse_Cow: yeah, it's weird. I don't know if you guys knew this, but your loved ones appreciate it when you, like, spend time with them in person. it's this new thing I've been trying out for the past month or two.

Apocalypse_Cow: works pretty well, actually.

Apocalypse_Cow: but she also plays world of warcraft with me three nights a week, so take from that what you will.

MirkerLurker: Ah, that makes me happy! I'm glad you're back together.

Apocalypse_Cow: how about you and mr. wallace?

Apocalypse_Cow: how'd he feel when he found out who you are?

MirkerLurker: I don't want to talk about Wallace, if that's okay.

MirkerLurker: Mostly I got on here to say how much I love you both. You do so much for me. I don't say that enough.

Apocalypse_Cow: no need to get sappy on us, e.

emmersmacks: You dont have to say it

MirkerLurker: Yeah, I do. I don't talk to you for weeks and you still let me come back. You always have time for my problems but I never make time for yours. I didn't know anything was wrong with Max and Heather at first, and I wasn't even around when Emmy put her teacher in his place.

MirkerLurker: I'm really sorry, you guys.

Apocalypse_Cow: you better stop that, or i'm gonna cry.

Apocalypse_Cow: and if i'm about to cry, what will poor emmy do?

Apocalypse_Cow: she's only twelve, for goodness' sake.

emmersmacks: IM NOT TWELVE

emmersmacks: Im fifteen now

On the day of her departure, Faren stayed awake with her. Neither of them spoke. When the crows outside began croaking—the signal of the early hours, since it was the winter months and the sun wouldn't rise for some time—they both pulled themselves out of bed and got dressed. During their breakfast of watery oatmeal, the alarm Amity had been given vibrated against the table, signaling that Sato would arrive shortly. The two of them stared at it. Amity set down her spoon. Her stomach had gone suddenly hollow.

Amity didn't want to meet Sato inside the house. She didn't want any excuse to have to invite him in, or stay here longer than necessary, so she went out to the stone courtyard and sat on one of the low benches there, surrounded by the blackwood trees, with a clear view of the path up the cliffside. Innumerable crows flocked in the trees around her, blackening her surroundings.

Faren disappeared into the house for a minute and returned with one of his chart papers. It was one of the small ones, the brown sheet creased with age; folded up, it fit neatly in his palm. He sat beside her on the bench and took her hand to press the thick paper into it.

"I know White said you wouldn't need anything, but I thought this might help."

She unfolded the paper. On it was an unfamiliar constellation. "Did you make this one up?"

He shook his head. "This is one of the Unnamed."

She turned the paper around to look at it from different angles. It had no particular shape; nothing jumped out at her. The Nocturnians divided constellations into two types: their own, and everyone else's. Theirs had names like Faren and Gyurhei; the others went Unnamed, because Nocturnians couldn't claim them. Amity had never quite understood—didn't you have to know what a constellation was before you could even call it a constellation? If it was some other culture's constellation, how could you know that without having spoken to them? But the Nocturnians knew.

"Why'd you draw this one?" she asked

"Because this one is yours." He took the paper and righted it in her hands. There was no correct direction for constellations, but at the bottom of the paper he'd scrawled AMITY. "I found it a few years ago. Before the Watcher. Amity isn't its proper name, of course. I don't know what it is. I wish I could tell you. But I thought . . . for this one, we could make an exception."

She looked again at the picture. "This is . . . you found my name in a constellation?" It was easy for Nocturnians to do, because they were named after the stars. But for her to be linked to one of the Unnamed . . . did that mean she came from whatever culture that particular constellation belonged to? If she could find out what it meant, where it came from, would she know where she came from too?

He had found her in a constellation.

She flung her arms around his neck. The pressure in her chest shut out all other feelings. He locked himself around her, one hand fisting in her hair. His lips pressed to her neck.

"I'll come back," she said. "I'll be back. I promise."

CHAPTER 43

I take Davy for walks every day. I sit on park benches and listen to birds sing. I watch my brothers' summer soccer conditioning. I help my parents with chores around the house, because as it turns out, Mom's clothes-folding yoga is actually really relaxing. Especially when combined with my new anxiety medication.

My therapist calls it a summer of discovery, and the first thing I discover is that I like being outside. In parks, in the woods, at lakesides, out in the country by cornfields. Wallace takes me to this place where his dad used to play football, a big open field in the middle of nowhere, edged by trees. There are no nearby roads or highways, and no electrical structures. The silence is so absolute it's eerie. I fall in love with it instantly.

Two months pass, and I think of Wellhouse Turn maybe every other day. The thought is still there, but the seriousness of it comes and goes.

I only go back on one of the nonserious days, and only with Wallace. We stand at the top of the hill, next to the cross and the offerings. I move the rock I put there months ago; in exchange, Wallace leaves the football jersey that once hung on his wall. WARLAND 73, shivering on the cross in a gentle summer breeze.

Wallace starts going to his own therapist. He doesn't tell me much about the visits other than the exercises he's supposed to do to get himself talking in front of strangers. He must talk to this therapist about his dad, and everything he told me in his email, but we don't talk about it, and I think that's okay. Instead we talk about the fact that he's going to college in the fall for business, with a minor in creative writing. We talk about how we're going to see each other while he's gone. And we talk about the new chapters he gives me of an original story of his he's been thinking about for a while.

We go to see his friends. He's talked to them plenty since the news came out, but I haven't. Megan, as I suspected, is the most understanding. Leece is just excited to know me. Chandra takes a bit to warm up, then gets flustered that I've seen her artwork. Cole takes the longest. We sit at our table at Murphy's, and he spends most of the first hour watching Wallace. When Wallace doesn't kick me out of the building, Cole glances at me and says, "So. Yeah. I guess this is pretty cool."

I don't know if they can be my friends too, after all this, but I hope they can.

Wallace convinces my brothers to start playing football with him in the afternoons. Mom and Dad join in, because they're Mom and Dad, and any form of physical exertion is a small form of happiness. It's strange, at first, to watch them play and realize for the first time that they do it for fun. This isn't a punishment for them, and it's not a way to pass the time. It makes them happy the same way drawing made me happy.

It's strangest with Wallace, because it's one thing to hear that he loves playing football, another thing to see it. And he's good at it too, which seems unfair. How can one person be so good at two drastically different things? How does he have enough love for both football and writing? But with him it seems there is no limit, that it's not a matter of picking and choosing, that he draws no lines between his sport and his art.

They get some of the neighborhood kids to play, and after a while they have a weekly thing going. One day in August, I walk Davy past the open lot where they play and hear Wallace yelling across the field.

I don't think it's him at first. I've never heard his voice that loud across so much space. But one hand is cupped to his mouth and the other points directions to some of the players—among them Lucy, who convinced the others to let her play and is now outrunning them all.

I stop to watch. Church runs past and sees me. He meets up with Sully at the other end, nudges him in the ribs, and nods his head my way. I politely pretend not to notice. Then Sully has the ball, and the two of them juggle it between them down the field in a way even I know isn't legal in football, weaving between the other players until they reach the trash cans—makeshift goalposts—at the other end of the lot. Wallace yells something at them, laughing when they launch into exaggerated touchdown dances.

He pulls them back into line. The other team gets the ball. Their quarterback has it, looking for an open pass. Wallace breaks through the line and charges at him.

I yell, "TAKE HIM DOWN!"

Both Wallace and the quarterback whip around with shock on their faces, but Wallace's momentum carries him straight into the other boy, and they tumble to the ground.

"Sorry!" I call.

Someone shouts for a time-out. Wallace picks himself up, helps the other boy, then jogs over to me. His shirt is stuck to his chest with sweat, and he smiles when I hold out my bottle of lemonade for him. He chugs half of it. Davy noses at Wallace's leg until Wallace pets him.

"It's supposed to be flag football, you know," he says. "I should ban you from the field for disrupting play."

"Nah, that would be way less fun." I reach out and pick at his sleeve. "You smell like hell."

"You should come play with us," he says. He hasn't moved away from me the few times I've reached out to touch him like that this week, but he goes still in a way that means he knows it's happening. He hasn't made any moves himself. There could be a lot of reasons for that, I guess, but for now I'm letting him keep them to himself.

"I don't think it'd work out." If I tried to play, I'd get trampled. It's good to know your limits, my therapist says. This is mine. "Lucy's killing them, though."

"She is."

"You're yelling."

"So are you."

Lucy appears at the edge of the field. "Hey, dummy! We're ready again!"

"Coming!" He hands me the lemonade bottle. Only a few dregs swirl at the bottom. I should probably go home and prepare for an empty refrigerator once Wallace and the rest of my family get back to the house.

Wallace stares at the field for a long second, then turns back and, before I can react, leans down to kiss me. He tastes like sweat and lemonade. It's quick. Easy. He pulls away, eyes down, voice soft.

"Surprise," he says.

The relief registers. I wrinkle my nose and laugh. "Like hell."

"Please, you know you love this." He flaps his sweaty shirt in my direction before turning and jogging back.

"I love *you*," I say, but he's too far away to hear it.

That's okay. He knows.

I finish Davy's walk and let him off his leash inside the house so he can trudge after me up to my room and collapse on my bed for a nap. My comforter has been covered in white fur for weeks, so what's a little more going to hurt? I throw the window open and turn on my oscillating fan to get some air circulating in the room, then push my desk chair out of the way and spend ten minutes doing stretches. Stretching makes everything feel better. My neck, my back, my legs. Everything that always cramped up when I sat at my desk for too long.

My parents have been looking into ergonomic desk chairs. Mom wants to buy me an exercise ball to sit on. I keep telling them I'll use whatever they get me, because they've been trying so hard this whole time to be helpful. They know they've done wrong, I can see it in their faces every time they talk to me. I don't want them to feel bad anymore. It might take a long time to get to that point, but it's worth it.

When the stretches are done and I feel like my mind is breathing, I climb up into my chair and turn on the computer.

For the past week or so, this has been a daily ritual. Sit. Look at the computer. Turn it on. Every day I try to go a little further, but not so far that it causes me distress. After I turn it on, I look at the desktop for a few minutes, or play a few games. The other day I used it to Google better walking harnesses for dogs. I talk to Max and Emmy again, but not anyone else. No one from the *Monstrous Sea* forums.

I haven't been back to the forums. Today I open up the browser and let the cursor hover over the bookmark for the forums, but I don't click it. I still feel that if I do, I'll only get upset. So I leave it alone.

I want to go somewhere, though. Somewhere that isn't a search engine, or a reference website. My attention wanders away from the computer monitor, to the books lined up beside it. The books that are the only things on the desk besides the monitor itself. I moved them there when I got tired of the desk being so empty. Children of Hypnos.

There. There is where I'll go.

My fingers remember the address like I'm thirteen again and I go to the Children of Hypnos fan forums every day. The page comes up right away. It's still there, after all this time. All the threads, all the posts. The fans may have fled, but the heart is still here, like a little fandom time capsule.

I only have to glance at the welcome thread and all those old emotions rush back into me. For a few years, this was where I belonged. I was a citizen in the city of the Children of Hypnos fandom, and I woke up every morning excited to talk with my fellow fans. I scroll through a few of the old role-playing threads where I once pretended to be a nightmare hunter in the Children of Hypnos world, wielding an oversized battle axe like one of my favorite characters, Marcia. Then I find the discussions where people argued about the meaning behind the symbols of the books and the pieces of the plot. Then conversations about favorite quotes from the four books. Then the endless speculations about that spectral fifth book and what became of Olivia Kane— the speculations that tore the fandom apart and killed this forum for good.

I don't want the *Monstrous Sea* fandom to collapse the same way the Children of Hypnos fandom did. I don't want my fans to float off the way I did. Not all of them will have the boon of their own creations to tether them down; not all of them will be able to create their own spaces where they can be who they want to be and love what they want to love without the fear of someone judging them. I don't want them to lose this story or this community. I don't know who they all are, but I know who I was, and I know what it would have meant to me.

I also know this isn't a good enough reason to force myself to finish the comic. If I don't have the motivation for it, it won't turn out well, and no one will be happy with the result.

But motivation doesn't come from nowhere. Like any good monster, you have to feed it.

I pick up the first Children of Hypnos book and run my hand along the war hammer embossed on the cover. The books never had the titles or Olivia Kane's name printed on the front cover. Only the weapons. My fingers graze along the spine and bump over the name KANE, and then, larger, DREAMHUNTER.

I crack the book open. Read the synopsis on the inside front flap. "Emery Ashworth's nightmares routinely try to kill her. . . ." Then flip inside, to the first chapter. As it always does, the first page entices me to read the next, and the next, and the next, until the front door bangs open and my brothers and Wallace tromp inside and I've blown through to the final chapter and sit pages away from finishing the book.

Wallace sticks his head through the doorway. "Hey. Thought you might be in here."

I look up. "What time is it?"

"Like four thirty. Your parents are making dinner."

"Oh."

"You rereading Children of Hypnos?"

"I . . . yeah, I guess." I didn't mean to, but now I really want to move on to the second book. "I'm almost done."

Wallace sits on the floor near the foot of my bed and pets Davy while I finish reading.

That night after dinner, I go back upstairs, get the second book, and start reading again. Then the third. I've read them so many times I breeze right through, and by five the next morning I'm halfway through the fourth book. When my parents get up, I'm done, and my emotions have been wrung out like a wet washcloth. Like someone cut me open, scrubbed my insides with a stiff brush, and sewed me back up again.

My brain is in high gear. My blood pumps hard through my veins, and my fingers twitch, and I *need* something. I need it, I need it, I need it. I need it right now, I need it worse than I've ever needed anything before.

I need my pencil.

CHAPTER 44

Monstrous Sea is mine.

I made it, not the other way around.

It's not a parasite, or an obligation, or a destiny.

It's a monster.

It's mine.

And I have a battle axe waiting for it.

MONSTROUS SEA FORUMS

LadyConstellation **

Admin

AGE: 18

LOCATION: Indiana

INTERESTS: Drawing. Walking my dog. Eggs. (Also, still riding sea monsters.)

Followers 6,340,228 | Following 0 | Posts 6,979

UPDATES

View earlier updates

Aug 25 2017

> Go here. Read this. Thank me later.
>
> *monstroussea.com*

EPILOGUE

I show Max and Emmy the pages before I put them up, of course. I'm not a completely terrible friend. Max demands I put them all up right away. Emmy is freaking out too hard about the ending to tell me to do much of anything besides fly out to California with a gallon of ice cream and hold her.

I don't look at the comments. I don't go to the forums. I don't want to see what people are saying about me or my story. I'm not ready for that yet, but I am ready for this to be finished.

Max and Emmy watch the boards, and Wallace reports back to me on the status of the fans.

"They're going fucking nuts," he tells me the night the pages go up. I have his webcam feed in one window and Minesweeper open in another. He looks off to the side, clicking through the *Monstrous Sea* forums. Behind him is a small dorm room, a bed lofted with his roommate's desk beneath it, and a TV perched precariously atop a dresser strewn with ramen noodles and open cereal boxes. I'd like to blame the mess on his roommate, but if it's food, it's probably Wallace's.

"More people are reading it every day. Way more than were ever in the fandom before. And the people who wrote articles about your identity back in May—they're talking about this now. That the comic's coming back, that it's ending. It's a thing, Eliza. Reading *Monstrous Sea* is a thing people do. Not just people who like comics but—but everyone. It's all over the internet."

I clear out a corner of the Minesweeper board. "Imagine what they're going to do when they hear about your transcription."

Wallace beams.

"My editor says we're in really good shape to have advance copies of the first book ready before the con." He starts clicking through something on his screen. "Here she said, 'Your chapters were already so clean, the line edits will be pretty light.' And she keeps asking if I think I'm going to have time to do my edits with all my homework." His smile grows. "Like my professors could even assign me enough homework to keep me away from this."

"If they do, I know some people who might be willing to help with that."

"I hope you're not talking about outsourcing my homework."

"Didn't you hear? I'm famous. I can do what I want."

Wallace laughs.

"Who's famous?" Wallace's roommate, Tyler, walks into the room behind Wallace carrying a hamper of laundry. Wallace explains the conversation quickly; when he mentions *Monstrous Sea*, Tyler bends into the webcam's sight.

"You made *Monstrous Sea*?" Then he looks back at Wallace. "Your girlfriend made *Monstrous Sea*?"

"Her name's Eliza," Wallace says.

"You have to be kidding." Tyler drops his laundry basket and hustles out of the room. A minute later, he returns with a flock of college students chattering about *Monstrous Sea*.

Wallace handles them well. He blocks them from the computer at first, letting them work through their preliminary questions, then lets them see me. Lets me see them.

They're not monsters. They're people. We greet each other, and they're polite, and they want to know how it feels to be me.

"A lot better than it used to," I say.

I think this will be okay. I think it will be strange, and probably scary, and I think there will still be times where I think I am the worst person on the planet. But I think I will also love myself and what I've made, and I'll know without doubt that those two things are separate.

I am Eliza Mirk, daughter and sister and friend.

I am Eliza Mirk, mother of a fandom.

I am Eliza Mirk.